Child Welfare Removals by the State

International Policy Exchange Series

Published in collaboration with the
Center for International Policy Exchanges
University of Maryland

Series Editors

Douglas J. Besharov
Neil Gilbert

United in Diversity?:
Comparing Social Models in Europe and America
Edited by Jens Alber and Neil Gilbert

The Korean State and Social Policy:
How South Korea Lifted Itself from Poverty and Dictatorship to Affluence and Democracy
Stein Ringen, Huck-ju Kwon, Ilcheong Yi, Taekyoon Kim, and Jooha Lee

Child Protection Systems:
International Trends and Orientations
Edited by Neil Gilbert, Nigel Parton, and Marit Skivenes

The Age of Dualization:
The Changing Face of Inequality in Deindustrializing Societies
Edited by Patrick Emmenegger, Silja Häusermann, Bruno Palier, and Martin Seeleib-Kaiser

Counting the Poor:
New Thinking About European Poverty Measures and Lessons for the United States
Edited by Douglas J. Besharov and Kenneth A. Couch

Social Policy and Citizenship:
The Changing Landscape
Edited by Adalbert Evers and Anne-Marie Guillemard

Chinese Policy in a Time of Transition
Edited by Douglas J. Besharov and Karen Baehler

Reconciling Work and Poverty Reduction:
How Successful Are European Welfare States?
Edited by Bea Cantillon and Frank Vandenbroucke

University Adaptation in Difficult Economic Times
Edited by Paola Mattei

Activation or Workfare? Governance and the Neo-Liberal Convergence
Edited by Ivar Lødemel and Amílcar Moreira

Child Welfare Systems and Migrant Children:
A Cross Country Study of Policies and Practice
Edited by Marit Skivenes, Ravinder Barn, Katrin Kriz, and Tarja Pösö

Adjusting to a World in Motion:
Trends in Global Migration and Migration Policy
Edited by Douglas J. Besharov and Mark H. Lopez

Caring for a Living:
Migrant Women, Aging Citizens, and Italian Families
Francesca Degiuli

Child Welfare Removals by the State:
A Cross-Country Analysis of Decision-Making Systems
Edited by Kenneth Burns, Tarja Pösö, and Marit Skivenes

SCHOOL of
PUBLIC POLICY

CHILD WELFARE REMOVALS BY THE STATE

A Cross-Country Analysis of Decision-Making Systems

Edited by

KENNETH BURNS

TARJA PÖSÖ

MARIT SKIVENES

OXFORD
UNIVERSITY PRESS

OXFORD
UNIVERSITY PRESS

Oxford University Press is a department of the University of Oxford. It furthers
the University's objective of excellence in research, scholarship, and education
by publishing worldwide. Oxford is a registered trade mark of Oxford University
Press in the UK and certain other countries.

Published in the United States of America by Oxford University Press
198 Madison Avenue, New York, NY 10016, United States of America.

© Oxford University Press 2017

Library of Congress Cataloging-in-Publication Data
Names: Burns, Kenneth, editor. | Pösö, Tarja, editor. | Skivenes, Marit, editor.
Title: Child welfare removals by the state : a cross-country analysis of decision-making systems /
edited by Kenneth Burns, Tarja Pösö and Marit Skivenes.
Description: New York : Oxford University Press, 2016. |
Series: International policy exchange series | Includes bibliographical references and index.
Identifiers: LCCN 2016008315 (print) | LCCN 2016011459 (ebook) |
ISBN 9780190459567 (alk. paper) | ISBN 9780190459574 (ebook)
Subjects: LCSH: Child welfare. | Child welfare—Government policy. |
Children—Legal status, laws, etc.
Classification: LCC HV713 .C39534 2016 (print) | LCC HV713 (ebook) | DDC 362.71—dc23
LC record available at http://lccn.loc.gov/2016008315

9 8 7 6 5 4 3 2 1

Printed by Sheridan Books, Inc., United States of America

CONTENTS

ACKNOWLEDGMENTS

This book was made possible through funding received from the Norwegian Research Council and the European Science Foundation, and support from the Department of Administration and Organisation Theory, University of Bergen (Norway); the School of Applied Social Studies, University College Cork (Ireland); and the School of Social Sciences and Humanities, University of Tampere (Finland).

This support facilitated the creation of a new multidisciplinary network of researchers and academics interested in child welfare removals by the state and related sociolegal decision-making bodies. This book arose out of the debates and activities of this new research network.

The editors would like to express their appreciation and gratitude to the chapter authors for sharing their knowledge and expertise to help bring this book to fruition. Finally, we would like to thank Ida B. Juhasz, University of Bergen, for assisting us with the preparation of the manuscript.

CONTRIBUTORS

KAREN BROADHURST is Professor of Social work and Socio-Legal studies, based in the Department of Sociology within the Faculty of Arts and Social Sciences at Lancaster University, England. She has led a number of research projects funded by research councils and government that have examined these topics. Broadhurst's most recent work is funded by the Nuffield Foundation England and is focused on repeat clienthood within public law proceedings, as well as the use of supervision orders. Broadhurst is a partner in the National Family Drug and Alcohol (FDAC) Development Unit in England, which is rolling out a problem-solving approach to family law proceedings. She is also Co-Editor-in-Chief of *Qualitative Social Work,* and her work is published extensively in social science, law, and health journals. Broadhurst's specialist research interests are in family law proceedings and family treatment courts.

KENNETH BURNS is a college lecturer and Deputy Director of the Master of Social Work programme at University College Cork, Ireland and a research associate with ISS21 (UCC). He has worked as a social worker and social work team leader in child protection and welfare. Burns is the Principal Investigator of the interdisciplinary Child Care Proceedings Research Group at UCC and has published widely on child protection and welfare, staff welfare and retention, social work, and community-based participatory research. Burns is a co-national lead for Campus Engage on Community-based Research and is a collaborator on a Horizon 2020 multicountry study on Responsible Research & Innovation (EnRRICH).

JANESE FREE is Assistant Professor of Sociology at Emmanuel College, Boston, Massachusetts. Free earned a PhD in Sociology (with a specialization in Criminology) at Northeastern University. She has worked as a victim advocate for the Massachusetts Department of Corrections and as a program coordinator with a nonprofit organization responding to intimate partner violence in the Boston area by coordinating the efforts of the police, the courts, hospitals, and health centers. Her research interests lie in the areas of alternative education for at-risk youth, migrant education, and street work targeting at-risk youth.

MONIKA HAUG is a research associate with the Criminological Research Institute of Lower Saxony and PhD-candidate at Kassel University in Germany. Monika studied law at Konstanz University and Cardiff Law School. After that she worked as research associate at Kassel University from 2010 to 2015, specializing in the field of "Law of Childhood and Youth." Since November 2015, she is research associate and head of a project on homicide of children aged 6–13 years in Germany at the Criminological Research Institute of Lower Saxony (Kriminologisches Forschungsinstitut Niedersachsen) in Hanover. Her research interests include physical abuse of children and criminal proceedings, and child protection from a legal and cross-national perspective, including the examination of legal practice.

RAIJA HUHTANEN is Professor of Public Law in the School of Management at the University of Tampere, Finland. Huhtanen, DSc (Admin) specializes in social law and administrative law and teaches students of administrative studies. Huhtanen has been involved in the research of child welfare law, especially from a fundamental and human rights' perspective. Huhtanen is the author of many articles on various branches of social law and her main research interests are social security law, social welfare law, and child welfare law.

STAFFAN HÖJER is Professor of Social Work at the University of Gothenburg in Sweden. His doctorate concerns knowledge in social work, and his research thereafter has focused on issues related to professionalization and organization in social work. Höjer has extensive international experience and has been a guest researcher in the United States and the United Kingdom and supervises PhDs in, for example, Uganda and Rwanda. His publication record is extensive. He is a board member of the *European Journal of Social Work*. He was awarded an Honorary Professorship at the University of Eastern Finland in 2015. He has been funded for several national research grants both as Principal Investigator and as co-applicant; for instance, in a three-year project on privatization in the service of professionalization, a project on laymen governance of professions, a study of political governance in child welfare, and an ongoing study on "the dilemma of work overload-survival strategies in the Swedish public sector."

THERESIA HÖYNCK is Professor Dr., LL.M. for Law of Childhood and Youth at Kassel University (Germany), teaching mainly courses for students of social work. Höynck studied law in Berlin and Passau (Germany) and Theory of Law in Brussels (Belgium) and Liverpool. She has worked for a nongovernmental organization (NGO) in the field of juvenile justice (German Juvenile Court Association, Deutsche Vereinigung für Jugendgerichte und Jugendgerichtshilfen) and the Criminological Research Institute of Lower Saxony (Kriminologisches Forschungsinstitut Niedersachsen). Her research interests have been comparative legal issues in victim's rights in criminal procedure, child homicide and maltreatment, child protection, sanctions in juvenile justice, and professionals in the juvenile justice system.

KATRIN KRIŽ is Associate Professor of Sociology at Emmanuel College, Boston, Massachusetts. She earned a master's degree in International Development and Social Change at Clark University and a PhD in Sociology at Brandeis University. She has published on the interactions between child welfare systems and minority ethnic and/or immigrant service users in England, Norway, and the United States, and on the Earned

Income Tax Credit. Her research interests lie in the areas of welfare policy, child welfare, comparative/international sociology, and the sociology of gender, race, and class.

GRANT KUEHL currently works as a teacher and Coordinator of English Language Learning Services and Advanced Student Reading at a private school in the Boston, Massachusetts area. Kuehl received his Bachelor of Arts degree from Emmanuel College, Boston, in elementary education. As an educator, Kuehl has worked with diverse populations of English language learning students and their families.

AISLING PARKES is a Lecturer in Law and Student Wellbeing Officer in the School of Law, University College Cork, Ireland. She lectures in child and family law, children's rights, disability and the law, and law for social workers. Furthermore, Parkes has completed in-depth research on the nature and scope of Article 12 of the United Nations Convention on the Rights of the Child and the extent to which it has been implemented under international law. This topic forms the subject matter of her book, *Children and International Human Rights: The Right of the Child to be Heard,* which was published by Routledge in 2013. She also has published on the rights of more vulnerable groups of children, including children with disabilities and those in care. Her research interests lie in the area of international children's rights, in particular the voice of the child and adoption law and practice.

CONOR O'MAHONY is a senior lecturer at the School of Law in University College Cork (UCC), Ireland, where he specializes in constitutional law, child and family law, and children's rights. He has written extensively on the evolution of the Irish Constitution and the European Convention on Human Rights in the context of family life, and on such topics as extramarital families, marriage equality, and children's rights. His work has been published in journals such as the *Child and Family Law Quarterly,* the *International Journal of Law, Policy and the Family,* the *Journal of Social Welfare and Family Law* and the *Irish Journal of Family Law.* He twice has spoken at the World Congress on Family Law and Children's Rights (South Africa 2005 and Canada 2009) and is a member of the organizing committee for the 2017 Congress in Dublin. He is also Deputy Director of the UCC Child Law Clinic, through which he works to support litigation and law reform on children's issues. This work includes the case of *O'Keeffe v. Ireland* in 2014, in which the European Court of Human Rights (ECHR) found Ireland's child protection measures in schools to be in breach of the ECHR.

TARJA Pösö is Professor in Social Work at the School of Social Sciences and Humanities, University of Tampere, Finland. She has long experience of more than twenty years in studying child welfare from various perspectives, with a keen interest in cross-cultural perspectives and exploring methods and ethics for child welfare studies.

STEFAN SCHNURR is a Professor and Head of the Institute for Studies in Children and Youth Services at the School of Social Work (Olten and Basel) and a member of the School's Management Board in Switzerland. Schnurr obtained his doctoral degree (PhD, Diplom-Pädagoge) from the Faculty of Educational Science, University of Bielefeld. He held an Honorary Professorship at the School of Health and Social Studies (now the Centre for Lifelong Learning/Social Work) at Warwick University (2009–2014) and has served as a specialist adviser in child welfare and child protection issues on federal, cantonal, and intercantonal bodies and committees. His teaching and research activities include international social work and social policy, children and family services, and child protection and participation.

CAROLINE SHORE is a college lecturer and year coordinator on the Master of Social Work programme at University College Cork, Ireland, and a research associate with ISS21 (UCC). She is a registered social worker and works as a Guardian *ad litem* in child care proceedings as an independent advocate representing the voice of the child. Shore has also been a member of a multidisciplinary research group at UCC examining child care proceedings in the District Court.

MARIT SKIVENES is Professor of Political Science at the Department of Administration & Organization Theory at the University of Bergen, Norway. She also holds a Professor II position at Bergen University College. Skivenes has extensive experience in comparative research on child welfare systems, and decision-making processes within these systems. Besides teaching and departmental obligations, she has managed and completed several large-scale, cross-country research projects and established an internationally renowned child welfare research network. She has contributed to the field with several coedited books, book chapters, reports and peer-reviewed journal articles, featuring both Norway-specific and cross-country comparisons of child welfare policies and practices.

KARL HARALD SØVIG (Dr. Juris) is Professor of Law at the Faculty of Law, University of Bergen, Norway. He previously served as a temporary judge at the district and high court and as ad hoc chairman of the county board. His research has focused on various forms of coercive measures within the welfare state, as well as on the rights of children. He has authored a report for the government on the implementation of the United Nations Convention on the Rights of the Child into the Norwegian legal system and chaired an expert committee drafting a new act on adoption (NOU 2014:9).

GUSTAV SVENSSON is a Doctor of Law and Senior Lecturer in Social Law at the Department of Social Work, University of Gothenburg, Sweden. His research in recent years has focused on the decision-making process in social matters at social welfare committees and administrative courts in Sweden. His work has examined examples of social assistance, such as cases of voluntary help and cases of coercive care of children and abusers.

Child Welfare Removals by the State

1

CHILD WELFARE REMOVALS BY THE STATE—COMPLEX AND CONTROVERSIAL DECISIONS

Kenneth Burns, Tarja Pösö, and Marit Skivenes

INTRODUCTION

The aim of this book is to examine how child welfare systems in modern, democratic states proceed when deciding whether to remove vulnerable children from their homes. Removing a child from her parents is one of the most significant and sensitive decisions a nation-state can make. It is an intervention into the private family sphere that is highly controversial because it threatens individual freedoms, along with the privacy and autonomy of family life. This is particularly so when the state seeks to place a child in out-of-home care, either with or without the consent of parents and/or children, through some form of decision-making process. Article 8 of the European Convention on Human Rights (ECHR) states, as phrased by the legal scholar Kilkelly, that such interference in family life,

> can only be justified where it is accordance with law, in pursuit of a legitimate aim and necessary in a democratic society . . . applying the principle of proportionality in a way that requires that such decisions are supported by 'relevant and sufficient reasons.' (Kilkelly 2008, p. 297)

This is undoubtedly a strong right that has its genesis in sociocultural practices that sought to protect the family unit. Interventions by the child welfare system and the placement of children in out-of-home care are interventions and decisions that are necessary, because children's welfare, childhood, and future opportunities are understood to be at stake.

Historically, children have been treated as dependents within the family, rather than as individuals with their own independent rights (Archard 2004). There is now a movement toward child-centric societies, in which, from 1989 on, children have their own Convention on the Rights of the Child (CRC), and children in modern societies are increasingly gaining status as individuals. These developments are recognized and so well put in James and Prout's (1997) conceptual distinction between perceiving children as *becoming* versus regarding them as *being*. The increased child-centrism in societies is clearly an advancement but also a challenge. The new position of children is not only a challenge to the traditional conception of the family unit, but also for the relationship between the state and the family: Now there is an even stronger (and contested) expectation that there shall be a relationship between the state and the child.

The proportionality principle urges states and welfare services to be mindful not to remove a child too "easily" from the family: Decision-makers must make a judgment based on complex and often conflicting information as to whether the benefits for a child of being in care outweigh the impact of removal from her parents (Corby et al. 2012; Kilkelly 2008). Only when a certain threshold has been met, can the decision-making systems in a country assent to the removal of a child from her family. As we will learn in subsequent chapters, there are differences between countries, and sometime within countries, as to where this threshold is set, how it is defined, and who decides whether a state's intervention to remove a child is proportionate.

Child welfare and protection agencies assess children's circumstances in the family home and make recommendations—sometimes in conjunction with the wider family and community—on whether a removal from the family home is necessary. As we will see in subsequent chapters, countries have different decision-making processes and systems to decide upon child removals, but it is common for there to be some blend of social-administrative and legal decision-making systems. It is often courts or court-*like* decision-making bodies that make the final decision on whether, for how long, and under what conditions, a child is removed from her parents and home. In some countries, the courts are involved in only some of these decisions concerning removals, because these countries also have administrative, voluntary processes, which are mostly social-work-led, whereby parents—and in some countries, children—can agree to the placement of a child in out-of-home care without a court process. State interventions into the private family domain are decided within legal and political orders and traditions that are shaped by a country's policies, welfare state model, child welfare system, and children's "status" and rights within that society. We firmly believe these social, political, economic, and systemic contexts matter for why and how decisions are made.

Despite the removal of children from their families being one of the most important and intrusive powers of the state, there is a scarcity of knowledge and research about decision-making systems that decide upon the removals of children. In many countries, little or nothing is known about what happens behind the closed doors of *in camera* child welfare court proceedings and social-work-led administrative processes. Few official or media case reports are available; few written judgments are made public; and there has been little empirical research, making it hard to build a picture of practices and trends. This results in an undesirable lack of transparency in the exercise of one of the state's most far-reaching powers, and a dearth of an adequate knowledge base on which to base discussions about potential legal, administrative, practice, and policy reforms and improvements. The Council of Europe (2015) also recently have passed a resolution on the removal of children from their families (Resolution 2049 [2015]).

This book seeks to address this lacuna in the research literature by comprehensively exploring sociolegal decision-making in child welfare and protection processes at the *exact point* where a decision is made to remove a child into out-of-home care. The book examines the legal and social contexts underpinning child removal decision-making systems in seven European countries and in the United States, with a specific focus on the state of Massachusetts. The range of countries represented in the book covers the social democratic Nordic countries (Finland, Norway, and Sweden), the conservative corporatist countries (Germany and Switzerland), the neoliberal countries (United States, England, and Ireland) (cf. Arts and Gelissen 2002, p. 149), and their related child welfare systems. Table 1.1 outlines the child populations in these countries, ranging from 16 percent in Germany to 25 percent in England, Ireland, and the U.S. state of Massachusetts.

Table 1.1. Child Population by Country (age 0–17 years)

Country	Population	Child population (Percentage of total population, year)*
Ireland	4.59 million	1.15 million (25%, 2011)
Norway	5 million	1.12 million (22.4%, 2014)
Finland	5.4 million	1.07 million (18.5%, 2012)
Switzerland	8 million	1.4 million (17.5%, 2012)
Sweden	10 million	2 million (20%, 2013)
England	54 million	12 million (25%, 2011)
Germany	80.5 million	12.9 million (16%, 2012)
United States	308 million	74 million (21%, 2012)
United States (Massachusetts)	6.6 million	1.4 million (25%, 2012)

*All population figures rounded up/down.

The term *sociolegal* typically is understood as denoting the relationship between law and society. In our context we emphasize the combination of legal and social factors, as is evident in the interdisciplinary nature of these decision-making systems, based on both legal and social methods and knowledge bases. Child welfare is regulated by law and adheres to the principles of the rule of law and due process, but is anchored in social work practice and knowledge about children's needs and development. The sociolegal dimension is furthermore evident in the composition of decision-makers, who can include judges, experts on child welfare and development, other professionals, and even laypeople. The term *sociolegal* also highlights that although the decisions are of a legal nature, they have a variety of social consequences for children, families, and society in general.

We use the term *child removals* in this book to denote processes—either court, social work, and/or police led—that seek to adjudicate on whether a child needs to be removed from her family into alternative/substitute care outside of the immediate family. Related terms common in the wider literature and in some of the chapters in this book include: "care," "alternative care," "care order," "looked after," or "out-of-home care," as a result of these removal decisions. We focus only on the removals for child protection reasons that are in most countries regulated by child welfare legislation. This focus excludes removals related to juvenile justice, health, custody disputes, or security under different legislation for different ambitions. Our focus also largely excludes an examination of decision-making theory and an analysis of how decision-makers make decisions; rather, the unique contribution of this book is to provide an in-depth description and examination of the nature of the child removal systems in these eight countries.

The key questions that guide the analysis in this and subsequent chapters include: What types of decision-making systems are used when alternative care for a child is under consideration? Who are the key participants in child removal decision-making systems? Who are the decision-makers, what powers do they have, and how do they ensure that decisions are proportionate? To what extent do children and young people participate, either directly or indirectly? What threshold standards are used when deciding to remove a child from the family home? What safeguards are in place to protect the rights of all parties, while also ensuring that the child's welfare is paramount? How do these decision-making systems balance parental rights with the rights of the child? A particular emphasis of this book is also to document what we *do not know* about these child removal systems.

REMOVAL OF CHILDREN IN VARIOUS CHILD WELFARE SYSTEMS

The countries represented in this book have organized their child welfare systems in various different ways, and individual chapters will briefly examine the underpinning welfare systems; however, it is beyond the scope of this book to comprehensively describe these systems. Nonetheless, it is important to provide a framework to understand how the underpinning welfare system influences a state's approach to deciding upon the removal of children to out-of-home care and how reunifications with family are facilitated. Child welfare systems in modern states can crudely be categorized into two types (Gilbert et al. 2011a; Gilbert 1997); namely, risk oriented or service oriented. A risk-oriented system has a relatively high threshold for intervention and a focus on mitigating serious risks to children's health and safety (Gilbert et al. 2011a). The United States is a typical example of this approach. In risk-oriented systems, there are high barriers for interference in the private sphere; thus, these systems have high thresholds for intervention. In service-oriented systems, the aims are to promote healthy childhoods as well as to mitigate serious risks, with an emphasis on the prevention of harm (Skivenes 2011). Thus, the state provides early intervention services to children and families in at-risk situations to prevent escalation to more serious risk and future harm to the child. The major differences between these two systems are found in their underlying ideologies and the ways they address children who are at risk.

Service-oriented systems provide services to families and are based on a therapeutic view of rehabilitation in which it is possible for people to revise and improve their lifestyles and behaviors through the provision of adequate services and help. A basic principle is that the child welfare system should be part of a broader child welfare system that provides services to prevent more serious harm and, as a result, prevent out-of-home placements. The aims and motivation for removals are thus different than in a risk-oriented system, because interventions are in principle a temporary means to support the family. The intervention threshold for these systems is low. The goal of risk-oriented systems is not to provide services to prevent possible harm, but to intervene when there is serious risk of harm to a child; thus, the threshold for intervention is high, and the ultimate goal is to provide services leading to possible reunification. Norway, Sweden, and Finland are typical service-oriented systems, whereas England has been categorized (in its actual practice) as a risk-oriented system (Berridge 1997), even though its legislation (Children Act 1989) places a duty on statutory services to support vulnerable families without removing children (compulsorily), unless assistance has been offered (Spratt 2001; Parton and Berridge 2011; Stafford et al. 2012, p. 145; Tunstill et al. 2010). In practice, Ireland has operated a high-threshold, risk-orientated system that in principle, through its social policies and legislation, should be more service-orientated. Fundamental changes to the delivery of Irish child welfare services with the establishment of the new Child and Family Agency in 2014 should result in a shift toward a service-oriented system (see Child and Family Agency 2013, 2014); however, concerns exist about the resourcing and implementation of this transformation process (Buckley and Burns 2015). Switzerland is classified as a risk-oriented child welfare system due to its legalistic approach and lack of a "universal" system of services for children and families. Germany is a family-service oriented child welfare system (Wolf et al. 2011) with traditionalist family leanings adding to the service orientation (Gilbert et al. 2011a). This being said, recent developments show that child welfare systems are now increasingly incorporating elements from one another (Gilbert et al. 2011b). Furthermore, a child-centric orientation is evident in welfare and child welfare policies and legislation, in which children are regarded as individuals with independent rights and interests, evidenced, for example, by countries such as Norway, Finland, and Ireland amending their Constitutions to recognize these rights. The move toward a child-centric orientation is only at the early stages of evolution, but it will inevitably challenge the established focus on the family unit and adult-centric practices. This emerging child-centric orientation in child welfare systems, its underlying principles, and how these principles are operationalized by decision-makers, is expected to have an impact on how decision-making is undertaken and carried out.

Child welfare systems often are not seen in relation to welfare state models, although the state and nature of child welfare systems is connected with the welfare provisions in society in general (Pösö et al. 2014; Blomberg et al. 2012; Forsberg and Kröger 2010). The eight countries represented in this book can be categorized according to different welfare regimes (cf. Arts and Gelissen 2002; Aspalter 2011) as we have presented previously. Finland, Norway, and Sweden— social democratic welfare states—have tight welfare safety nets and offer numerous universal welfare services. The United Kingdom was categorized as a liberal welfare regime by Esping-Andersen (1990), but today, scholars note that it is only an approximation of this type of system (Aspalter 2011). The latter argument is supported in empirical testing of welfare states in which the United Kingdom was not categorized as a liberal welfare state, but rather as a radical or undefined type (Arts and Gelissen, 2002). Germany and Switzerland are both conservative welfare states with universal services and a moderate degree of decommodification (i.e., social welfare is a right-based service and the citizens have some independence from the market). They are grounded in employment-based insurance systems and consider families the vital providers of solidarity and services to family members (Esping-Andersen 1990).

Considering the welfare of children specifically, UNICEF has made an overall well-being index for high-income countries, measuring the situation for children on such variables as "material well-being," "health and safety," "education," "behavior and risks," and "housing and environment" (UNICEF 2013). The measurements have been undertaken three times (UNICEF 2007, 2010, 2013) and the results for these years show that Sweden, Norway, and Finland were among the top five countries to provide the most for children on the measured variables, followed by Germany, Switzerland, and Ireland. England is in the mid-category in providing for children's well-being, whereas the United States is toward the bottom of the league table. However, the most recent poverty report by UNICEF (2014) charts the dramatic deterioration in selected child well-being indicators in countries worst hit by the recession. Of the countries examined in this book, Sweden, Norway, and Switzerland were assessed as being least affected by the recession. Germany, Finland, the United Kingdom, and the United States were assessed as being moderately affected by the recession, and Ireland as most affected (UNICEF 2014, p. 14). Child poverty rates[1] in Ireland soared from 18 percent in 2008 to 28.6 percent in 2012 and the median incomes of households with children in Ireland were eroded to the same level as a full decade earlier.

A premise for this book is that different welfare state models, the economic health of a nation, and political and well-being arrangements for children and families influence their exposure to risk and social problems and their opportunities to receive services and help in vulnerable situations. Therefore, the welfare state and child welfare system helps ameliorate, or contributes to, the challenges families experience in parenting. Thus, families in each country who interact with decision-making systems when a state body is seeking to remove a child from her family and place her in alternative care will have had vastly different experiences of support and early-intervention. In our view, this is likely to influence not only the format and approach of the decision-making systems to decide upon a child's removal, but how removal decisions are made, the numbers of families who are under strain, the extent to which alternative solutions to prevent entry to care are resourced, and approaches to reunification after removal. Furthermore, the degree of child-centrism in a society, the prevailing attitudes of political and legal systems toward "the family" and "childhood," and whether these are expressed explicitly or implicitly through moral reasoning and normative claims, inform the culture and operation of child welfare decision-making systems.

SOCIAL WORK, COURT, AND COURT-LIKE DECISION-MAKING SYSTEMS

An underpinning principle for all child welfare systems in modern, democratic states is that children and parents have a right to family life and should be protected against arbitrary and unwarranted state interventions. A state's responsibility for children who are mistreated, neglected, or lack protection is delegated to the child welfare system and front-line child welfare workers, who are often social workers by training. They are responsible for assessing children's needs and risks to their welfare; providing advocacy, support, and intervention; and strengthening the connection between children and their families, communities, and community services. In a small number of cases, if it is considered necessary and proportionate and all other options are exhausted, child welfare workers may recommend that a child should be taken into care.

The guidelines for assessments, the criteria for risk, and the nature of child welfare practices differ significantly between countries (see, for example, Berrick et al. 2015); yet, it is these front-line assessments and decisions that initiate emergency removals, voluntary care by "consent," or some form of contested process in a court or court-like proceeding. There are two options to consider at this point of decision-making. Firstly, the child can remain within the home with state or community service and/or be kept under close supervision. Secondly, the child welfare system and/or community and family members that out-of-home care is required to protect a child. In the latter situations the case is then usually brought to some form of court or court-like decision-making body. Some countries have a social-work-led administrative system whereby parents can request or agree to voluntarily place a child, by consent, into alternative care. As subsequent chapters will show, there are significant differences between countries as to the format and operation of these "voluntary," administrative systems as well as to the length of time in such voluntary placements. A core achievement of this book is to describe and analyze these "voluntary" systems, and we find that a surprisingly large percentage of children are coming into state care through "voluntary" processes and very little is known about how they operate (see, for example, the Ireland, Finland, and Conclusion chapters for more detailed discussions on voluntary care). In particular, we raise some questions about the voluntariness of "voluntary" care through a discussion on the "soft coercion" of parents and children to participate with voluntary removal processes.

All countries have some form of court, or court-like, judicial system to make child removal decisions, this being a requirement when parents dispute the state's contention that a child should come into care. There are different legal systems in place, however, and an important distinction is made between the common law systems in which the court itself is the one making "laws"—judicial precedent—and the civil law systems, in which statutory laws are imperative. Norway, Finland, Germany, Switzerland, and Sweden belong to the latter system, whereas the United States, England, and Ireland belong to the common law system. The basic principles, fundamental legal concepts, and legal reasoning differ in the common law and civil law systems (Bogdan 2013; Schweppe 2002). Similarly, we can anticipate that the relationships between the judiciary and political systems will be quite different in these two systems, and this also has an impact on how system reforms and changes are developed and implemented. In civil law systems, changing the law is likely to influence the judiciary, whereas this is not as straightforward in common-law systems. Another complicating factor for how a child welfare court proceeding is handled relates to the location of the child welfare proceedings in the legal system: Child welfare belongs to public law or private law, and it may be regarded as an administrative or a civil issue. Different sets of logics and procedures will apply within different spheres of the judiciary, and this again will influence the child welfare proceedings.

In summary, the message we bring forward is that the context and setting for decision-making, that is, the institutional and organizational frameworks, matters, along with the decision-making model (or lack of thereof) and political-legal and practice-level cultures and normative platform. A considerable number of factors influence, and are of importance in, child welfare proceedings, and our position is that decision-making in removal proceedings must be understood within the political, institutional, and structural contexts in which it is undertaken.

DECISION-MAKING IN CHILD WELFARE: SUBJECTIVE AND INTERSUBJECTIVE PRACTICE MODELS

Decision-making in child welfare systems is complex and made with a high degree of uncertainty (cf. Mnookin 1973; Elster 1989; O'Sullivan 2011). In child welfare practice, decision-makers must take into account: multifaceted normative issues, a wide range of and various types of research knowledge, competing legal and human rights, the unique needs and interests of children and their parents, the consequences of parenting practices and maltreatment for the child later in adult life, multiple narratives and meanings attributed to children's behavior and parenting, the impact of poverty and structural issues on parenting, and the prioritization of scarce resources. All these issues, among many others, need to be considered, weighed against one another, reckoned with, and finalized in decisions.

The theoretical distinction between a subjective and an intersubjective decision-making model provides us with a conceptual framework to grasp some of the dynamics that take place in care order proceedings in courts. A subjective model of decision-making is based on the idea of the individual making decisions, after carefully considering and reviewing the case evidence, facts, and information. The "rational man model" or the "administrative man model" (Simon 1965) are two examples of this type of thinking. The intersubjective model of decision-making is based on the idea that rationality is to be found in the reasoning and argumentation between people, in the intersubjectivity with which communication provides us. In this perspective, rationality is to be found in the argumentation processes that are conducted (Alexy 1989). A deliberative model of decision-making is an example of this type of thinking (Eriksen & Weigård 2003). The basic premise for most decision-making practice models is that decisions should rest on good information regarding the contents of the case and the parties' situations, that possible choices of action and their consequences must be explored, and that possible results should be ranked in relation to overall goals. The deliberative model of decision-making underscores the importance of involving those concerned, children and parents in particular, in open and reasoned discussions. In child welfare, the overarching goal is the child's best interests, and when these interests remain for the most part undefined, the decision-making process is about finding out what a particular child's best interests might be.

Decision-making proceedings in child welfare systems are organized with more or less emphasis on the involvement of parents and children, and collaborative discussions as a method for developing solutions. Countries have introduced various methods to involve parents and children directly or indirectly via legal or other representatives. Some countries trust one decision-maker; others require several decision-makers. Some states have one judge to make decisions on involuntary removals; others use three-to-four-member panels comprising a judge, professional/expert, and/or a lay-person. Subsequent chapters will describe and examine the decision-making models or approaches that individual countries employ, and critically analyze the strengths and shortcomings of the present sociolegal decision-making model adjudicating on child removals.

CURRENT CHALLENGES FOR SOCIOLEGAL DECISION-MAKING MODELS

Sociolegal decision-making systems are not static systems; rather, they are constantly evolving over time. At the time of this writing, several challenges exist for these systems and make this book particularly topical. We address three major challenges here. First, the Council of Europe introduced new guidelines for child-friendly justice, approved by the Ministers of the Council of Europe. The guidelines aim

> to ensure that, in any such proceedings, all rights of children, among which the right to information, to representation, to participation and to protection, are fully respected with due consideration to the child's level of maturity and understanding and to the circumstances of the case. Respecting children's rights should not jeopardise the rights of other parties involved. (Council of Europe, 2011, p. 16)

These guidelines include recommendations on the use of child-friendly language and child-friendly methods to gather evidence from children. These guidelines should be implemented in care order proceedings and court-based decision-making in child welfare (Council of Europe 2011). The notions of child-friendly justice are similar to the emerging child-centric orientation in child welfare systems because they both emphasize the rights of children. Do we see any evidence yet of best practice in child-friendly justice in the various sociolegal decision-making models of child removals examined in this book? The literature demonstrates many weak points in the practices of children's views and wishes being taken into account in court-related child welfare decision-making (e.g.,

Cashmore and Parkinson 2007; Hill et al. 2007; Archard and Skivenes 2009; Vis and Fossum 2013; de Godzinsky 2014; Magnussen and Skivenes, 2015; Parkes et al. 2015). The systems of decision-making and their approaches to gathering, examining, and weighing information were built for adults. In child welfare, decisions do not only pertain to the adults, and there is increasing impetus and pressure to find ways to involve children in all aspects of decision-making. However, as subsequent chapters will demonstrate, although there is a broad spectrum of approaches concerning the involvement of children in these decision-making systems, a significant research gap remains in this area of practice.

Second, the analysis of child welfare systems in ten Western countries (Gilbert et al. 2011a) demonstrates that child welfare systems are expanding in all countries involved. The range of tasks and numbers of users of these services has increased during the last ten years. This expansion raises questions regarding the efficiency of the present systems and whether the growing numbers of child welfare referrals and interventions are improving children's welfare, particularly in the context of fiscal retrenchment and growing income inequality in certain countries. Indeed, professionals and institutions are challenged by the public, advocates, and politicians to make the "right" decisions for children in families—in a timely, transparent, and accountable manner. This should particularly apply to decisions that may restrict parental rights. Professional and social services' accountability is an ongoing priority for public policy. Although motives for accountability may start with cost-awareness and cost saving, they also include ethics-awareness (see, for example, Banks 2004). Eileen Gambrill (2011) argues that it is the ethical duty of child welfare practitioners to make the best possible decisions based on the best available knowledge. Evidence-based assessment and structured decision-making tools are increasingly playing an important role in present child welfare systems, which suggests that they address somehow the call for accountability. The courts play an important role in this: How do courts value various types of knowledge in the complex decisions of child removals? Consequently, it is important to gain an understanding of how different socio-legal decision-making models address accountability, including the somewhat thorny issue of the accountability of courts and judicial decision-makers, given their independence and resistance to regulation in some countries.

Third, due to the increasing number of migrating families and transnational families, the decision-making systems are challenged by families' and children's "right" to be a part of the nation-state's welfare state and child welfare system. In a recent analysis of eleven child welfare systems meeting migrant children and families, it was concluded that,

> The child welfare systems are at their strongest in protecting children and providing services to settled migrant communities—families and children who are documented and recognized by nation-state legislation and bureaucracy. However, the countries under study lack the ethos, policy,

and practice to effectively work with migrant children and families who do not meet those criteria. This is a major problem as those groups of children may be in an extremely vulnerable position because they or their parents are undocumented. (Barn et al. 2014, p. 274)

This is to say that there are some vulnerable groups of children, such as undocumented and unaccompanied children, whose needs are not fully met by welfare states and child welfare systems. Child welfare systems tend to be bound to the nation-states and related positions of children and families. Most legislation is also national and is poorly useable in situations in which children and families move across the national boundaries (Barn et al. 2014). For child welfare systems, the challenge is to rethink the role of the boundaries of nation-states and the rights of children and to make decisions in which the children's best interests are paramount.

STRUCTURE AND SCOPE OF THE BOOK

When state interventions in family life lead to a recommendation for the removal of a child, the systems that adjudicate on the state's recommendation must be transparent, robust, fair, and accountable, and they must include and weigh the views of all affected parties. The quality of child, family, and parental participation, professional assessments and training, legislative and policy frameworks, and the resourcing of these systems, all contribute to the legitimacy of the child welfare system. The increasing child-centeredness in societies in combination with public and political demands that the "correct" decisions must be reached when exercising this form of state power further emphasize the high expectations concerning legitimacy.

In this book we undertake a comprehensive examination of the formats, range of participants, powers, thresholds for removal of children into state care, statistical data, supporting social policies and legislation, and child-centeredness of these administrative, court, and court-like decision-making bodies. One of the contributions of this book is to describe, examine, and critique the decision-making systems at the *exact point* at which a decision is made regarding the removal of a child from the home. As a growing number of children come into state care, it is imperative that we know about, learn from, understand, and critique the bodies and systems that are empowered to make these decisions.

The genesis of the book, and the selection of its contributors, was a colloquium funded by the Norwegian Research Council held at the University of Bergen, Norway, followed by a European Science Foundation Explorative Workshop on Socio-Legal Models of Care Order Proceedings in Europe at University College Cork, Ireland. These colloquia sought to lay the foundations for the establishment of a multidisciplinary network of European researchers in this field. A key finding of these colloquia was that there was very little up-to-date written material on the decision-making systems in each country, which limited knowledge sharing, comparisons, and opportunities to learn from good practices. To achieve our aim of a comprehensive analysis of these decision-making systems, we have intentionally sought to limit authors by excluding discussions of earlier decision-making processes (e.g., case conferences and family welfare conferences), as well as debates on outcomes and processes after the decision to remove a child [or not] from the family home has been made. Due to the comprehensive, global analysis of welfare systems undertaken in the Gilbert et al. book (2011a), authors were asked to include only limited contextual information on their welfare state and child welfare system. Therefore, this book should be read in conjunction with the analyses in Gilbert et al. (2011a) and Skivenes et al. (2015). A series of short supporting country-profile videos, funded by the Irish Research Council, are available to view online at:http://www.ucc.ie/en/appsoc/cs/videoresources/ccpsvideos/.

A limitation of this book is its overemphasis on Northern European countries. Although the comprehensive focus on these decision-making systems is a strength, a limitation of this approach is that authors had limited space to describe their welfare state in detail and present their own empirical research findings.

Finally, the challenges with terminology should not be overlooked in any cross-country analysis. In an analysis like ours, the country practices and rationalities of child removal are presented in the English language. There is good reason to be mindful of actual or perceived loss of meaning and inaccurate messages due to translation. The translations of the terminology of child removal in the countries using Finnish, Norwegian, German, Swedish, and French languages include, unintentionally, the Anglophone system of child removals—terms related to *child protection* ideology rather than *child welfare/family service* ideology—because the terms used in those countries are the ones available in English (see Pösö 2014). Even within the Anglophone systems, however, terms such as child welfare do not travel problem-free across borders (Thoburn 2007; Stafford et al. 2012). In fact, this book originally set out to explore care order decision-making. Defining a "care order" proved, however, to be a considerable challenge for translation and comparison purposes. A "care order" is a particularly European, Anglophone concept and is most commonly used in the way the Anglophone European countries suggest: It refers to court-ordered removals of children from their birth family. The court is the decision-making body, guided by common law, and there is an assumption that the state makes these decisions against a family's wishes. The term "care order" is not used to describe the removals of children in the United States (cf. Berrick 2011; Križ et al. in this book). We find that the Swedish and the Finnish chapters make the distinction between voluntary and involuntary care orders, which differs from the English and Irish use of the term. Furthermore, care orders in the Nordic countries are not necessarily ordered by the courts and decided by judges, but rather by court-like bodies with a team of decision-makers including judges, lay people, and experts on child welfare and development. Therefore, instead of the term "care orders," the book addresses the removals of children. Using the word "removal" makes us more sensitive to the translation of the countries' specific terminology and to the width of sociolegal decision-making systems across these countries. The following country chapters are structured with the Nordic countries appearing first, starting with Finland, followed by Norway and Sweden. Germany is next, then Switzerland, Ireland, and England. The United States, with a particular emphasis on the state of Massachusetts is the last of the country chapters. In the concluding chapter we draw together the findings and key tendencies from the country chapters.

NOTE

1 UNICEF (2014, p. 9) calculated child poverty changes between 2008 and 2012 by using a "fixed reference point, anchored to the relative poverty line in 2008, as a benchmark against which to assess the absolute change in child poverty over time" rather than using a relative poverty line each year.

REFERENCES

Archard, D. and Skivenes, M. (2009). "Hearing the Child." *Child and Family Social Work*, 14(4), 391–399.

Archard, D. (2004). *Children: Rights & Childhood* (2nd ed.). New York and London, United Kingdom: Routledge.

Arts, W. and Gelissen, J. (2002). "Three Worlds of Welfare Capitalism or More? A State-of-the-Art Report," *Journal of European Social Policy*, 12 (2), 137–158.

Aspalter, C. (2011). "The Development of Ideal-Typical Welfare Regime Theory," *International Social Work*, 54 (6), 735–750.

Banks, S. (2004). *Ethics, Accountability and the Social Professions*. Basingstoke, United Kingdom: Palgrave.

Barn, R., Križ, K., Pösö, T., and Skivenes, M. (2014). "Migrant Children and Child Welfare Systems: A Contested Challenge." In Skivenes, M., Barn, R., Križ, K., and Pösö, T. (Eds.), *Child Welfare Systems and Migrant Children*. New York, NY: Oxford University Press, 263–280.

Berrick, J., Peckover, S., Pösö, T., and Skivenes, M. (2015). "The Formalized Framework for Decision-Making in Child Protection Care Orders: A Cross-Country Analysis." *Journal of European Social Policy*, 24 (4), 366–378.

Berrick, J. (2011). "Trends and Issues in the U.S. Child Welfare System." In Gilbert, N., Parton, N., and Skivenes, M. (Eds.), *Child Protection Systems:*

International Trends and Emerging Orientations. New York, NY: Oxford University Press, 17–35.

Berridge, D. (1997). "England: Child Abuse Reports, Responses and Reforms." In Gilbert, N. (Ed.), *Combatting Child Abuse: International Perspectives and Trends.* New York, NY: Oxford University Press, 72–104.

Blomberg, H., Kroll, C., and Meeuwisse, A. (2012). "Nordic Social Workers' Assessments of Child Welfare Problems and Interventions: A Common Model in Child Welfare?" *European Journal of Social Work,* 16 (3), 311–326, http://dx.doi.org/10.1080/13691457.2012.685700.

Buckley, H. and Burns, K. (2015). "Child Welfare and Protection in Ireland: Déjà Vu All Over Again." In Christie, A., Featherstone, B., Quin, S., and Walsh, T. (Eds.), *Social Work in Ireland: Continuities and Changes.* Basingstoke, United Kingdom: Palgrave Macmillan.

Cashmore, J. and Parkinson, P. (2007). "What Responsibility Do Courts Have to Hear Children's Voices?" *International Journal of Children's Rights,* 15(1), 43–60.

Children Act (1989). *Children Act 1989.* The National Archives. Available at: http://www.legislation.gov.uk/ukpga/1989/41/contents

Child and Family Agency. (2014). *Tusla, Child and Family Agency Corporate Plan 2015–2017,* http://www.tusla.ie/uploads/news/Tusla_Corporate_Plan_2015_-_2017.pdf. Accessed June 17, 2015. Dublin: Child and Family Agency.

Child and Family Agency. (2013). *Suite of Policy and Guidance Documents for the Child and Family Agency.* http://www.childandfamilyresearch.ie/publications/policy-practice. Accessed February 5, 2014. Dublin, Ireland: Child and Family Agency.

Corby, B., Shemmings, D., and Wilkins, D. (2012). *Child Abuse: An Evidence Base for Confident Practice.* Maidenhead, United Kingdom: Open University Press.

Council of Europe (2015). *Social Services in Europe: Legislation and Practices on the Removal of Children from Their Families in Council of Europe Member States,* http://assembly.coe.int/nw/xml/XRef/Xref-DocDetails-EN.asp?FileID=21679&lang=EN. Accessed January 29, 2016. Strasbourg: Council of Europe.

Council of Europe (2011). *Guidelines of the Committee of Ministers of the Council of Europe on Child-Friendly Justice.* http://www.coe.int/t/dghl/standardsetting/childjustice/. Accessed August 20, 2014. Strasbourg: Council of Europe.

De Godzinsky, V-M. (2014). *Lapsen etu ja osallisuus hallinto-oikeuksien päätöksissä* [The best interest of the child and the child's right to participate in administrative court proceedings]. Reports 267. Helsinki, Finland: Oikeuspoliittinen tutkimuslaitos.

Elster, J. (1989). *Solomonic Judgements: Studies in the Limitations of Rationality.* Cambridge, United Kingdom: Cambridge University Press.

Esping-Andersen, G. (1990). *The Three Worlds of Welfare Capitalism.* Princeton, NJ: Princeton University Press.

Forsberg, H. and Kröger, T. (Eds.). (2010). *Social Work and Child Welfare Politics. Through Nordic Lenses.* Bristol, United Kingdom: The Policy Press.

Gilbert, N. (Ed.). (1997). *Combatting Child Abuse—International Perspectives and Trends*. New York, NY: Oxford University Press.

Gilbert, N., Parton, N., and Skivenes, M. (Eds.). (2011a). *Child Protection Systems: International Trends and Emerging Orientations*. New York, NY: Oxford University Press.

Gilbert, N., Parton, N., and Skivenes. M. (2011b). "Changing Patterns of Response and Emerging Orientations." In Gilbert, N., Parton, N., and Skivenes, M. (Eds.), *Child Protection Systems: International Trends and Emerging Orientations*. New York, NY: Oxford University Press, 243–258.

Gambrill, E. (2011). "Evidence-based Practice and the Ethics of Discretion." *Journal of Social Work* 11(1), 26–48. doi: 10.1177/1468017310381306.

Hill, M., Lockyer, A., and Stone, F. (Eds.). (2007). *Youth Justice and Child Protection*. London, United Kingdom: Jessica Kingsley.

James, A. and A. Prout. (1997). *Constructing and Reconstructing Childhood*. London, United Kingdom: Falmer Press.

Kilkelly, U. (2008). *Children's Rights in Ireland: Law, Practice and Policy*. Sussex: Tottel Publishing.

Magnussen, A-M and Skivenes, M. (2015). "The Child's Opinion and Position in Care Order Proceedings: An Analysis of Judiciary Discretion in the County Boards Decision-making." *International Journal of Children's Rights*, 23(4), 705–723.

Mnookin, R. H. (1973). "Foster Care: In Whose Best Interest?" *Harvard Educational Review*, 43(4): 599–638.

O'Sullivan, T. (2011). *Decision-Making in Social Work*. Basingstoke, United Kingdom: Palgrave.

Parton, N. and Berridge, D. (2011). "Child Protection in England." In Gilbert, N., Parton, N., and Skivenes, M. (Eds.), *Child Protection Systems—International Trends and Orientations*. New York, NY: Oxford University Press, 60–88.

Parkes, A., Shore, C., O'Mahony, C., and Burns, K. (2015). "The Right of the Child to Be Heard? Professional Experiences of Child Care Proceedings in the Irish District Court." *Child and Family Law Quarterly*, 27 (4), 423–444.

Pösö, T., Hestbæk, A. D., and Skivenes, M. (2014). "Child Protection Systems in the Danish, Finnish and Norwegian Welfare States—Time for a Child Centric Approach?" *European Journal of Social Work*, 17(4): 475–490. **DOI**:10.1080/ 13691457.2013.829802

Pösö, T. (2014). "Translation as a Knowledge Transformation Practice—The Ambiguous Case of Presenting Finnish Child Welfare in English." *European Journal of Social Work*, 17(5): 616–626.

Simon, H. (1965). "The Logic of Rational Decision," *The British Journal for the Philosophy of Science*, 16 (63), 169–186.

Skivenes, M. (2011). "Norway: Towards a Child-Centric Perspective." In Gilbert, N., Parton, N., and Skivenes, M. (Eds.), *Child Protection*

Systems—International Trends and Orientations. New York, NY: Oxford University Press, 154–182.

Spratt, T. (2001). "The Influence of Child Protection Orientation on Child Welfare Practice," *British Journal of Social Work,* 31(6), 933–954.

Stafford, A., Parton, N., Vincent, S., and Smith, C. (2012). *Child Protection Systems in the United Kingdom—A Comparative Analysis.* London, United Kingdom: Jessica Kingsley.

Tunstill, J., Aldgate, J., and Thoburn, J. (2010). "Promoting and Safeguarding the Welfare of Children: A Bridge Too Far?" *Journal of Children's Services,* 5 (3), 14–24.

UNICEF (2007). Innocenti Report Card 7: *Child Poverty in Perspective—An Overview of Child Well-being in Rich Countries.* Available at: http://www. unicef-irc.org/publications/pdf/rc7_eng.pdf

UNICEF (2010). Innocenti Report Card 9: *The Children Left Behind.* Available at: http://www.unicef-irc.org/files/documents/d-3796-The-Children-Left-Behind-.pdf

UNICEF (2013). Innocenti Report Card 11: *Child Well-being in Rich Countries— A Comparative Review.* Available at: http://www.unicef.org.uk/Images/ Campaigns/FINAL_RC11-ENG-LORES-fnl2.pdf

UNICEF (2014). Innocenti Report Card 12: *Children of the Recession: The Impact of the Economic Crisis on Child Well-being in Rich Countries.* Retrieved November 4, 2014 from: http://www.unicef-irc.org/publications/series/16.

Vis, S. and Fossum, S. (2013). "Representation of Children's Views in Court Hearings about Custody and Parental Visitations—A Comparison between What Children Wanted and What the Courts Ruled." *Children and Youth Services Review,* 35(12), 2101–2109.

2

REMOVALS OF CHILDREN IN FINLAND

A MIX OF VOLUNTARY AND INVOLUNTARY DECISIONS

Tarja Pösö and Raija Huhtanen

INTRODUCTION

In a recent cross-country analysis of child welfare systems (Gilbert et al. 2011), Finnish child welfare is seen to belong to the welfare and family service model, with an emerging focus on children's rights in the system. It shares many principles with other Nordic countries—such as universal welfare services and benefits for children and families to support children's upbringing and education. In Finland, child protection services are by law a part of the social services to which children and families are entitled and which the municipalities are obliged to provide. Most of the child protection services are voluntary in-home services, which aim to support the parents and children in their everyday environments. The removals of children from their homes comprise only a fraction of the array of child protection services.

In short, decision-making in the Finnish child protection system could be described as possessing the following features: On the one hand, the majority of child protection decisions are about voluntary services provided to support children and families, resting on social work discretion; on the other, the decision-making also includes involuntary measures of social control, which are treated as administrative judicial matters by the administrative courts. The removals of children out of their homes could belong to either decision-making approach.

This chapter describes in more detail the distinctive mix of voluntary and involuntary measures and the character of the court and its decision-making rationale in Finland, a country of 5.4 million inhabitants, including 1 million children under the age of eighteen years. The first sections describe three types of out-of-home removals of children and then focus on care order decision-making, first in the social welfare agencies and then in the regional administrative courts. The descriptive section is followed by a chart of the numbers of children and decisions made in the child protection system for removal in the period between 2008 and 2013. The latter sections of the chapter highlight the tensions and critical tendencies in the Finnish decision-making system.[1]

THREE TYPES OF REMOVALS

Since the early 1980s Finnish child welfare legislation has recognized three different types of removals of children out of their homes: as part of in-home services, as an emergency measure, or as a result of care order.[2]

In-home services constitute the core of the child protection system and are widely used. They should always be given the first priority and other measures such as care orders should be introduced only in case the in-home services are not relevant. In order to gain in-home services, the child's need for child protection services should be assessed. This assessment is initiated either by a child welfare notification or by the child's or parents' request for child protection services. The variety of in-home services is wide. They may include family work, financial support, peer-support families, counseling, and intensive youth work, among many other forms of support. In-home services also may include out-of-home placement of the child or, preferably, the whole family (family rehabilitation, family assessment).

Removals as part of in-home services are carried out when there is a reason to think that they are needed to support the family and the child. The relevance of the removal should be assessed every three months. As in all the in-home services, the removal of the child under this paragraph is based on the consent of the custodians and the child (twelve years of age or older). The decision is made by a social worker.

Children (and their families) are placed in residential institutions or foster families as part of in-home services. These substitute homes also serve other types of removals. If the child is placed as part of in-home services, however, the residential institution is not allowed to carry out any restrictive measures against the child as is the case in the two other types of removals. Further, the parents (custodians)[3] keep full custody over the child during this type of placement. This type of placement also can be used for after-care services to which the children are entitled after they have been in care. This option is also available to children who are older than eighteen years.

The second type of removal is an *emergency placement*, which is introduced if the child is in urgent need of protection and alternative care. An emergency placement decision is valid for thirty days. The decision-maker has to be a social worker employed by the local authority either in social welfare or emergency social services. A social work manager can make a decision to continue the emergency placement for another period of thirty days. The maximum time for an emergency placement is thus sixty days. When making the decision, the opinions of the parents and child should be solicited; such consultation may only be waived in cases of serious emergency or of special conditions. The administrative court makes an emergency placement decision only on the appeal of a parent or a child twelve years of age or older. The legal implications of the emergency care order are similar to those of a care order and thus they differ considerably from removals carried out as part of in-home services.

The third type of removal is a *care order*. A care order decision should be considered only if the in-home services are not relevant or appropriate (condition number one) and if the child's health or development is at risk of being seriously endangered (condition number two). The endangerment may be due to lack of care or other circumstances in which the child is being brought up; or due to the child seriously endangering his/her health or development by the abuse of intoxicants, by committing an illegal act other than a minor offense, or by any other comparable behavior. The third condition for the care order and related alternative care is that it should serve the child's best interest (condition number three). The principle of the child's best interest, as defined by legislation, covers a wide array of children's rights to caring relationships and rights to participate in decisions concerning themselves (see more about the criteria for care orders in Pösö 2011).

The care order is meant to be temporary with the aim of family reunification. The child welfare legislation does not recognize any permanent placement; yet, it is known that many children stay in care for all of their childhood. The care order implicates shared custodianship between the custodians and the social welfare authorities. The social welfare authorities have the right "to decide on the child's whereabouts and care, upbringing, supervision and other care and the instruction and health care necessary for the provision of these" (Child Welfare Act 417/2007). Social welfare authorities should cooperate with the parents as much as possible in order to support the child's best interests in care. While the child is in care, however, the authorities have the right to restrict contact between the parents and child. Other restrictive measures are possible as well, and they are based on decisions, which, in general, may be appealed.

Similar to the removal as part of in-home services and emergency placements, children may be placed into residential care, foster homes, or other relevant substitute homes as a result of a care order. In 2014 (on a set day), 53 percent of children in care were in foster care (of which 13 percent were kin placements) (Lastensuojelu 2014, 5). Previously more than half of the children in care had been in residential care and professional family homes. Due to the change of legislation in 2012, foster care should now always be considered as the first option (Pösö and Laakso 2014). The implications of this change are now visible in the placement profile.

Given that the decisions contained in care orders legally and socially comprise the most important type of removals, we will describe this decision-making process in detail. We first will present the preparations for a care order decision on the municipal level and the decision-making process in the cases of voluntary care orders. We then will present the decision-making process in the administrative courts, which decide on involuntary care orders and appeals against voluntary care orders. We are aware of the problems inherent in translation (see the introduction of this book) and that the term "voluntary care order" might not travel well across borders. Nevertheless, we have decided to remain faithful to the Finnish terminology and to use the term "care order" (huostaanotto) to cover both voluntary and involuntary care orders, which have the same legal implications for the child's and family's rights.

CARE ORDER DECISIONS IN THE SOCIAL WELFARE AGENCIES

In general, the Child Welfare Act (417/2007) describes the decision-making process in child protection. The Act is interrelated with many other acts and should be read only in conjunction with them. The Finnish Constitution sets the principles of human rights and equality, and the Act on the Status and Rights of Social Welfare Clients (812/2000) sets the rights of the service-user for good client-centered service in social welfare; further, the Act of Administration (434/2003) describes the norms of "good public administration," which all statutory child welfare decisions should follow. This set of legislation requires the public authorities, such as social workers, to provide good and equal services and to practice transparent and well-documented decision-making. It also gives service-users the right to good service and administration. Children are seen as any other service-users, with the distinction that they should have an additional right to protection.

Child protection decision-making has gone through some major changes recently. Prior to the present Child Welfare Act (2007), introduced into practice in 2008, the decisions regarding care orders were made only on the municipal level. The major decision-makers were social workers and social welfare boards, politically chosen lay-organizations among local authorities, very similar to the local social welfare boards in Sweden (see Svensson and Höjer in this book). The courts were involved if there were formal appeals. In addition, involuntary care order decisions had to be submitted to administrative courts for approval. One of the main objectives of the present Child Welfare Act (2007) was to reform the decision-making process in order to improve a child's and his/her parent's legal protection. Municipal social welfare boards were considered to be lacking in legal knowledge as well as expertise in child welfare. Moreover, dependency on municipal resources was likely, at least in some cases, to endanger the impartiality of the decision-making of the boards. (Hallituksen esitys 252/2006, 95). The present Act extensively re-regulates the decision-making process and, related to it, the participatory and procedural rights of the child and the custodian.

Care orders are meant to be the intervention of last resort and they may be carried out only if no other measure is applicable. In addition to the delivery of in-home services, the preparatory process prior to actual care order decision-making includes negotiations with the child, with the parents, and with their close personal network. There are relatively few formal regulations or professional assessment schemes concerning how the preparatory work should be done together with the child, parents/custodians, and other close people. It is, however, stipulated that there should always be two professionals working with the case during the preparatory process. The Act requires multiprofessional views to be present as well as the views of individuals in the close personal network. Furthermore, there should be a plan to present the aims for alternative care and the placement should be chosen to meet the aims for a care order, prepared together with the child and parents if possible.

The Child Welfare Act emphasizes a child's right to be heard throughout the child protection process. According to the Act, the child's wishes and views must be ascertained and taken into account in a way that is "appropriate for the child's age and level of development." In addition, the Act requires that children aged twelve years or older must be given an opportunity to express their views in matters affecting them. The minimum age is quite low compared with many other administrative law matters in which the corresponding age is fifteen years. When aged twelve years or older, the children are considered competent to legally represent themselves separately and parallel with their custodians; their opinion influences the care order decision in the same way as that of the custodians'.

The child, twelve years of age or older (but also younger children if appropriate) and custodians have to be heard formally in a "hearing" and consulted about the care order and placement as part of the preparatory process. Hearings are a common practice in other fields of public administration as well, with the aim of guaranteeing that the persons in question have the right to express their opinion about the matter at hand, and that they have the right to access all the material the public authorities have regarding the case. A hearing provides the formal forum for the child and custodians/parents to express their view about the relevance of the care order and the placement. The hearing may take place as a face-to-face meeting or through exchange of documents. The various parties are allowed to have legal representation during the hearing process.

In the event that the custodians and a child of twelve years of age or older do not oppose the care order and the placement, the decision is made by the leading authority in child protection. In many municipalities, the leading authority refers to the social work manager/team leader. After this decision, the child is "in care." The custodians, parents, and child retain the right to appeal to the administrative court.

The legal consequences of the voluntary care order are the same as for an involuntary care order; only the decision-making body differs. In general, the share of voluntary care orders is estimated to be more than three-quarters of care orders. (Heino 2009; see also the fifth section in this chapter). In cases of involuntary care orders, the social worker submits "an application for care order" to the administrative court, including all the preparatory material and the documents of the hearing.

CARE ORDER PROCEEDINGS IN ADMINISTRATIVE COURTS

Regional administrative courts play an important role in the Finnish child protection system as they decide at first instance on the involuntary taking of a child into care and related placement in alternative care. The role of the Supreme Administrative Court is that of an appellate authority. Due to the position of administrative courts in the Finnish legal system, compared with that of general courts of law deciding civil and criminal matters, their task is to make decisions about disputes that fall within the sphere of public law. These mainly concern appeals against administrative decisions of public authorities. The administrative court's jurisdiction also covers administrative litigation over disputes between a public authority and individuals.

A regional administrative court usually consists of three members. In child protection cases, they would include two legally trained judges and an expert member who usually represents expertise in social work, psychology, or education and who serves only part-time. The work of professional judges covers all the issues of the administrative courts' jurisdiction and, therefore, there is no specialization, such as in child protection matters. The responsibility for preparing cases for main hearings or for decisions upon presentation belongs to the referendaries of the court, who usually are legally trained as well.

Care order proceedings may be initiated in a regional administrative court either on application by a municipal social worker as described in the previous section or on appeal by a child aged twelve years or older or his/her custodian/parent. The right to appeal belongs to a wider group of people than the right to oppose the care order: the noncustodial parent, for example, has the right to appeal, but only the custodial parent's opposition is judicially effective, which is to say that it transfers the decision-making power from a social worker to a court. In practice, administrative courts deal more with involuntary care order applications than appeals against voluntary care orders.

In regional administrative courts, the procedures for involuntary care order proceedings (first-hand decisions), on the one hand, and voluntary care order proceedings (appeals), on the other, are nearly identical. The differences are more procedural than substantial, concerning, for instance, the role of the public party (the municipality) in the proceedings. That is why we describe these proceedings in parallel.

Investigating the case

The procedure followed by administrative courts must satisfy the requirements of a fair trial laid down in the Constitution of Finland (1999) and the European Convention on Human Rights (ECHR). These include, inter alia, the right to be heard and the right to receive a reasoned decision. The procedure is regulated in more detail by the Administrative Judicial Procedure Act (586/1996).

When dealing with a case an administrative court is responsible for its investigation and for the lawfulness of the decision. It is under a general obligation to actively conduct the procedure and to obtain evidence and factual information also on its own initiative (*the investigation principle*). The court's reasoning is not bound by the demands, claims, admissions, or repudiations of the parties in the same way as it is in civil disputes in general courts of law. In administrative matters the public party (e.g., a municipality) is perceived to have a superiority of power as compared with the private party (e.g., a custodian and/ or a child). Its superior position is based on several factors, usually including expertise in legal and administrative issues and broader access to government-held data and information (Mäenpää 2012, 200–201). This also applies to child protection cases. In consequence, administrative courts are required to balance the advantage of the social welfare authority by actively obtaining evidence in favor of the child's and/or the parents' interests if that evidence is not presented by the private parties themselves (*the equality of arms principle, the fair balance principle*).

The involuntary care order procedure in a regional administrative court is based on the factual information produced in the application by municipal social workers (the criteria for care order: see section 2 in this chapter). According to the Child Welfare Act, the application must include, inter alia, justifications for the demand that the child be taken into care and placed in alternative care and a description of the place of alternative care, including a variety of reports prepared by social workers or other professionals as described in the section above. The evidence provided in the application does not, however, prevent the court from also taking into account other relevant information presented to it or obtained by it during the proceedings (Aer 2012, 282).

If the evidence presented by the parties is insufficient, the court shall inform them of the additional evidence needed. The court also may ask for information from relevant authorities or hear witnesses or experts. There are, however, certain restrictions on this, due to confidentiality and the private nature of the matter. For example, the child and the custodians are not obliged to produce information about their private or family life, even if they oppose the care order proposed by social workers (Aer 2012, 287). In any case, when making a decision to take a child into care, the court must make sure that the requirements for the decision are satisfied; namely, that the child's health or development is seriously endangered. The causes of the endangering are less important because it is not the guilt but the child's best interest that is decisive for the care order.

Hearing the parties of the proceedings

In care order proceedings, the child and the custodians are the primary parties to be heard. The court may hear other private parties, too; for instance, the person responsible for the care and upbringing of the child (e.g., the child's grandparent). In order to support the child's participation and legal representation in care order proceedings, the court may appoint a guardian[4] and/or a legal advisor for the child. A guardian's task is to deputize for the custodian and represent the child if the custodian is unable to supervise the child's interests without prejudice, and the designation of a guardian is necessary to safeguard the interests of the child. In a typical case, the child is under twelve years of age. If, on the other hand, the child has reached the age of twelve years and exercises the right to be heard alone, she or he may need a legal advisor. Administrative courts have, however, thus far seldom appointed guardians or legal advisors in care order proceedings[5]. Legal advice for the child and the custodians is available through the public legal aid; the cost for advice is income-related.

The court also is obliged to hear the municipality responsible for arranging child protection. This is usually a social worker who represents the municipality in question. In Finland, the public authority is not usually considered to have its own rights to defend in administrative–judicial proceedings. Procedurally, it is a party, but it is bound by the principles of legality and objectivity as well as by the obligation to protect the general interest. It must act in a detached and impartial manner in the judicial procedure. For instance, it must provide all the evidence at its disposal even if it might be compromising for the authority's case (Mäenpää 2012, 200–201). This applies also to care order proceedings. Yet, proceedings concerning involuntary care orders are of special interest here, due to their distinctive nature. The fact that the procedure is initiated on application by a public authority and not on appeal by a private party, might emphasize the party role of the public authority as an applicant defending its own rights. There is, indeed, certain empirical evidence supporting this hypothesis (de Godzinsky 2012, 82; Heinonen and Hiitola 2009), but unfortunately the research on the issue is thus far barely sufficient to draw any conclusions.

Proceedings in administrative courts are generally based on written statements but the court also may decide on an oral hearing. An oral hearing is conducted if the private party so requests, or the court conducts it for the purposes of establishing the facts of the case. The hearing in care order proceedings is usually closed (in camera), because of the confidentiality of the matter. Insofar as the court's decision identifies the persons concerned, secrecy applies to it as well. In recent years, administrative courts have conducted oral hearings in ever-increasing numbers, and this particularly concerns care order proceedings. Nowadays, an oral hearing is conducted in approximately one in every three care order proceedings, which is more than in any other proceedings in the administrative courts. Indeed, 77 percent of all oral hearings conducted by regional administrative courts in 2013 concerned child protection cases (de Godzinsky 2012, 77–79; Hallinto-oikeuksien toimintakertomus 2013, 15).

Presumably, the frequency of oral hearings depends, at least to some extent, on the use of legal representatives and counsels, which has become more common in care order proceedings. Legal representatives and counsels most often are used by parents, especially by mothers, but even the public party (the municipality) resorts to them more and more frequently (de Godzinsky 2012, 87–88). In 2011, it was prescribed by law that only lawyers are permitted to act as representatives and counsels of private parties in care order proceedings. The reason was the demand for legal expertise to safeguard the legal protection of a child and his/her custodian (Hallituksen esitys 318/2010, 18).

In order to protect children from serious conflicts, the Child Welfare Act confirms certain restrictions regarding hearing them in oral proceedings. For instance, a child may be heard in person only if he or she consents to it. In practice, children aged twelve years or older often participate directly in these hearings, whereas younger children are heard only exceptionally, and when this happens it is indirectly through guardians. Accordingly, especially small children are estimated to be at risk of remaining invisible in care order proceedings (de Godzinsky 2012, 93–94, 138–139; Note 5 this chapter). Nevertheless, de Godzinsky's (2012, 82–83) interviews with judges suggest that oral hearings provide a child and the parent an opportunity to describe in their own words the conditions at home and in the family. Consequently, and especially because the applications by social workers sometimes include little evidence for the family, oral hearings are found to act as an important guarantee of procedural fairness in involuntary care order proceedings.

The decision of the court

With regard to involuntary care orders, the regional administrative court has two options for its decision: either to accept the application by social workers or to dismiss it. When accepting the application the court is obliged to confirm the place of alternative care for the child. In 2013, there were 608 applications, of which 579 (95 percent) were accepted and only 29 (5 percent) dismissed (Suomen virallinen tilasto: Hallinto-oikeuksien käsittelemät asiat 2005–2013). Regarding voluntary care orders, the administrative court may, on appeal by a parent, for example, uphold the decision of a social worker or overrule it. It also may return the case to the social worker (if, for example, the care order is poorly justified) or dismiss an appeal without considering its merits (if, for example, the appeal has not been lodged within the prescribed time limit). In most cases (nearly 99 percent in 2013) the social worker's decision is upheld by the administrative court (ibid). This may generally prove the lawfulness of the decisions made at the local level. Yet, one must be very careful when drawing any conclusions, because, on the whole, relatively few appeals (fewer than 100 in 2013) are lodged against voluntary care order decisions.

The decision of the regional administrative court concerning a care order may be appealed to the Supreme Administrative Court. The right to appeal belongs to a child aged twelve years or older, a child's parent and custodian, or a person in charge of the care and upbringing of the child during or immediately before the preparation of the case (e.g., the grandparent). The municipality concerned also may lodge an appeal if the regional administrative court has dismissed the application or overruled the decision of the social worker.

The judicial review exercised by the Supreme Administrative Court is focused on whether the decision made by the regional administrative court conforms to the law. According to the investigation principle, the court is responsible for comprehensively scrutinizing the contested decision. As part of this responsibility, it is required to review all evidence available and to examine the facts and considerations on which the decision is based (Mäenpää 2012, 201). In 2013, there were 201 care order proceedings in the Supreme Administrative Court, in most (93 percent) the decision of the regional administrative court was upheld (Suomen virallinen tilasto: Korkeimman hallinto-oikeuden käsittelemät asiat 1991–2013).

According to the Child Welfare Act, child protection cases must be processed as urgent by the administrative courts. In 2013, care order proceedings took 5.3 months on average in the regional administrative courts and 10.9 months in the Supreme Administrative Court (from the arrival of the application/appeal to the decision-making of the court). The length of the proceedings has been criticized because it is in the child's interests to decide these matters without undue delay. There might also be the need to place the child outside his/her home while waiting for the court's decision. To shorten the total duration of the proceedings the Supreme Administrative Court has proposed that a leave should be required for appeal in the highest instance in child protection cases (Korkeimman hallinto-oikeuden esitys oikeusministeriölle, 17.9.2013). If that is realized, only the most legally complex cases will be decided by the Supreme Administrative Court.

According to the ECHR, the European Court of Human Rights may receive applications from any person, organization, or group of individuals claiming to be the victim of a violation by a member state of the rights set forth in the convention. Finland ratified the ECHR in 1990. Since then, the Court has given six judgments concerning involuntary care of children in Finland. In five judgments, it has found a violation of Article 8 (the right to respect for private and family life). One case, *K. and T. v Finland* (2001), was dealt with twice by the Court, first by the Chamber and then by the Grand Chamber of the Court. Most violations have concerned the access rights of custodians during alternative care or the reunification of family (The HUDOC database, Pellonpää et al. 2012, 269).

OVERVIEW OF THE STATISTICS OF REMOVALS

As a general trend, the number of children in the child protection system has increased since the mid-1990s. The number of children receiving in-home services has increased from 5.4 percent to 7.5 percent of the total child population between the years 2008 and 2014 (Lastensuojelu 2014). In 2013, this proportion was 7.4 percent (ibid.) The number of children in out-of-home care has increased so that it is estimated that the costs of out-of-home care are three times more in 2011 than they were in 2000; the growth is estimated to be 400 million euros (Enemmän ongelmien ehkäisyä 2013). In 2008, 9.7 children per 1,000 children were placed out of their home on a given day whereas in 2013 the same number was 10.5 children. Table 2.1 demonstrates the number of various removals in detail.

Table 2.1. The number of children younger than eighteen years of age in out-of-home care on a given day/per 1,000 children

Type of Removal	2008	2009	2010	2011	2012	2013
Part of in- home services	1,341 (1.2)	1,291 (1.2)	1,304 (1.2)	1,324 (1.2)	1,385 (1.3)	1,395 (1.3)
Emergency placement	355 (0.3)	514 (0.5)	560 (0.5)	590 (0.5)	698 (0.6)	784 (0.7)
Care order: Total of which	8,893 (8.1)	8,764 (8.0)	8,894 (8.2)	9,118 (8.4)	9,108 (8.4)	9,177 (8.5)
Voluntary	7,202 (6.6)	7,032 (6.4)	7,038 (6.5)	7,178 (6.6)	7,121 (6.6)	7,103 (6.6)
Involuntary	1,691 (1.6)	1,732 (1.6)	1,856 (1.7)	1,940 (1.8)	1,987 (1.8)	2,074 (1.9)

Source: THL 2016[i].

[i]The material for tables 1 and 2 was provided by the child welfare register keeper THL by request in January 2016.

Table 2.2. The age of children in three types of removal in 2013 (on a given day)

The age of children	Part of in-home services (%)	Emergency placement (%)	Voluntary care order (%)	Involuntary care order (%)
0–2	250 (18)	90 (11)	255 (4)	107 (5)
3–6	195 (14)	102 (13)	785 (11)	359 (17)
7–12	271 (19)	185 (24)	2217 (31)	708 (34)
13–15	375 (27)	238 (30)	1953 (27)	487 (23)
16–17	304 (22)	169 (22)	1893 (27)	413 (20)

Source: THL 2016 (see Footnote 6).

Table 2.1 demonstrates that the removals, emergency placements in particular, have increased during the period between 2008 and 2013. In that time, the majority of children in out-of-home care were there based on a voluntary care order decision: In 2013, 6.6 children per 1,000 children were in voluntary care following a care order decision, and 1.9 children per 1,000 children were in involuntary care (care order decision).

Most of the children in out-of-home care are seven years of age or older and frequently are teenagers (Table 2.2). Small babies (two years or younger) are rarely taken into care by a care order decision. The age profile is similar to that of the receivers of in-home services, suggesting that Finnish child protection works mainly with children in the middle childhood and teenage years.

The number of care order decisions by the administrative courts is presented in Table 2.3. The first category includes the court decisions of care order applications as well as appeals of voluntary care orders; the former make the majority of the decisions. In 2013, the number of appeals was seventy-seven. We also list the number of emergency placements (and their continuation) and termination of care. The substantial fall-off in 2010 of the decisions concerning emergency placement or its continuation is due to an amendment to the Child Welfare Act that came into effect in 2010. According to the amendment, it is no longer a court but rather a social worker who decides on the continuation of the emergency placement. The court gets involved only when the decision is appealed. The table also demonstrates that decisions to terminate care are rarely

Table 2.3. Decisions by the regional administrative courts in 2008–2013

Decisions by the administrative courts	2008	2009	2010	2011	2012	2013
Care orders (involuntary and voluntary)	328	691	743	735	676	685
Emergency placements and their continuation	679	1041	516	280	274	381
Termination of care	27	57	101	93	78	72

Source: Suomen virallinen tilasto (SVT) (2013).

done by the courts. No national statistics exist to inform us about the number of decisions on the municipal level to terminate care.

CHALLENGES AND BLIND SPOTS IN FINNISH DECISION-MAKING ON REMOVALS

The challenges and critical points of the decision-making system are based on our reading of the existing research as well as policy and legislation initiatives. It is important to stress that there is a considerable lack of research on child protection decision-making on the municipal and court level. Only a couple of studies have highlighted social workers' decision-making process regarding the removals of children (e.g., Saurama 2002; Pösö and Laakso 2013); thus, very little is known about the process. Whereas the decisions of the courts have been studied to some extent (e.g., Kuula and Marttunen 2009; Hiitola 2015), the courts rarely have been studied as decision-making bodies in action (e.g., de Godzinsky 2012, 2014; Heinonen and Hiitola 2009; Korpinen 2008). This lack of research is the result, firstly, of Finnish legal studies focusing on legal dogmatics (thus being more interested in the law in books than the law in action), and secondly, of the limited number of studies in child protection in general (Pekkarinen 2011).

Although still in the shadows of research, child protection recently has gained much public and media attention in Finnish society (e.g., Forsberg and Ritala-Koskinen 2012). Most interestingly, the numerous recent policy reports analyzing the state of child protection do not raise decision-making in care orders as an issue needing more policy attention. Although the field of public child protection services is understaffed in relation to the number of children and families involved, and though it is to some extent occupied by unqualified staff, the impact of such factors on the quality of care order decision-making has not been on the mainstream agenda of public concern. If care orders are considered at all in the recent policy reports, it is mainly with regard to the costs of alternative care and the high number of children in care, the lack of monitoring practices of alternative care, and the concerns of the poor outcomes of out-of-home care (e.g., Toimiva lastensuojelu 2013; Enemmän on vähemmän 2013; Tuloksellisuuskertomus: Lastensuojelu 2012). The growth of emergency placements has been reflected in the recent change of legislation in 2015 making the threshold higher; again, the decision-making practices remain unchanged.

Despite the lack of policy and academic interest, some developments in recent child protection decision-making need further consideration. We will map out three major issues in the following subsections and will discuss the categories of voluntary and involuntary decisions, the diffusion of care order decision-making, and finally the dynamics between social work and legal reasoning in the matter under study.

INVOLUNTARY AND VOLUNTARY CARE ORDERS—WHAT IS THE DIFFERENCE?

The Finnish child welfare system is characterized by a mix of voluntary and involuntary measures. Interestingly, in research and in statistics these interventions usually are dealt with as a uniform whole without distinguishing between voluntary and involuntary measures (Alastalo and Pösö 2014). On the other hand, the existing research on care orders tends to focus on the decisions of the administrative courts without explicitly recognizing their involuntary characteristic (Helavirta et al. 2014). For this reason very little is known, for instance, about how the assessment processes on the local level differ regarding various measures and whether the activity of the administrative courts in conducting the proceedings and obtaining evidence varies depending on the nature of intervention. Further, we do not have any solid body of research describing how the children, families, and their psychosocial situations differ in voluntary and involuntary care orders (Helavirta et al. 2014) or what "consent" means in these contradictory decisions.

Voluntary and involuntary care orders share many important qualities. Their prerequisites are identical, excepting the requirement of consent in the context of a voluntary care order, as are their legal impacts. With regard to the wording of the Child Welfare Act, the only difference between the two care orders concerns the decision-making body. When examined closely, however, there are also other differences. An involuntary care order signifies interference in a child's and/or his/her custodian's fundamental and human rights, such as the right of respect for family life and the right to self-determination. These rights are guaranteed to everyone by the Finnish Constitution and international human rights conventions, such as the ECHR. As a result, the prerequisites of an involuntary care order must be interpreted strictly by the decision-maker, so that the threshold for the interference remains high. The same requirement does not apply to voluntary care orders, at least not to the same extent. A voluntary care order is a kind of borderline case between voluntariness and coercion: Because of its voluntary nature, it resembles consent-based public services but is, on the other hand, also comparable with an involuntary care order with which it shares identical legal implications, namely, the restrictions on parental responsibilities. When interpreting the prerequisites in a concrete situation, this twofold nature of voluntary care orders must be taken into account.

In practice, it sometimes may be difficult to know whether the care order is opposed or not if, for example, a child aged twelve years or older does not want to express his/her view. A social worker must then, during the preparation process, try to conclude the child's opinion from his/her behavior or consult the views provided by the child's guardian. In the case of uncertainty, the opposition—and not the consent—must be assumed, and the decision must be made by a court. This aims to safeguard the legal protections afforded the child and his/her custodian/parent.

THE EMERGING PARALLEL DECISION-MAKING SYSTEM INTRODUCING "LIGHT" DECISIONS

A particularly complex recent tendency has been the growth of emergency placement. It is estimated that since the introduction of the new Act in 2008, emergency placements have grown by 60 percent (Toimiva lastensuojelu 2013, 18). Although the number of emergency placements has increased, the number of children taken into care without any emergency placement has decreased (Toimiva lastensuojelu 2013, 18). In 2009, 22 percent of children who were taken into care had not had any emergency placement before the care order, while in 2002 the corresponding number was 39 percent. The majority (57 percent) of children in emergency placements in 2011 were between the ages of twelve and seventeen, making the emergency placements predominantly a practice with youth (Toimiva lastensuojelu 2013). Again, there is a lack of research on emergency placements and related decision-making. Practice suggests, however, that the growth of emergency placements cannot be exhaustively explained by a changing number of emergencies for children and families but rather by the child protection practice itself (Lamponen 2014).

The legal implications of an emergency placement and care order are similar for the child, parents, and local authorities. The decision-making process, however, differs considerably between care orders and emergency placements as described earlier in this chapter as the decision-making process of emergency placements is much lighter (the decision is made by one social worker). The "lightness" of emergency placement decisions may threaten the rights of the parents and children as they have the right only to make an appeal. Furthermore, while the children are in emergency care and there is reason to start to prepare a care order, the social workers have to complete the care order preparations within the time limits of an emergency placement (maximum sixty days). Such time limits are nonexistent in care order proceedings otherwise. Even then, the care order preparation process may thus be "lighter" because there is less time to involve parents and children or to consult other experts.

The "lightness" of the decision-making process together with the growth in care orders preceded by emergency placement may suggest that there are some fundamental hidden changes in the decision-making practices taking place after implementation of the Child Welfare Act in 2007. Indeed, the emergency placements tend to have created *parallel decision-making systems for care orders*: one that is carried out with time and attention paid to careful assessment and involvement of relevant parties, and the other one carried out in a short period of time with little involvement of children, parents, and (multi-) professional assessment teams. This means that there is some diffusion, if not even dilution, of the principles and guidelines of care order decision-making.

THE INTERPLAY BETWEEN SOCIAL WORK AND LEGAL REASONING IN THE DECISION-MAKING

Legislation as well as other sources of law, such as the Convention of Children's Rights and the case law of the European Court of Human Rights, set the framework for decision-making on care orders at both the local and court level. The decision-maker, whether a social worker or a judge, is obliged to recognize this framework. Within the legal framework, there is still plenty of space for interpretation and discretion, the use of which mainly requires expertise other than judicial, namely expertise in professional social work and child welfare. The interplay between social work and legal expertise in decision-making was significantly increased by the present Child Welfare Act.

The interplay between social work and legal reasoning can be illustrated with the three prerequisites for care orders set down in the Child Welfare Act (section 2 in this chapter), which are described in very flexible terms open to various interpretations. One of these prerequisites says that taking a child into care and the provision of alternative care may only be resorted to "if alternative care is estimated to be in the child's interests." To guide the interpretation, the Act confirms seven principles that must be taken into account when assessing the best interests of the child, but even these are formulated in a discretionary way and may lead to different conclusions (Pösö 2012). For instance, consideration must be given to the extent to which the alternative measures and solutions safeguard "balanced development and wellbeing, and close and continuing human relationships" for the child. With all these open and future-orientated phrases, as well as many others in the Child Welfare Act, it is manifest that the legislators' aim was to ensure that there is enough space for professional social work and child welfare expertise to influence the decision-making. Consequently, the challenge to decision-making is, in short, to combine professional (social work) expertise based on individual discretion, on one hand, with objective and predictable legal reasoning on the other.

The very fact that social work reasoning has to be presented to the administrative court in the cases of involuntary care orders is reported to have influenced social work practice. In particular, documentation—writing the case notes and decisions throughout the intake, in-home services, and actual preparatory process of the care order—is carried out with an awareness of the legal reader in mind (e.g., Huuskonen 2014). Therefore, documentation is, on the one hand, more exact and detailed than before, but on the other, it takes more time away from actual client work and may not include issues such as professional doubts and hypotheses to be tested, which may be important for actual case work (Huuskonen 2014). Consequently, the possibility of the legal decision-making body is interwoven into social work practice.

Further, when the decisions are made in administrative courts, both legal and social work reasoning are at stake. It is not known exactly how the interplay between social work and legal reasoning is put into practice by the courts.[6] Yet it can be carefully estimated that the courts give preference to judicial materials and principles, such as the rule of law and the fair trial principles, in their decision-making. It is, important, however, to note that in care order proceedings the decision-making body of a regional administrative court consists, contrary to a general rule, of an expert member representing expertise in child welfare (section 3 in this chapter). This, again, suggests the need for interplay between judicial and psychosocial knowledge of child welfare. In very complex and contested child protection cases administrative courts may even have to employ a high level of nonlegal reasoning, even that of lay knowledge (Korpinen 2008), demonstrating, again, the interweaving of various types of reasoning in decision-making. More should be known about how this interplay actually influences decisions, and what the position of children and families is at the juncture of various traditions of knowledge.

CONCLUSIONS

We have seen that the decision-making practices in Finnish child protection follow the idea that child protection is one form of social service. Most of the care order decisions are made by social workers on the municipal level as voluntary decisions and the court becomes involved only when there is disagreement about the need for the removal of the child. In this sense, the decision-making system is based very much on social work discretion and on the idea of voluntarism. This mix of voluntary and involuntary decisions and different decision-making bodies, at its best, is sensitive and flexible enough to meet the complex sociolegal issues of child protection and to serve the best interests of children. At its worst, it may dilute the nature of some child removals by the state as a measure of social control against human rights. The tendencies and blind sports recognized in this chapter suggest that the strengths and weaknesses of the present system cannot be thoroughly highlighted based on existing research and, therefore, there is an urgent need to explore the functioning of the system in more detail.

An emerging critical view on the quality of care order decision-making underlines the children's position and agency. Although the rights of children, that of participation in particular, and the wide notion of the principle of the best interest of the child make the system principles "child-centric" (Pösö 2011), children's involvement is not yet strongly embedded in care order decision-making. When de Godzinsky (2012) studied the decision-making of the administrative courts soon after the introduction of the present Child Welfare Act, she concluded her study with her doubts about whether the children's views were genuinely heard and examined by anyone involved in the decision-making process. Similar doubts were expressed in her later study in 2014. Similarly, child protection practice on the municipal level is criticized for not acting in a "child-centred manner" (e.g., Toimiva lastensuojelu 2013). Consequently, there is a clash between the ideology of the Finnish decision-making principles and practice: the children should be involved in decision-making as service-users and as legal parties (at a certain age) but there tends to be barriers to hinder such a practice. This clash suggests that the sociolegal agenda of the system and its implications for children and families should be thoroughly revisited.

NOTES

1   We are grateful to Elina Pekkarinen, Tuuli Lamponen, Rosi Enroos, and Susanna Helavirta for their careful and encouraging comments on different versions of the present chapter.
2   Adoption is not classified as a child protection measure and thus is not considered as a type of removal. It is regulated by the Adoption Act (22/2012). Most adoptions in Finland are "international adoptions" and adoptions within the family due to new family arrangements.
3   A child's parents usually have custody of the child, but custody can be awarded to other persons, too. When parents are married to each other at the time of the birth of the child they both have custody. If they are not, the custody belongs to the mother. The parents may, however, agree on joint custody. To be valid the agreement must be confirmed by a public authority. In the case of divorce, the parents may agree that one of them has sole custody or they may agree on joint custody. According to the Act on Child Custody and Right of Access (361/1983), the purpose of custody is to ensure the welfare and balanced development of a child in accordance with his/ her individual needs and wishes as well as to secure a close and affectionate relationship in particular between the child and his/her parents. For this purpose the custodian has the right to decide on a child's personal matters, such as his/her upbringing and place of residence.
4   Guardians also may be appointed during the process on the local, social welfare agency level.
5   In the care order proceedings analyzed by de Godzinsky (2012, 101–103), a guardian was appointed in only 3 percent and a legal advisor in 4 percent of the cases. Some of the appointments of guardians were made by the administrative courts while some were made on the local level. The data analyzed

consisted of 159 decisions of regional administrative courts from a three-month period in 2010 (de Godzinsky 2012, 46–47).

6 It is important to recognize the trusted role of the court system in Finland. In the European comparisons, the trust of citizens toward the court system was 34 percent higher in Finland than in the European Union countries in general in 2008. In the case of administrative courts, it is noteworthy that the authorities trusted the legitimacy of the court decision-making more than private parties in 2012; nevertheless, trust was high in both groups (de Godzinsky and Aaltonen 2013).

REFERENCES

Aer, J. 2012. *Lastensuojeluoikeus. lapsi- ja perhekohtaisen lastensuojelun oikeudelliset perusteet* [Child protection law. The legal basis of child-specific and family-specific child welfare]. Helsinki, Finland: Sanoma Pro Oy.

Alastalo, M. and Pösö, T. 2014. "Number of Children Placed Outside the Home as an Indicator—Social and Moral Implications of Commensuration." *Social Policy & Administration* 48(7), 721–738. doi: 10.1111/spol.12073

Child Welfare Act 417/2007 (unofficial translation). Retrieved May 5, 2014 from www.finlex.fi.

Convention on the Rights of the Child (CRC). United Nations 1989. Retrieved May 5, 2014 from http://www.ohchr.org/en/professionalinterest/pages/crc.aspx.

De Godzinsky, V-M. 2012. *Huostaanottoasiat hallinto-oikeuksissa. tutkimus tahdonvastaisten huostaanottojen päätöksentekomenettelystä* [Taking a child into care. Research on decision-making in administrative courts]. Research Report 260. Helsinki, Finland: Oikeuspoliittinen tutkimuslaitos.

De Godzinsky, V-M. 2014. *Lapsen etu ja osallisuus hallinto-oikeuksien päätöksissä* [The Best Interest of the child and the child's right to participate in administrative court proceedings]. Report 267. Helsinki, Finland: Oikeuspoliittinen tutkimuslaitos.

De Godzinsky, V-M. and Aaltonen, M. 2013. *Koettu oikeudenmukaisuus hallintoprosessissa* [Experienced legitimacy in administrative processes]. Tutkimustiedonantoja 121. Helsinki, Finland: Oikeuspoliittinen tutkimuslaitos.

Enemmän ongelmien ehkäisyä, vähemmän korjailua? [More prevention of problems, less mending]. 2013. Report 11. Helsinki, Finland: Valtiovarainm inisteriö.

European Convention on Human Rights (EHCR). Council of Europe 1950. Retrieved May 5, 2014 from http://www.echr.coe.int/Pages/home.aspx?p=ba sictexts&c=#n1359128122487_pointer.

Forsberg, H. and Ritala-Koskinen, A. 2012. "Lastensuojelun sosiaalityö muutoksessa [Changing child protection social work]" In Jahnukainen, M. (Ed.),

Lasten erityishuolto- ja opetus Suomessa [Special education and care of children in Finland], pp. 153–179. Tampere, Finland: Vastapaino.

Gilbert, N., Parton, N., and Skivenes M. (Eds.). 2011. *Child Protection Systems: International Trends and Orientations.* New York, NY: Oxford University Press.

Hallinto-oikeuksien toimintakertomus 2013. [The annual report of administrative courts 2013] Retrieved June 10, 2014 from http://www.kho.fi/fi/index/julkaisut/hallintotuomioistuintenyhteisettoimintakertomukset.

Hallituksen esitys 252/2006 lastensuojelulaiksi ja eräiksi siihen liittyviksi laeiksi [Government proposal 252/2006 concerning the Child Welfare Act and certain other acts related to it]. Retrieved May 5, 2014 from http://www.eduskunta.fi.

Hallituksen esitys 318/2010 laiksi luvan saaneista oikeudenkäyntiavustajista ja eräiksi siihen liittyviksi laeiksi [Government proposal 318/2010 concerning the Act on the Licensed Attorneys and certain other acts related to it]. Retrieved May 5, 2014 from http://www.eduskunta.fi.

Heino, Tarja. 2009. "Lastensuojelu—kehityskulkuja ja paikannuksia [Child protection—tendencies and locations]." In Lammi-Taskula, J., Sakari Karvonen, S., and Salme Ahlström, S. (Eds.), *Lapsiperheiden hyvinvointi 2009* [The well-being of Families with Children], pp. 198–213. Helsinki, Finland: Terveyden ja hyvinvoinnin laitos.

Heinonen, H. and Hiitola, J. 2009. *Huostaanotto ja oikeudellinen päätöksenteko* [Care order and juridical decision-making]. Report 46. Helsinki, Finland: Terveyden ja hyvinvoinnin laitos.

Hclavirta, S., Laakso, R., and Pösö T. 2014. Huostaanoton kuva suomalaisen tutkimuksen valossa [Care orders as seen by Finnish research]. *Janus* 3 (22) 288–298.

Hiitola, J. 2015. *Hallittu vanhemmuus. Sukupuoli, luokka ja etnisyys huostaanottoasiakirjoissa* [Governed parenthood. Out-of-home placements and gender, class and ethnicity]. Acta Universitatis Tamperensis 2026. Tampere, Finland: Tampere University Press.

Huuskonen, S. 2014. *Recording and Use of Information in a Client Information System in Child Protection.* Acta Universitatis Tamperenses 1904. Tampere, Finland: Tampere University Press.

Korkeimman hallinto-oikeuden esitys oikeusministeriölle lainsäädäntötoimeen ryhtymisestä [A proposal of the Supreme Administrative Court to Ministry of Justice concerning starting law drafting] (unpublished). 17.9.2013.

Korpinen, J. 2008. *Istuntoja institutionaalisen katseen alla: lastensuojelun suulliset käsittelyt hallinto-oikeudessa* [Sessions under the institutional gaze: child protection oral hearings in the administrative courts]. Acta Universitatis Tamperensis 1322. Tampere, Finland: Tampere University Press.

Kuula, T. and Marttunen, M. 2009. *Laitoksessa rikosten vuoksi. Selvitys alaikäisenä vastentahtoisesti huostaan otetuista* [In institution due to crime. A report of minors taken into involuntary care]. Helsinki, Finland: Oikeuspoliittinen tutkimuslaitos & Humanistinen ammattikorkeakoulu.

Lamponen, T. 2014. *Kiireellisten sijoitusten päätöksenteko* [Decision-making of emergency placements]. Research plan (unpublished). Tampere, Finland: University of Tampere.

Lastensuojelu 2014 [Child Welfare 2014]. Statistical report. Helsinki: Terveyden ja hyvinvoinnin laitos, Suomen virallinen tilasto, Sosiaaliturva 2015. Helsinki: Terveyden ja hyvinvoinnin laitos.

Mäenpää, O. 2012. "The Rule of Law and Administrative Implementation in Finland." In Nuotio, K., Melander, S., and Huomo-Kettunen, M. (Eds.), *Introduction to Finnish Law and Legal Culture..* Helsinki, Finland: Faculty of Law, University of Helsinki.

Pekkarinen, E. 2011. *Lastensuojelun tieto ja tutkimus—Asiantuntijoiden näkökulma* [Knowledge and research in child protection—the view of the experts]. Helsinki, Finland: Nuorisotutkimusverkosto/Nuorisotutkimusseura.

Pellonpää, M., Gullans, M., Pölönen, P., and Tapanila, A. 2012. *Euroopan ihmisoikeussopimus* [The European convention on human rights]. Liettua: Talentum.

Pösö, T. 2011. "Combatting Child Abuse in Finland: From Family to Child-Centered Orientation." In Gilbert, N., Parton, N., and Skivenes, M. (Eds.), *Child Protection Systems. International Trends and Orientations*, pp. 112–130. New York: Oxford University Press,

Pösö, T. 2012. "Lapsen etu, oikeudet ja näkökulma moraalisina kannanottoina" [The best interest, rights and view of the child as moral standpoints]. In Forsberg, H., and Autonen-Vaaraniemi, L. (Eds.), *Kiistanalainen perhe, moraalinen järkeily ja sosiaalityö* [Contested family, moral reasoning and social work], pp. 75–97. Tampere, Finland: Vastapaino.

Pösö, T. and Laakso, R. 2014. "Matching Children and Substitute Homes: Some Theoretical and Empirical Notions." *Child & Family Social Work*. doi:10.1111/cfs.12144

Saurama, E. 2002. *Vastoin vanhempien tahtoa* [Against the will of the parents]. Research 7. Helsinki, Finland: City of Helsinki Urban Facts Research Series.

Suomen virallinen tilasto (SVT) (2013) Hallinto-oikeuksien käsittelemät asiat 2005–2013. Helsinki: Tilastokeskus [Official statistics in Finland 2013: The proceedings in administrative courts in 2005–2013]. Retrieved December 29, 2015 from http://pxnet2.stat.fi/PXWeb/pxweb/fi/StatFin/StatFin__oik__haloikr/010_haloikr_tau_101_fi.px/?rxid=4736c235-66d3-4e7d-bd51-709c8da2d937.

Suomen virallinen tilasto (SVT) (2013) Korkeimman hallinto-oikeuden käsittelemät asiat 1991–2013. Helsinki: Tilastokeskus [Official statistics in Finland 2013: The proceedings in Supreme Administrative Court in 1991–2013]. Retrieved December 29, 2015 from http://pxnet2.stat.fi/PXWeb/pxweb/fi/StatFin/ StatFin__oik__khaloikr/?tablelist=true&rxid=4736c235-66d3-4e7d-bd51-709c8da2d937.

The Constitution of Finland 731/1999 (unofficial translation). Retrieved May 5, 2014 from www.finlex.fi.

Toimiva lastensuojelu. Selvitysryhmän loppuraportti. [Functioning child welfare. The final report]. 2013. Raportteja ja muistioita 2013:19. Helsinki, Finland: Sosiaali- ja terveysministeriö.

3

NORWAY

CHILD WELFARE DECISION-MAKING IN CASES
OF REMOVALS OF CHILDREN

Marit Skivenes and Karl Harald Søvig

INTRODUCTION

One of the most invasive and consequential decisions a state can make is to terminate or severely restrict the bonds between parents and children. Through the action and preparations by the child welfare agency and formal decisions by the courts or independent administrative bodies, the state takes over the care of the children or revokes all parental rights when parents are unable or unwilling to perform their parental responsibilities and obligations. In such cases, children are removed from their homes and placed in foster homes or residential units, and they may ultimately be adopted. Clearly, these interventions are some of the most intrusive decisions a state can make, because family is a core unit in our society. Care orders or termination of parental responsibility simultaneously challenges the freedoms of individuals and the privacy and autonomy of family life, but these decisions may be absolutely necessary when children's welfare, childhood, and future are at stake.[1]

In child welfare[2] the child's best interests is a paramount consideration (cf. Article 3 in the Convention of the Rights of the Child [CRC, 1989]; see also Sandberg [2014] on the incorporation of CRC into Norwegian law). Due process, legitimacy, and the quality of child protection decisions are, therefore, key issues. These are, however, decisions that are legislated for, with court decision-makers authorized to exercise discretion when parents' rights and responsibilities for their children are restricted or terminated. Child protection decision-making is a unique field of research (van Thiel 2007), because of its complexity and value-laden character, the extent to which discretion is needed, and the strong use of state power that it represents. There is a scarcity of knowledge and research regarding judicial reasoning and decision-making concerning the removal of children in child protection cases in Norway and, more generally, throughout Europe. In 2013, child welfare agencies in Norway sent 1,799 care order applications to the County Social and Child Welfare Boards (county boards), which made decisions in 1,554 cases about involuntary removal of children. Of a total population of approximately 5 million people, the child age population in Norway is 1,125,161 as of January 1, 2014.

In this chapter, we present the basic features of the proceedings related to the removal of children by the Norwegian child welfare system and address some of the challenges faced by the Norwegian system. The chapter begins with a brief outline of the general system features of the Norwegian welfare state, child welfare system, and legal system, followed by a description of the recent policy context. Then, descriptions of the processes of care orders/removals (or pre-proceedings processes) in child welfare cases are presented, including the decision-making bodies and available statistics. Finally, the chapter identifies and discusses possible blind spots and challenges in care orders/removals decision-making systems.

THE NORWEGIAN SYSTEM

Child welfare systems in modern states can crudely be categorized into two types (Gilbert, Parton, and Skivenes 2011; Gilbert 1997): risk-oriented and service-oriented. Norway belongs to the latter category and has a child welfare system that is family-service-oriented and child-centric (Skivenes 2011). In service-oriented systems, the aims are to provide for children's needs and promote healthy childhoods and through this mitigate serious risks and prevent harm (Skivenes 2011). The state therefore provides early intervention services to children and families in at-risk situations to prevent future harm to the child. The major differences between risk oriented system and a service oriented systems reside in their underlying ideologies and the ways in which they address children who are at risk. Typical for service-oriented systems that are in place in the Nordic countries and many other countries, is a therapeutic view of rehabilitation in which it is possible for people to revise and improve their lifestyles and behaviors. A basic attitude is that the child welfare system should be part of a broader welfare system that provides services to prevent more serious harm and, consequently, prevent out-of-home placements. The intervention threshold for providing services in these systems is low. Although child welfare systems are not often seen in relation to welfare state models (Pösö et al. 2013), common ground seems to exist between the family-service system and the Norwegian social democratic welfare state, which is characterized by tight welfare safety nets and numerous universal welfare services (Pösö et al. 2013). The type of child protection system, its underlying premises, and type of welfare state model are important contextual components for understanding the challenges that at-risk families and children face, the thresholds for intervention, and the features that are likely to have an effect on how decision-making is undertaken within the child welfare system. A detailed presentation of the Norwegian child welfare system is presented in Skivenes (2011), and thus only a brief overview is given here.

The last twenty years have seen a steady increase in the responsibilities and services provided by the child welfare system in Norway and in other countries (Gilbert et al. 2011). In Norway, more children receive services, more children are placed out of their homes, and more workers are employed by the system. There also has been a juridification (for example more-detailed statutory provisions) of the system, an emphasis on education and knowledge, and a steady stream of reforms. Today's system has high ambitions for children who may be at risk, and a child-centric policy is evident in the way that children are addressed as individuals who deserve respect and dignity as children and not only as future adults who may contribute to, and provide for, the welfare state (Skivenes 2011, 2014). Child welfare work is undertaken by child welfare workers in 428 municipalities in Norway (an ongoing reform will reduce the number of municipalities). Because municipality sizes differ (the smallest have around 200 inhabitants), agency sizes differ; however, the responsibility for at-risk children is identical across these municipalities, and the services and quality of casework and decision-making should adhere to the same standards. About 43 percent (n = 183) of the municipalities have organized their child welfare services in collaboration with other municipalities, and an additional handful (n = 14) have organized their child protection services under the joint social welfare, unemployment, and social security services (Statistics Norway 2013).

The three main reasons for the provision of child services or interventions from the child welfare system are as follows:

1. At the least intrusive level, the child welfare system intervenes when a child has a particular need for assistance, as defined in the Child Welfare Act of 1992, section 4-4 (1), by providing in-home services.
2. If the agency is unable to help the child with in-home services or if in-home services are inappropriate (if the child is maltreated or abused, for example, as described in the Child Welfare Act, section 4-12), out-of-home placement is sought.

3. If a child behaves destructively or violently (e.g., substance abuse), the child welfare agency may provide in-home services or an out-of-home placement under the Child Welfare Act, section 4-24 and section 4-26.

Interventions may be voluntary or compulsory, and most in-home services are voluntary, although involuntary measures such as supervision or mandatory day care may be put in place (a wider selection of compulsory out-of-home measures was introduced by amendment June 7, 2015, No. 81). Intrusive interventions, such as involuntary measures and care orders are decided by the county boards, of which there are twelve in Norway. (We return to the organization of the county boards and the court system below.) In the Norwegian system, there are four ways a child can be placed out of the home: First, the parents may place the child for up-bringing by other persons for a short or longer period of time. The parents may at any point request that the child be returned home to them. If the placement lasts for more than two months, however, the child welfare agency may seek to approve the placement. The county board is also vested with the competence to issue a temporary moving ban (cf. section 4-8[2]). Second, there is voluntary placement, in which the child welfare agency places a child with the consent of the parents and without any interventions for the parents. Third, there is emergency place-ment, in which there is an incident that requires the protection of the child. The child welfare agency has the authority to place a child without the parents' consent until such time as the county board is able to review the emergency removal and make a decision. Emergency removals either end with the child's return to her/his parents or with the preparation of a care order application. Fourth, the child wel-fare agency can prepare and submit a care order application to the county board.

In 2012, 2.7 children per 1,000 children lived out of home, having been placed by the child protection agency in accordance with the voluntary place-ment provision. Also in 2012, 1.4 children per 1,000 were placed out of home as emergency removals, and 1,408 care order decisions were made. The ideology in Norway is that care orders, whether voluntary or involuntary, are to be treated as "involuntary interventions," due to the seriousness of the intervention. The decision-making process should, therefore, be undertaken in accordance with fair trial principles. Adoption is also an alternative in the Norwegian system, but it is ruled out as a first option because of the legal requirement that prospec-tive parents must have been fostering the child prior to adoption. A recently established provision also allows the police and/or the child welfare agency to place a child who is involved in human trafficking in a residential unit, without consent (Child Welfare Act, section 4-29). Although defined as deprivation of liberty, the aim is to care for and protect the child, and decisions must be in ac-cordance with the best interests principle. Table 3.1 below presents an overview of basic statistics concerning the number of children who are involved in our system and which services and interventions are undertaken:

Table 3.1. Statistics on children and the child welfare system

	2008	2009	2010	2011	2012	2013	2014
Child population, end of year, N = children	1,103 481	1,109 156	1,114 374	1,118 225	1,122 897	1,125 161	1,125 604
Referrals investigated, per 1 000 children	25.2	26.5	28.8	30.6	30.1	36.1	36.6
Children receiving services (all types), end of year, per 1 000 children	28.4	29.5	30.4	30.5	30.6	29.7	29.6
Children receiving in-home services, end of year, per 1 000 children	22.6	23.6	24.1	24.0	23.7	22.5	22
Children placed out of home (with *and* without care order), end of year, per 1 000 children	8.2	8.4	9.0	9.3	9.7	10.1	10.4
Children with a formal care order decision, end of year, per 1 000 children	5.8	6.0	6.3	6.5	7	7.2	7.6
Children placed out of home without a formal care order decision, end of year, per 1 000 children	2.4	2.5	2.8	2.8	2.7	2.9	2.8
Emergency placements, during the year, per 1 000 children	0.9	0.9	1	1.2	1.4	1.4	1.3
Reunification cases decided by county boards, # N = cases	191	208	203	214	220	286	324
Adoptions of foster children (0–18), N = persons	. (14)	30 (17)	29 (16)	40 (17)	40 (20)	57 (36)	62 (41)
Adoption cases decided by court, # N = cases	24	23	34	38	55	62	88
Young persons (18–22) receiving child welfare services, end of year, N = persons	2,570	2,922	3,459	3,899	4,331	3,844	3,787
New children in the system, N = children*	11,760	12,386	13,231	13,695	13,583	10,212	13,746

Sources: Statistics Norway 2014; Skivenes 2011, 2014; Central Unit of the County Boards 2015.

. Statistics not available

* This statistic may include several young adults (18–22 years old).

Outcome of decision is not known.

POLICY AND LEGISLATION

The Norwegian child welfare system has been fairly stable in its legal and political orientation, with a steady increase in recent decades in its focus on children's rights and children's place in society. The latter focus is one of several things reflected in the new provision in the Norwegian Constitution, implemented May 11, 2014, in which children are given a clear and prominent place in our society that puts them on equal footing with other individuals. The article reads in translation as follows:

> **Article 104.**
> Children are entitled to respect for their human dignity. They have a right to be heard on issues that affect themselves, and their opinion should be given weight in accordance with their age and development.
> Regarding actions and decisions concerning children, the child's best interests should be a primary consideration.
> Children are entitled to protection of their personal integrity. Government authorities should facilitate the child's development, including ensuring that the child receives the necessary economic, social and health security, preferably in his own family.

The wording of this article is inspired by Article 3 of the CRC. The committee drafting the provision emphasized that the preference for raising children in their own birth family must be read in conjunction with the best interest of the child and the child's right to be heard (Dok. 16 (2011–2012), 194–195). The revised Constitution now also protects the right to family life (Article 102), which may be invoked by parents in child welfare cases.

This view, that children are individuals within the family context, is also evident in the policy changes that weaken the biological principle to give more weight to the child's actual attachment and the psychological impact of parental relations (The Ministry of Children and Equality 2009; cf. NOU 2012, 40–48; 118–121). An implication is that the threshold for reunification is raised due to new interpretations of the material content of provisions. These changes are combined with an increased attention to younger children (and an increased attention to the effects of the in-home services that are provided to ascertain whether they are actually effective in changing the situation for the child (The Ministry of Children, Equality and Social Inclusion 2013). Although each change may be minor, together these changes are redirecting the child welfare system toward a more child-oriented approach in which children's interests are regarded as separate from their parents.

In addition, from June 1, 2014 on, children's right to participate in decisions regarding their situation in child welfare cases is clarified and made explicit.

That is, the child's involvement is now included as part of the best interests principle (a new section Two) on which the child welfare law rests. In other words, children's participation is an important component in the interpretation of the best interests principle, and the revised section reads as follows:

Section 4-1. The child's best interests standard

In applying the provisions of this chapter, it is of decisive importance to find measures that are in the best interests of the child. This shall include emphasis on providing the child stable and good contact and continuity of care.

The child must be given the opportunity to participate and conversations with the child must be facilitated. Children whom child welfare services have under care orders may be allowed to bring a person in which they have special confidence. The Ministry may issue further regulations on participation and the "confidence person's" duties and functions.

Although, there is currently a strong emphasis in Norway on the position of children, based in legislation and policies, we do not have sufficient knowledge of how children's participation actually plays out in practice. Certain studies on children's participation at the agency level (Stang 2007; Križ and Skivenes 2014; Skivenes 2015; Berrick et al. 2015) and the court-level (Archard and Skivenes 2009; Skivenes, 2010; Vis et al., 2013; Magnussen and Skivenes 2015) indicate that there is a discrepancy between the ambitions of legislation and how it is implemented in the child welfare system.

As a family-service-oriented child welfare system, the Norwegian system aims to provide in-home services, and only removes children from their parents as a last resort. Legislators have outlined two *main* reasons for the removals of children, related to the child's own behavior or the parents' harmful care and neglect of the child's needs. The latter is the dominant reason for removing children in Norway, and the legal criteria are stated in section 4-12 in the Child Welfare Act, which reads in translation as follows:

A care order may be made

  (a) if there are serious deficiencies in the everyday care received by the child, or serious deficiencies in terms of the personal contact and security needed by a child of his or her age and development;
  (b) if the parents fail to ensure that a child who is ill, disabled or in special need of assistance receives the treatment and training required;
  (c) if the child is mistreated or subjected to other serious abuse at home; or
  (d) if it is highly probable that the child's health or development may be seriously harmed because the parents are unable to take adequate responsibility for the child.

An order may only be made pursuant to the first paragraph when necessary due to the child's current situation. Hence, such an order may not be made if satisfactory conditions can be created for the child by assistance measures pursuant to section 4-4 or by measures pursuant to section 4-10 or section 4-11.

An order pursuant to the first paragraph shall be made by the county social welfare board pursuant to the provisions of chapter 7.

As noted above, there are three criteria for the removal of a child. First, in circumstances where harm or neglect may occur. Second, in-home services are unable to provide satisfactory conditions. Third, removal is considered to be necessary based on an overall assessment and is in the child's best interests. It is also possible to undertake a care order based on the child's own destructive behavior, section 4-24, or to withhold a child who is placed voluntarily by the parents (section 4-8). Section 4-8(2) also allows for care orders of newborn babies who are still in the hospital.

The county board can without the parents' consent, order medical treatment for a child (section 4-10), and also order that assistance is provided for children with particular training or treatment needs (section 4-11). We will not go into detail, however, on the legal criteria for these types of interventions, given that the criteria in section 4-12 quoted above establish the general threshold for removals of children by the Norwegian state.

THE REMOVAL PROCESSES

In almost all cases of removals of children by the child welfare system, it is the child welfare agencies and child welfare workers that prepare and provide documentation for removals. (The police can make temporary decisions in some situations.) As noted above, there are three routes that can be pursued for removals of children in the Norwegian child welfare system: voluntary removals, emergency removals, and care orders. The baseline is that the county boards have the formal authority to make decisions on any serious intervention. The child welfare agency, however, has the authority to facilitate voluntary placements and the temporary authority to place children who are in an emergency situation until such time that the county board is able to review and authorize a placement decision. In the following sections, we outline each of the three different removal options, starting with the formal care orders that are made by the county board.

Care orders
Care orders are the most frequently used legal basis when the child welfare system removes children. A care order is rendered either because the child is

not properly cared for (section 4-12) or because of the young person's own be-havior (section 4-24). These decisions are prepared by the child welfare agency and decided upon by the county board. When Norway enacted the Child Welfare Act of 1992, it was with the explicit aim of improving the legal frame-work of the system, anchoring the system in an independent body, securing the rights of parents and children, ensuring due process, and ensuring that the system and its decisions were in accordance with the rule of law (Skivenes 2002; cf. Benneche 1987; Andersland 2011). Thus, legislation was changed ac-cordingly. A new administrative body—the county social welfare board—was also established. This was a somewhat unique solution for Norway, given that our system is a unitary court system that is reluctant to establish specialist courts (Andersland 2011). The establishment of the county board in force from 1994 constituted an exceptional undertaking because the county board is not formally regarded as a court, but instead as a "court-like" decision-making body, which leaves it outside of the ordinary judicial system. The county board is a part of the executive branch, although with an independent position. The chairman is a civil servant and not a judge with special privileges according to the constitution.

One of the implications of its status outside of the formal judicial system as such, which we return to in the final discussion, is that appeals of decisions made by the county board are brought in front of the district court for yet another full trial on all issues at the time of the court date. Regardless of the county board's status as an administrative body within domestic law, the board will likely be considered as a "court," according to ECHR Article 6, due to its independent position and procedural guarantees.

Figure 3.1 presents an overview of the judiciaries that would be involved in a care order case if appealed all the way up to the Norwegian Supreme Court. Appeals to the courts of appeal and to the Supreme Court will be screened; for example, if it is proved that the decision by the district court has serious flaws, or there are important new pieces of evidence in the case. We have also included the European Court of Human Rights in Figure 3.1, because cases concerning human rights—as child protection cases often do—can be referred for exami-nation by this supranational court.

The county boards make the decisions in care order cases. Typically, there are three decision-makers on the board: a lawyer (the board's chair), an expert member, and a lay member. The main principles for the county social welfare board are outlined in the Child Welfare Act of 1992, section 7-3:

> The county social welfare board shall address cases in a satisfactory, expeditious and confidence-inspiring manner. Its proceedings shall be adapted to the measure in question and the nature, scope and complex-ity of the case and shall underpin the fundamental considerations of the Act.

The Court System in Norway

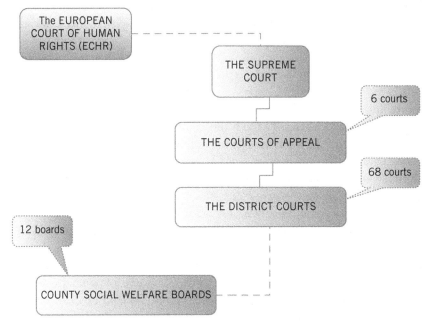

Figure 3.1. Court systems for child welfare cases in Norway.

To achieve the goals set out in the first paragraph,

(a) the county social welfare board shall ensure that the evidence sub-mitted provides an adequate factual basis for decision-making;

(b) the parties to the case shall be heard, normally by means of oral statements made directly to the boards;

(c) steps shall be taken to ensure that both sides are heard;

(d) the parties to the case shall be treated equally and receive the neces-sary guidance;

(e) the county social welfare board shall conduct an independent and genuine assessment of the basis for decision-making; and

(f) the grounds for decisions on measures and other important deci-sions shall be stated.

The board chair is responsible for ensuring that cases are handled in ac-cordance with the first and second paragraphs and to this end shall plan and direct the preparatory proceedings, negotiation meeting and delib-erations and shall ensure that the proceedings are proportionate to the case that is to be decided.

A care order case is normally presented to the county board only after it has been in the child welfare system for a while. This is one of the features that characterize a family-service-oriented system (Skivenes 2011). The child welfare agency attempts to prevent out-of-home placements by providing services and assistance to the child and the family, and it is only when it is impossible to provide for the child when she or he is living with her or his parents, that a care order may or should be suggested. If the child welfare agency believes that a care order should be applied for, it informs the parents and assists the parents (and the child when she or he is fifteen years old or older) to find a lawyer. At this stage, the child welfare agency initiates an investigation, in which it collects additional information. In some cases, the agency may already have sufficient evidence and information to write a care order application. The average processing time to prepare a care order application varies greatly among municipalities, from an average of sixty-nine days in Telemark to 117 days in Rogaland (Office of the Auditor General of Norway 2015, 53–54). The main reasons for care orders being sought in the Norwegian system are parental abuse or parental neglect, in which the child's needs are not being recognized and met (NOU 2012, 67). In December 2015, the Ministry of Children, Equality and Social Inclusion presented new guidelines (Q-42/2015) on proceedings in cases with children affiliated to other countries, emphasizing collaboration with both the family and the authorities in the child's home country.

The care order application prepared by a child welfare agency is a written statement that consists of the names of the parties, a brief description of what the application concerns, a presentation of the case, a list of evidence and witnesses, and a proposal for a decision. The head of the child welfare agency sends the application to the county board. Upon receipt of a care order application, the county board assigns the case to a county board chair, who reads the case quickly and initiates the *preparatory proceedings* (section 7-12). This includes specifying the composition of the board, taking care of practical matters, conducting prenegotiation meetings, appointing a spokesperson for the child, and examining whether additional evidence is needed; for example, whether an independent expert should be appointed (in which case, the hearing is likely to be postponed for three to four months). The chair of the county board has the responsibility to ensure that the case has all the necessary information and evidence. Thus, the chair may require the parties to provide summaries, closing statements, and additional documents before a hearing is held. The county board only has direct contact with the legal representatives of the parents and of the child welfare agency. Typically, the municipality lawyer handles care order cases, and, although it is formally given notice of a care order application by the county board, the child welfare agency is most likely also to have informed the municipality lawyer of the upcoming case. The municipality lawyer can assist the child welfare agency with legal advice if the agency requires it. The parents will have appointed a lawyer according to their preferences and will be granted free legal aid.

The pre-proceeding meeting, in which the chair of the county board goes over the preparations of the case with the lawyers, is conducted in person or over the phone. In this meeting, the main aspects of the case are sorted out, including agreements and disagreements, which witnesses are to be called in, and most likely a discussion on whether an independent expert is necessary.

The county board hearing (or the *negotiation meeting* as it is known in Norway) is held as soon as possible, preferably no later than four weeks after the county board has received the care order application. The average processing time from when the county board receives an application until the first day of the negotiation meeting has increased by about 20 percent during the last four years, from seventy-five days in 2010 to approximately eighty-nine days in 2014 (Office of the Auditor General of Norway 2015, 53–54). The negotiation meeting is an *in camera proceeding* in which the parties lawyers orally present arguments, opinions, and evidence in private. Both parties may call in witnesses who may be cross-examined by the lawyers, and the chair and co-decision-makers also may ask questions. Typically, these hearings last approximately two to three days. If the parties agree, and additional requirements are fulfilled, the case can be decided by the chairman alone, and/or without a hearing. This simplified process is typically used in cases where the parents consent that their child should be taken into care.

The chair and the co-decision-makers meet after the last day of the negotiation meeting to discuss the case and make a decision. Typically, these decisions are unanimous. The written decision should be ready as soon as possible, no later than two weeks after the conclusion of the negotiation meeting. The written decisions consist of four parts: an objective (noncontested) summary of the case; the two (usually) contesting parts, each with a presentation of the viewpoints and the arguments of the parties (public and private); and finally, the county board's considerations and conclusion(s). Typically, these written decisions contain in total approximately eight to twelve full written pages.

There is a scarcity of research regarding the county board's decision-making (or the court's decision-making, for that matter) in child welfare cases (cf. literature review undertaken January 2015.) Table 3.2 presents an overview of the removal cases (Child Welfare Act sections 4-12, 4-8, 4-24), adoption cases that may include termination of parental responsibility rights (4-20), and reunification cases (4-21) that the county boards have received and decided on over the last seven years. The county board made a decision on approximately 85 percent of the applications they received.

In care order cases, the county boards' conclusions are usually to grant a care order. For example, for care order cases based on section 4-12 for the years 2008–2010, 84 percent to 88 percent of the cases resulted in a care order. In the Norwegian system, nine out of ten children with a care order are placed in foster homes. In 2010, 6,980 (6.3 children per 1,000 children) were placed out-of-home by a care order by the end of the year: Of these children, 6,294 were in foster homes, 149 in

Table 3.2. Care order, adoptions, and reunification cases (sections 4-8, 4-12, 4-20, 4-21, and 4-24), received and decided by the county boards in Norway for 2007–2013. N = cases

Case type	2007 n (%)	2008 n (%)	2009 n (%)	2010 n (%)	2011 n (%)	2012 n (%)	2013 n (%)
Section 4-12 received	812	885	910	1,122	1,191	1,363	1,333
Section 4-12 decided	655 (80%)	732 (82%)	779 (85%)	807 (72%)	876 (73%)	995 (73%)	1,135 (85%)
Section 4-8 received	152	149	154	181	185	206	200
Section 4-8 decided	147 (96%)	142 (95%)	135 (87%)	169 (93%)	161 (87%)	179 (86%)	192 (96%)
Section 4-20 received	16	26	22*	50	52	60	78
Section 4-20 decided	11 (68%)	24 (92%)	23	34 (68%)	38 (73%)	55 (91%)	62 (79%)
Section 4-21 received	210	243	258	261	252	323	360
Section 4-21 decided	174 (82%)	191 (78%)	208 (80%)	203 (77%)	214 (85%)	220 (68%)	286 (79%)
Section 4-24 received	304	352	275	288	292	292	266
Section 4-24 decided	219 (72%)	264 (75%)	214 (78%)	227 (78%)	212 (72%)	234 (80%)	227 (85%)

Source: Central Unit of the County Boards.

*The discrepancy between received and decided cases is probably due to one case being received in 2008.

contingency homes, 484 in residential units, 36 in treatment residential units, and 17 in bedsits or housing with follow-up services (NOU 2012, 67).

A county board's care order decisions may be appealed to the district court and further up in the court system (cf. Figure 3.1), and although it is not a part of the Norwegian Court system, removal cases can be applied to be reviewed by the European Court of Human Rights (ECtHR). The appeal courts can examine all parts of the case, such as evidence, procedures, and discretion (cf. the Norwegian Civil Procedure Act, Chapter 36). In practice, however, these reviews are oftentimes less about the use of judiciary discretion and more about the use and interpretation of legal sources, especially before the Supreme Court. One particularity of the Norwegian child protection decision-making system is that a county board is not defined as part of the judicial system. In other words, a specialized county court makes the first decision and a generalist district court—also considering all evidence and all arguments—makes the appeal decision. Further appeals can be made; see the overview of courts in Figure 3.1, but are dependent on being declared admissible. When examining only the care order

Table 3.3. Overview of care order decisions based on the Child Welfare Act, section 4-12, by the county boards and appealed to the district courts

Year	Decisions	Decisions pursuant to the child welfare agency	Decisions appealed to the district court
2008	732	85.8%	331 (45.2%)
2009	778	84.2%	374 (48%)
2010	807	88.4%	390 (48.3%)

Source: NOU 2012, section 6.3.2.

decisions based on section 4-12 of the Child Welfare Act, we see that a little less than half of decisions were appealed. Table 3.3 presents an overview of the decisions, decisions pursuant to the child welfare agency, and number of appealed cases. We do not know the result of the decisions made in the district courts, and statistics for the later years are not available.

By the end of 2013, the Supreme Court had screened out (Supreme Court Appeals Selection Committee) or made decisions in about 180 child welfare cases since the Child Welfare Act of 1992 was implemented. The Norwegian state has been brought in front of the ECtHR in three child welfare cases. These cases were two adoption cases (Johansen in 1996;[3] Aune in 2010[4]), and one child protection investigation case (K. T. 2007[5]). The ECtHR concluded that in one of the cases (1996), the Norwegian state had violated the concerned parents' "Right to Respect for Private and Family Life" (cf. European Convention on Human Rights, 1950, Article 8). The ECtHR is not an appeals court, and only four percent of all the cases they receive are actually accepted for further proceedings. The ECtHR can review all aspects of a case as long as they concern a right enshrined in the convention, although states are admitted a margin of appreciation. In child protection cases, however, due to the necessity for discretion (cf. the ECHR ruling Olsson vs. Sweden, 1988[6]), the ECtHR has the tendency to focus on the procedural aspects of cases and on how the decision was implemented, rather than on the actual intervention and the judicial discretion exercised. A stricter scrutiny, however, is called for in situations where the bonds between children and parents are being curtailed, such as in cases of adoption (cf. Johansen vs. Norway), and in cases concerning especially harsh measures, like removal of newborns (cf. K. and T. vs. Finland, 2001[7]). Even a care order can be found to be in violation of the parents' human rights (cf. Kutzner vs. Germany 2001[8]). The Court has stressed the necessity of separate assessments of orders; removing children into care and emergency orders, given that they are different kinds of decisions, call for different kinds of legal safeguards. The child welfare cases presented for the ECtHR are most often about the possible misuse of state power while there are rarely any disputes about the cases in which the child welfare system facilitates voluntary removals.

Voluntary removals

In section 4-4 (4), the Child Welfare Act of 1992 creates leeway for voluntary placements in the event of temporary parental problems. The conditions are that a child must be in need of particular assistance and that a placement may not last for an "extended period." Legislators underscored that this type of placement is an exception, and that the rationale for this possibility was the example of a parent who had to be hospitalized, leaving no family or friends who would be able to care for the child (Skivenes 2002). These types of removals are categorized as voluntary services, and they include no restriction on parental rights. In principle, parents may at any time require that their child be returned to live with them again. Of course, if the child welfare agency disagrees, they have the opportunity to bring the case to the county board, and the child may be withheld for three months "if there are no reasonable grounds for removing the child, or if removal may be harmful for the child" (Child Welfare Act section 4-8 [1]). During this period, the child welfare agency must decide whether the criteria for a care order (see section 4-12 cited earlier) have been met. However, even if the criteria for a care order according to section 4-12 have not been met, a care order may be made as is laid out in section 4-8 (3):

> Even if the conditions pursuant to section 4-12 are not satisfied, a care order may be made if the placement has lasted more than two years and the child has become so attached to the persons and the environment in which he/she is living that it must be assumed, on the basis of an overall assessment, that removing the child may lead to serious problems for him/her.

The statistics show that these types of removals have steadily increased since the Child Welfare Act was implemented in 1993, from 1.9 per 1,000 children in 2000 to 2.7 children per 1,000 in 2012 (cf. Table 3.1). There is scarce research and knowledge concerning why this increase has occurred, how long children are placed out of home anchored in the parents' authority, and how the children are doing. There is concern in the practice field and among researchers (Skivenes 2002, 2011; Bache-Hansen and Havik 1997) that these removals occupy a gray area of voluntary–involuntary interventions, and that they are chosen as measures based on convenience rather than on the best interests of the child after a careful assessment of the child's situation and an examination of the evidence and facts. Thus, due to the deficits in the proceedings and the lack of external oversight, these removals may represent violations of the rule of law for both the child(ren) and parents involved.

In an attempt to regulate this area, a new section (4-5) was passed in 2009. It required that a time-limited plan of measures shall be made, that the child welfare agency shall monitor these placements and the measures implemented, and that this plan shall be evaluated on a regular basis. Table 3.4 displays an

Table 3.4. Overview of the section 4-8, clause two decisions and percentage "in favor"

Year	Decisions	Decisions pursuant to the child welfare agency	Decisions appealed to the district court
2008	142	94.5%	49 (34.5%)
2009	134	98.0%	36 (26.9%)
2010	169	97.4%	51 (30.2%)

Source: NOU 2012, section 6.3.2.

overview of care order cases that started as voluntary removals and ended in involuntary removal decisions (including removals of newborns). The rate of appeals of these decisions is quite similar to the rate for ordinary care order decisions of the county board.

Emergency removals

The third route for the removal of children is when an interim order is issued due to an emergency. Emergencies may include situations in which the parents are not present or are incapacitated due to, for example, substance use, and situations in which there are reasons to believe that a child may be harmed. The criterion reads: "If there is a risk that a child will suffer material harm by remaining at home . . . ." The authority to remove resides, first, with the head of the child welfare agency (or the police) and, second and finally, with the county board, because the child welfare agency must submit an application to the county board as soon as possible, that is, no later than six weeks after the removal (section 4-6 [4]). The chairman of the county board should within forty-eight hours of having received the application approve the decision (section 7-22), and the parents may appeal the decision, which then will be decided by the county board after a hearing (section 7-23). About 98 percent of the emergency cases are handled within the legally set timelines (Office of the Auditor General of Norway 2015). Approximately 40 percent of emergency removals result in a care order application or another application to the county board (Bufetat 2014). As with ordinary care orders, there has been an increase in emergency removals, from approximately 500 children in 1994 to approximately 1,000 children in 2004 (Oppedal 2008). These statistics only recently have become accurate. In 2008, 0.9 per 1,000 children were removed through an emergency removal, and in 2012, this figure increased to 1.4 per 1,000 children (Bufetat 2014, 22). There are substantial differences in the use of emergency placements across municipalities (Bufetat 2014). The total increase in emergency placements is greater than the increase in care orders (Bufetat 2014). Approximately 70 percent of emergency removals are placements that last up to three months. The reasons for emergency removals can only be indirectly determined by assessing the serious reasons for the first entry into the care system (Bufetat 2014,

34), and in a report, the Norwegian Directorate for Children, Youth and Family Affairs emphasizes the following five reasons for entry: parents' inability to care for the child; the child's behavior; parents' substance abuse; the child having mental problems; and physical mistreatment.

As in the case of voluntary placements, the Ministry[9] and researchers (Oppedal 2008; Christiansen and Havnen 2003) are concerned that the emergency orders represent a violation of the rule of law for children and parents. According to the wording of the provision and the preparatory work, emergency decisions are to be the exception and only used in extraordinary circumstances. In practice, the exception has become the rule. For example, emergency orders may often be "eligible" care order cases that are overdue, where the child welfare agencies are not making decisions, but rather "waiting" for an emergency, to ensure that the care order application is "clear cut," that is, substantiated with the evidence from the emergency removal. Research on this subject is also scarce, however, and we cannot know what the actual primary concerns are in this area. The increase in emergency removals also may be due to an increase in family problems, an increased police focus on family problems, or other reasons. The Norwegian Directorate for Children, Youth and Family Affairs is focusing on this topic and recently (2013) initiated research on this subject to increase the knowledge base.

DISCUSSION, POSSIBLE BLIND SPOTS AND CHALLENGES

This chapter focuses on removals of children by the child protection system. Norway has been criticized by international forums on several occasions, regarding its high numbers of child welfare removals. In 2005, the Committee on the Rights of the Child (cf. CRC article 43) stated: "The Committee is concerned at the number of children who have been removed from their families and live in foster homes or other institutions. In this regard, the Committee notes the State party's willingness to review its practices concerning the removal of children from their family environment" (CRC/C/15/Add. 263, section 23-24; cf. also Søvig 2009, 159). Although the Committee did not raise a similar critique in 2010, the Committee on Economic, Social and Cultural Rights (E/C.12/1/Add. 109, section 14 and 32) criticized the Norwegian state for similar reasons. Apparently, the critique raised by these two committees is based on the understanding that the child welfare system does not provide sufficient in-home and preventive services for families and children (op cit). Thus, the critique questions the system's family-service orientation, which is considered to be a core element of the child welfare system in Norway. We lack knowledge concerning why Norway has comparatively high removal rates within its system, and these rates are puzzling given the generous and universal welfare state in place in Norway (cf. Pösö et al. 2013; Conclusion chapter in

this volume). A reason for Norway having comparatively fewer voluntary placements of children than other countries (e.g., England), is that the legislative
definition of removals of children as involuntary intrusions results in statistics
that report on a comparatively high numbers of care orders even though some
of these are voluntary. We also can speculate, however, that a child-centered approach that regards children as individuals experiencing a time-limited period
of childhood encourages the system to make decisions in favor of removals. The
Ombudsman for Children has consistently argued that children's rights should
take precedent over those of parents (and the family) (www.barneombudet.no;
cf. Andersland 2011).

The Norwegian child welfare system is family-service oriented and considered to be child-centric. The latter is particularly evident in the strong position
children are accorded in legislation and policy; this is particularly emphasized
in administrative cases and court proceedings. The challenge, in Norway as
in many other countries, is that children are not participating to the degree
envisioned in legislation. We lack persuasive explanations for why it is difficult to balance the aims of protection and participation in child protection
cases. One explanation that we believe must be further considered in the literature and research is the child welfare workers' understanding of participation: Child welfare workers' perceptions of participation are reflected in how
participation is implemented in practice. For example, in a paper comparing
child welfare workers in Norway, the United Kingdom, and the United States,
Križ and Skivenes (2014) report that the American workers displayed a one-
dimensional perspective on children's participation; namely, the purpose is to
gather information and evidence. However, both the British (in particular) and
the Norwegian workers displayed a multidimensional understanding of participation. Studies on the child's position and role in care order cases treated by the
county board clearly demonstrate that there are several blind spots (Vis et al.
2011; Magnussen and Skivenes 2015; cf. Archard and Skivenes 2009). These
studies indicate that children's views are frequently not included in the county
boards' decisions, and only in a few cases are the children's views accorded due
consideration.

We lack research on decision-making concerning child welfare, on the
county boards in particular, and in the courts in general. Norway, a member
of the Nordic law family, is a civil law system. The primary distinction in legal
traditions is between common law systems, in which the court itself is the entity
making "laws"—judicial precedent—and civil law systems, in which statuary
laws are imperative. The basic principles, fundamental legal concepts, and legal
reasoning differ between these two main systems (Bogdan 2013), although the
development in recent years may have blurred the differences. The literature
on comparative law has identified groups of legal families (Bogdan 2013; Husa
et al. 2007). The major families include English law (the common law system)
and German law (the civil law system). A particular Nordic legal family (and

civil law system) also has been identified (Husa et al. 2007), which is a branch of the German legal family but is substantially more pragmatic. In this system, the important sources of arguments and reasoning that are presented in courts are the following, ranked in descending order of importance (Eckhoff 1971): legislation, the preparatory papers for an act, court decisions, governmental practice, practice among private parties, legal theory and reasoning, and perceptions of fairness/justice. We can only speculate, but we wonder how decision-making would have been affected if children occupied a more prominent role in removal cases, for example, by being present at the county board or being able to directly present their views and interests by other means. A further issue is the balance of power between the courts and the political institutions and how supranational courts such as the ECtHR are considered to increasingly accumulate power and establish demands that may be at odds with the democratic system. This debate is not as prominent in the Norwegian public debates as in other countries, as for example, in England. Recently, a former Lord Chief Justice referred to the, in his opinion, highly problematic democratic issues involved when the ECtHR demanded that England and Wales follow a recent ECtHR decision concerning the political rights of prisoners (Daily Mail, October 1, 2014).

A related issue concerning decision-making power is the status of the county board, and the fact that a specialist county board renders the decisions in care order cases, whereas the appeals court is a generalist decision-making body. Concern exists that this arrangement reduces the quality of decision-making because the presumption is that a decision-making body with expertise in child development and social issues would be better equipped to make reasonable decisions in child protection cases than institutions lacking such expertise. In addition, there is a time issue involved, because all cases decided by the county board can be appealed to the district court for a full hearing involving all aspects of the case. This implies that the child welfare agency and the parents will have to prepare their cases again, including new evidence, children's participation, etc., all while the child is unaware of what the outcome will be. One solution is to make the county board a specialist court, namely a family court, as some have argued (Andersland 2011), to ensure that appeals must be directly filed with the appeals court. This suggestion was proposed by the Ministry of Children, Equality and Social Inclusion back in 2004, but was strongly opposed by the appeal courts (Ot. Prp 64, 2004–2005). The government now has appointed an expert committee to discuss the possibility of introducing specialized courts.

Child-protection decisions are *discretionary decisions*, in which legislation authorizes court decision-makers to exercise discretion when parents' rights and responsibilities for their children are restricted or terminated. Judiciary discretion is necessary in child protection, but is problematic, because it challenges the principles of the rule of law, democratic control and influence, and the legitimacy and quality of decisions (Herring 2014; Molander et al. 2012; Dworkin 1967). Child welfare workers and court decision-makers enjoy a high degree of discretion in the Norwegian child welfare system compared with several other child welfare systems. The legal scholar Dworkin distinguishes between strong and weak discretion. Strong discretion concerns decisions that are not "bound by any standards set by an authority" (Dworkin 1967, 33). An example of this would be when judges are given the authority to determine the best interests of the child, but are offered no instruction on how to do so. Weak discretion is when decision-makers have some authority to exercise judgment, such as when the English Children Act provides instructions on what aspects are relevant to consider in a child well-being assessment and allows judges to decide how to regard and weigh these aspects (cf. Archard and Skivenes 2009). Thus, discretion concerns the instructions that the relevant authorities provide to decision-makers. An empirical study of the "discretionary space" in child welfare systems in the United Kingdom, Finland, Norway, and the United States (California), demonstrates that the United States and the United Kingdom have established much more stringent regulations (or "standards" in Dworkin's terminology) for the exercise of discretion by decision-makers in care order preparations than have Norway and Finland (Berrick et al. 2015).

CONCLUSION

The Norwegian child welfare system, being family-service-oriented and child centric, shifts its orientation toward a legalistic order when removals of children are at stake, but is also distinguished by an undefined gray zone concerning implementation that needs to be addressed. In the Norwegian system, provision of services and working together with the family on a voluntary basis are key, but a shift happens when the risk for the child is considered to be too high. The child welfare system then takes steps to intervene by applying for a care order, which makes it clear that they will use the full provisions of the law to make sure the child's needs are met. Per definition, all removal applications to the county board are considered to be involuntary and representative of the use of State power toward the individual. Recent policy currents indicate that greater use of state/coercive power will be allowed for in the child welfare system, illustrated by the Government's recent proposal stating that in-home services can be implemented against the parents' will (The Ministry of Children, Equality and Social Inclusion 2014). This will give the child welfare system and the front-level child welfare workers authority to use more power. The increase in removals performed by the child welfare agencies that we have witnessed, with many children being removed from their homes without the county boards' thorough and vetted decision-making process, is a concern. The expansion of emergency placements and voluntary placements clearly require further investigation regarding the reasons for these developments, in conjunction with research on the well-being of children facing removal by the state. From the position of the child welfare agencies, the fact that so many children are being removed voluntarily or by an emergency removal, may indicate that an alternative legal route for removals of children that does not involve the county board is needed. However, the high number of these removals also can be due to a lack of resources, or other reasons. A final point to be made is that the issues of transparency and accountability in removal cases are cause for concern. In principle, 20 percent of all cases decided by county boards should be anonymized and made public, thereby providing the press, universities, researchers, and the general public insight into decisions made in the child welfare system. The reality is that only 2 percent to 5 percent of the decisions are made available publically (own data). A legitimate child welfare system rests upon high-quality decision-making and a transparent system.

NOTES

1   Many thanks to the editors Tarja Pösö and Kenneth Burns for insightful and important comments to this chapter, thanks also to Guri Jordbakke and Hege B. S. Helland for providing statistics. Furthermore, thanks to Nikolai Bratteli and Annette Pedersen for providing information about emergency placements and voluntary placements. As always, Ida Juhasz has been of great help.
2   The term *child welfare* characterises systems that are responsible for children at risk of harm or neglect from their caregivers or who may be at risk of harm to themselves or others. In some countries, these may be referred to as *child protection* systems.
3   Appl. No. 17383/90, judgment 7 August 1996.
4   Appl. No. 52502/07, judgment 28 October 2010.
5   Appl. No. 26664/03, judgment 25 September 2008.
6   Appl. No. 10465/83, judgment 24 March 1988, paras 60–65.
7   Appl. No. 25702/94, judgment [Grand Chamber] 12 July 2001.
8   Appl. No. 46544/99, judgment 26 February 2002.
9   The Ministry of Children, Equality and Social Inclusion sent a letter to all municipalities in 2006 regarding its concern regarding the use of emergency placements (Bufdir 2014).

REFERENCES

Andersland, K. (2011) "Mot et bedre barnevern?" [Toward a better child protection agency]. *Tidsskriftet Norges Barnevern*, 88 (3), 158–169.

Archard, D. and Skivenes, M. (2009) "Balancing a Child's Best Interest and a Child's Views." *International Journal of Children's Rights*, 17 (1), 1–21.

Bache-Hansen, E. and Havik, T. (1997) *Barnevern på barns premisser* [Child protection on the childs premise]. Oslo: Ad Notam Gyldendal.

Benneche, G. (1987) *Barnevernet i Norge* [Child welfare in Norway]. Oslo: Norwegian University Press.

Berrick, J., Pecover, S., Pösö, T., and Skivenes, M. (2015) "The Formalized Framework for Decision-Making in Child Protection Care Orders: A Cross-Country Analysis." *Journal of European Social Policy*.

Bogdan, M. (2013) *Concise Introduction to Comparative Law*. Groningen: Europa Law Publishing.

Central Unit of the County Boards (2013) *Årsrapport* [Yearly rapport]. Central Unit of the County Boards, Available from: http://www.regjeringen.no/upload/BLD/Fylkesnemnda/Arsrapport_2013.pdf, Retrieved November 12, 2014.

The Child Welfare Act (1992) *Act of 17 July 1992 No. 100 Relating to Child Welfare Services*. Available at: http://www.regjeringen.no/upload/BLD/Lover/Barnevernloven%20engelsk%2001%2001%202010.pdf. Retrieved October 21, 2014.

Christiansen, Ø. and Havnen, K. S. (2003) "Plassering utenfor hjemmet—Sammenbrudd eller gjennombrudd" [Placement outside the home, success or failure]. In Hansen, B. (Ed.), *Barn utenfor hjemmet. Flytting i Barnevernets regi*" [Children outside of the home. Placements organized by the Child Care Services]. Oslo: Gyldendal Norwegian Publishers.

Conventions of the Right of the Child (1989): United Nations Convention of the Rights of the Child. Available at: http://www.ohchr.org/en/professionalinterest/pages/crc.aspx. Retrieved October 10, 2014.

Daily Mail, October 1st, 2014. Newspaper article.

Dworkin, R. M. (1967) "The Model of Rules." *The University of Chicago Law Review*, 14, 14–46.

Eckhoff, T. (1971) *Rettferdighet ved utveksling og fordeling av verdier* [Fairness in the exchange and allocation of assets]. Bergen: Universitetsforlaget.

European Convention On Human Rights (1950) European Convention on Human Rights as amended by Protocols Nos. 11 and 14, supplemented by Protocols Nos. 1, 4, 6, 7, 12, and 13. Available at: http://www.echr.coe.int/Documents/Convention_ENG.pdf. Retrieved October 21, 2014.

European Court of Human Rights (ECtHR) judgment: Olsson [1] vs. Sweden, appl. no. 10465/83, judgment March 24, 1988.

ECtHR judgment: Johansen vs. Norway, appl. no. 17383/90, judgment August 7, 1996.

ECtHR judgment: K. and T. vs. Finland, appl. no. 25702/94, judgment (Grand Chamber) July 12, 2001.

ECtHR judgment: Kutzner vs. Germany, appl. no. 46544/99, judgment February 26, 2002.

ECtHR judgment: K.T. vs. Norway, appl. no. 26664/03, judgment September 25, 2008.

ECtHR judgment: Aune vs. Norway, appl. no. 52502/07, judgment October 28, 2010.

Gilbert, N. (1997) *Combatting Child Abuse: International Perspectives and Trends,* New York: Oxford University Press.

Gilbert, N. Parton, N., and Skivenes, M. (2011) *Child Protection Systems: International Trends and Orientation,* New York: Oxford University Press.

Herring, J. (2014) "The Welfare Principle and the Children: Presumably It's About Welfare?" *Journal of Social Welfare and Family Law,* 36 (1), 14–25.

Husa, J., Nuotio, K., and Pihlajamaki, H. (2007) "Nordic Law—Between Tradition and Dynamism." Ius Commune: European and Comparative Law Series, Volume 66, Intersentia.

Kriz, K. and Skivenes, M. (2015) "Child Welfare Workers Perception of Children's Participation: A Comparative of England, Norway and the United States (California)." *Child and Family Social Work.* DOI: 10.1111/cfs.12224

Križ, K. and Skivenes, M. (2014) "Street-level Policy Aims of Child Welfare Workers in England, Norway and the United States: An Exploratory Study." *Child and Youth Services Review,* 40, 71–78.

Magnussen, A-M and Skivenes, M. (2015) "The Child's Opinion and Position in Care Order Proceedings: An Analysis of Judiciary Discretion in the County Boards Decision-making." *International Journal of Children's Rights,* 23(4), 705-723.

The Ministry of Children and Equality (2009) *Om Lov om endringer i Barneloven,* Ot. prp. 69 (2008–2009) [Proposition to the Odelsting, nr 69(2008–2009) about changes in the Children Act]. Oslo. Available at: http://www.regjerin-gen.no/nn/dep/bld/dok/regpubl/otprp/2008-2009/otprp-nr-69-2008-2009-.html?id=556260. Retrieved: October 21, 2014.

The Ministry of Children, Equality and Social Inclusion (2013) *Endringer i barnevernloven,* Prop. 106 L (2012-2013) [Proposition 106 L, (2012–2013) Changes in the Children Act]. Oslo. Available at: http://www.regjeringen. no/en/dep/bld/documents/propositions-and-reports/prop/2012-2013/prop-106-l-20122013.html?id=720934. Retrieved October 21, 2014.

The Ministry of Children, Equality and Social Inclusion (2014) Paper for public hearing of October 20, 2014. Suggestion to change the Child Welfare Act to make it possible to implement involuntary in-home services (Forslag om å utvide adgangen til å pålegge hjelpetiltak med hjemmel i lov om barneverntjenester).

The Ministry of Children and Family (2005) Om lov om endringer i lov 17. juli 1992 nr. 100 om barneverntjenester og lov 13. desember 1991 nr. 81 om sos-iale tjenester (sosialtjenesteloven) m.v., Ot. prp. 64 (2004–2005) [Proposition to the Odelsting, 2004–2005 regarding changes in law of the 17th of July

1992, nr. 100 about Child Welfare Services, and law of the 13th of December 1991, nr. 81, about social services (The Social Services Act)]. Oslo. Available at: http://www.regjeringen.no/nn/dep/bld/Dokument/proposisjonar-og-meldingar/Odelstingsproposisjonar/20042005/otprp-nr-64-2004-2005-.html?id=398514, Retrieved November 12, 2014.

Molander, A., Grimen, H., and Eriksen, E. O. (2012) "Professional Discretion and Accountability in the Welfare State." *Journal of Applied Philosophy*, 29(3), 214–230.

Norwegian Directorate for Children, Youth and Family Affairs (Bufetat) (2014) *Akuttarbeid i kommunalt barnevern* [Emergency work in child welfare in the municipalities]. Norwegian Directorate for Children, Youth and Family Affairs. Available at: http://www.bufetat.no/Documents/Bufetat.no/Nett_Bufdir_Akuttrapport_2014_TRYKK.pdf Retrieved October 21, 2014.

NOU (2012) *Bedre beskyttelse av barns utvikling* [Better protection of child development]. Official Norwegian Report (NOU), Oslo. Available at: http://www.regjeringen.no/nb/dep/bld/dok/nouer/2012/nou-2012-5.html?id=671400. Retrieved October 21, 2014.

Office of the Auditor General of Norway (2015) Riksrevisjonens undersøkelse av saksbehandling i Fylkesnemndene for barnevern og sosiale saker. Dokument 3:10 (2014–2015). Fagbokforlaget. Available at: https://www.riksrevisjonen.no/rapporter/Documents/2014-2015/SaksbehandlingFylkesnemndeneBarnevern.pdf. Retrieved July 2, 2015.

Oppedal, M. (2008) *Akutthjemlene i barnevernloven [Emergency Authorizations in the Child Welfare Act]*. Oslo: Gyldendal Akademisk.

Pösö, T., Skivenes, M., and Hestbæk, A. D. (2014) "Child Protection Systems in the Danish, Finnish and Norwegian Welfare States—Time for a Child Centric Approach?" *European Journal of Social Work*. 17(4), 475–490.

Q-42/2015. *Guidelines on the Treatment of Child Welfare Cases in Which Children are Affiliated to Other Countries*. Oslo: Ministry of Children, Equality and Social Inclusion.

Sandberg, K. (2014) "The Role of National Courts in Promoting Children's Rights: The Case of Norway," *The International Journal of Children's Rights*, 22(1), 1–20.

Skivenes, M. (2002) "Lovgivning og legitimitet: en evaluering av lov om barneverntjenester av 1992 i et deliberativt perspektiv" [Legislation and legitimacy: An evaluation of the Child Welfare act of 1992 in a deliberative perspective]. Dissertation for the degree of *philosophiae doctor* (PhD), University of Bergen.

Skivenes, M. (2010) "Judging the Child's Best Interests: Rational Reasoning or Subjective Presumptions?" *Acta Sociologica*, 53(4), 339–353.

Skivenes, M. (2011) "Norway—Toward a Child Centric Perspective," In Gilbert, N., Parton, N., and Skivenes, M. (Eds.), *Child Protection Systems: International Trends and Emerging Orientations*, pp. 154–179. New York: Oxford University Press.

Skivenes, M. (2014) "How the Norwegian Child Welfare System Approaches Migrant Children," In Skivenes, M., Barn, R., Križ, K., and Pösö, T. (Eds.), *Child Welfare Systems and Migrant Children—A Cross Country Study of Policies and Practices*, pp. 154–179. New York: Oxford University Press.

Stang, E. G. (2007) *Det er barnets sak. Barns rettsstilling i sak om hjelpetiltak etter barnevernloven § 4-4* [It's the childs' case. The legal position of the child in cases concerning voluntary measures according to the Child Welfare Act section 4-4]. Oslo: Universitesforlaget.

Statistics Norway (2013) Child Welfare 2012. Available at: http://www.ssb.no/sosiale-forhold-og-kriminalitet/statistikker/barneverng/aar. Retrieved October 9, 2014.

Søvig, K. H. (2009) Barnets rettigheter på barnets premisser [The rights of the child on the childs own premise]. (Det juridiske fakultets skriftserie (UiB) nr. 115 [2009]).

van Thiel, S. (2007) *Research Methods in Public Administration and Public Management*. London: Routledge.

Vis, S. A., Strandbu, A., Holtan, A., and Thomas, N. (2011) "Participation and Health – a Research Review of Child Participation in Planning and Decision-making." *Child & Family Social Work*, 16 (3), 325–335.

4

PLACING CHILDREN IN STATE CARE IN SWEDEN

DECISION-MAKING BODIES, LAYPERSONS, AND LEGAL FRAMEWORK

Gustav Svensson and Staffan Höjer

INTRODUCTION—THE POLICY CONTEXT

In various comparisons of child welfare/child protection systems, Sweden is normally categorized as a family-service-oriented system in a Scandinavian welfare model (Gilbert et al. 2011; Cameron and Freymond 2006; Gilbert 1997). This categorization can be questioned, at least to some extent, because, as the following chapter will discuss, many child protection elements have been emphasized over the last decade. In classic welfare theory, Sweden is one of the "ideal" types of a Scandinavian welfare state built on universal values, high taxation, and involving substantial state involvement and responsibility in welfare provisions (Esping Andersen 1996). Welfare activities are characterized by proactive state involvement in the lives of individuals and families, with a willingness to identify certain groups and individuals in difficult life situations in order to prevent more severe problems later on. There are a number of primary prevention strategies (e.g., general prenatal supporting measures in public health care), secondary prevention strategies for groups at risk for negative development (e.g., open-care activities such as contact families for families in need of support), as well as tertiary interventions in order to, for example, support and treat those who misuse substances.

The family-service orientation considers the various problems found among parents and families as central to the understanding of the child's situation. In a family-service orientation, services should always focus on alleviating these problematic conditions within the family. Hence, out-of-home care placements for children only should be considered as a last resort, and when out-of-home placements are carried out, the overarching goal should always be to sustain contact with the child's birth family in order to facilitate the child's move back to the family home, whenever this proves to be possible and safe. As much as possible, all interventions should be done in cooperation or partnership with the family. It has been argued, in Sweden and elsewhere, that this approach has led to too much of an emphasis on the views of parents and not enough focus on the needs and wishes of children (e.g., Mattsson 2008). However, since January 1, 2013 in Sweden, there have been changes in the Social Services Act (SoL), which aim at strengthening the focus on and the rights of children.[1] For example, this Act prescribes that the views of the child shall always, independent of age, be made clear as far as possible and if a decision concerns care or treatment for the child, the best interest of the child shall be paramount.

In this chapter we will examine the social and legal decision-making systems concerned with the removal by the Swedish state of children from their family homes. Section 2 describes the relevant Swedish decision-making bodies; section 3 examines the various ways to remove a child from his/her own home in Sweden, and this is followed in section 4 by a description of the relevant statistics on children, child protection, and child removals. Sections 5 and 6 provide an analysis and commentary on the strengths, weaknesses, and distinctive features of the Swedish system. In particular, we will emphasize some of the unique traits of the Swedish system, such as the role of laypersons in these decision-making bodies, the use of Social Welfare Boards, and the rights of children in these decision-making processes.

THE DECISION-MAKING BODIES

Social Welfare Boards

To contextualize the discussion on care orders and decision-making bodies in Sweden, we will first briefly outline the context for child protection in Sweden. Social services in Sweden are organized at the local level in 290 municipalities. The national state has regulated general directions within a legislative framework of the Social Services Act (SoL) (2001: 453) and related laws (see below); however, it is the responsibility of the municipalities to create social services in line with this framework. The law requires every municipality to have a board that deals with the tasks that are mentioned in the social legislation (e.g., the welfare of children).

In practice this means that each municipality normally has a Social Welfare Board (SWB) even if the actual name can vary across municipalities. Political parties, in response to the results of the local and general elections, nominate the members of these boards. In the larger cities there are several SWBs, divided along geographical lines. A board can have up to twenty delegates and normally a specific Social Welfare Committee (SWC) is formed from a subsection of the SWB. Decision-making in individual cases that are under the jurisdiction of the board is normally handled in the SWC committee, which often consists of five to eight delegates. The committee members are all laypersons and no one has special knowledge in social and child welfare/child protection matters. These laypersons are older and more educated than the public in general, but they generally do not have any specific education in a welfare profession, such as social work, psychology, nursing, or medicine (see Höjer et al. 2014). In this chapter, we will consider both the SWB and the SWC, because the role of the SWB is determined in the law, but in practice, the work is delegated to the SWCs.

The members of the SWC are not supposed to act according to their political ideology; instead, they are instructed to follow the law and act in the best interests of the child. These laypersons are understood to represent the "good citizens" in their constituencies, using sound judgment based upon social-service social workers' assessments and their own common sense (Forkby et al. 2014). The majority of decisions are delegated to the social workers in the local social services according to the discretion of the local board.[2] Independent of who is the decision-maker (professionals, committee, or board), a board's decisions can be appealed by parents to an administrative court.

Administrative Courts

The court of first instance is the county administrative court, the second the regional administrative court, and the third, the Supreme administrative court. Voluntary measures always can be appealed to the county administrative court. To appeal to the regional and to the Supreme administrative court, a *prövningstillstånd* (trial permission) is required. Coercive measures start in the county administrative court and these decisions can be appealed to the regional administrative court. To appeal to the Supreme administrative court in the coercive cases, a trial permission also is required. Laymen appear in both the county and the regional administrative courts. The Supreme administrative court only consists of professional judges.[3]

REMOVALS OF CHILDREN OUTSIDE THEIR OWN HOME

Removals of children outside their own home can be done in one of two ways. Either the removal is a voluntary action or it is done through a court-based process. These two different ways will be described in more detail in the following sections.

Voluntary removals

When the removal of a child from his or her own home is a voluntary action, the decision is taken by the SWB within the framework of social assistance outlined in SoL. Social assistance is the basic form of voluntary help, financial and otherwise, that the SWB provides to individuals. The crucial criterion is that there exists a reasonable need of care for the child, a need that cannot be responded to in any other way than by social assistance.

A precondition for a decision of social assistance is an application. The application is usually made by the parent(s)/custodian(s) and is an application for care of the child either in a family home (foster care) or in an institutional HVB [home for care or residence].[4] An application also can be made by a child, and we will discuss this in greater depth later in the chapter. In practice, however, it is very seldom that the first contact between the family and the social service is an application for assistance from the custodians (see, for example, Wiklund 2006). Instead, most cases of voluntary removal are initiated by a report, from either a professional or a private citizen. According to the provisions in the 14 chap 1 § of the SoL, professionals working with children have an obligation to report to the SWB if they learn or a suspect that a child is at risk. According to the 14 chap 1 c § SoL, a private citizen is requested to report to the SWB if he or she has similar knowledge or suspicion; however, unlike for professionals, this is not a legal obligation.

When a report is received by the SWB, the board has to assess, out of the information in the report, whether a case of child maltreatment is likely.[5] If this preliminary assessment, which must be done within fourteen days, shows that a case of child maltreatment is *not* likely, the SWB will take no action and the report will simply be saved at the office. If, on the other hand, the preliminary assessment shows that such a case is likely, an investigation must be opened. The aim of such an investigation, carried out by social workers, is to find a solution that all parties involved can accept. If the proposed solution is a removal of the child outside her or his own home and all parties involved agree, the parent/custodians can apply for social assistance. This decision has to be made by the SWC (or in rare cases by the SWB), because the law prohibits such a decision from being made by a single social worker.

If the custody of the child is common, and the application is made by just one of them, the other parent must consent to the application.[6] In addition, the child, if he/she is more than fifteen years old, must consent to the application. If all of the parties do not consent, then the removal, if still considered necessary, has to be decided upon by the administrative court, upon application by the SWB and involves coercion. If the child is younger than fifteen years of age, his or her consent is *not* a precondition for the removal. If a child of any age, however, opposes his or her removal from the biological family, this may contradict that the removal is in the best interest of the child. This is perhaps especially true if the child is just below the age of fifteen.[7] A child older than fifteen years can apply on his/her own to be removed from the biological home and has the right to plead his/her own case (see 11 chap 10 § SoL). In such cases, however, the custodians also have to consent to the application. If the custodians do not consent, again the decision of removal must be a decision of coercion in the administrative court (more about this in section 3 below).

As was remarked earlier the decision about an out-of-home placement is a decision about social assistance. The application will be judged in light of the prerequisites for such assistance. The prerequisites are described in the 4 chap 1 § of the SoL, which says:

> A person who cannot provide for his/her needs or have them provided in any other way is entitled to assistance from the social welfare board towards his livelihood and other aspects of living.
>
> . . .
>
> The individual shall by the assistance be assured a reasonable level of living . . .

Applied to this situation this means that the applicant has to show:

(1) That there is a reasonable need for a placement of the child outside his/her own home; and,
(2) that this need cannot be fulfilled in any other way than with social assistance.

If the application is a result of talks between the social workers and the parents (and the child) the SWC most likely will consent to the application (Forkby et al. 2014). This is a consequence of the fact that the social workers generally are seen as the experts and it is difficult for the members of the SWC to have an opinion that deviates from the one held by the social workers. *If* the application is rejected by the SWC, however, the custodians can appeal this decision to the county administrative court. The county administrative court will then examine the application in light of the same prerequisites as the SWC.

The county administrative court consists of one judge and three laypersons. The municipal council appoints the laypersons in the court after suggestions from the political parties. They shall represent "the ordinary citizen" and they have no special education either in law or in social matters. The three laypersons will, if they are unanimous, dictate the decision even if the judge does not agree. Otherwise, the decision will reflect the view that the judge is expressing. Of course, the opinions of the laypersons in the court must be grounded in the law, and they are not allowed to let their political view determine their decision. Whether this happens or not is, however, an empirical question. For example, lately it has been debated whether persons representing a specific right-wing party critical of immigration should be chosen as laypersons given that their judgment in some cases can be questioned.

If the county administrative court assents to the appeal, the decision by the court should be executed at once by the SWB (16 chap 3 § SoL). The SWB can, however, appeal this decision to the regional administrative court. A precondition for the regional administrative court to examine the case is then "trial permission" (prövningstillstånd). Trial permission only is given if the case is a matter of principle. Both the board and the applicants have as a last option the right to appeal the decision of the regional court to the Supreme administrative court. A precondition for this, however, is that the case is an obvious matter of principle and that means that this will only happen in very rare cases. The Supreme Administrative court consists in these cases of five professional judges.

After the out-of-home care placement, the work by social services shall be directed toward a reunion between the child and the rest of the family. The SWB shall at least every sixth month reconsider whether there still is a need for out-of-home care (see 6 chap 8 § SoL). Since 2003, however, in order to grant permanency and stability for the child, Swedish legislation states that when the child has lived for three years in the same family home, the SWB shall consider whether the custody of the child shall be transferred to the foster parents (6 chap 8 § SoL).

The decision about transferring custody to the foster parents is taken up by the district court. A prerequisite is that such a decision should be made in the best interest of the child (6 chap 8 § of the Parental code). In 2012, custody was transferred to foster parents in 246 cases (Socialstyrelsen 2014a). If custody is transferred to foster parents, the stay of the child in the foster family is no longer a social services placement and the foster parents no longer receive the normal economic payment from the SWB. The SWB, however, still has the right to pay some money to the family each month as a kind of compensation (6 chap 11 § SoL). The board also is obliged to give the new custodians special advice and support. If custody is transferred to the foster parents, they can later proceed with an adoption. This is a private action, however, and investigations have shown that the SWB very seldom initiates adoptions. In 2012, only fourteen children placed in foster care had been adopted (Socialstyrelsen 2014a). Thus, in Sweden, transfer of custody rather than adoption is the alternative to placement by the SWB.

Removals by coercion

The question of removal by coercion can arise if it is impossible to find a voluntary solution to the problem, and the SWB still considers it necessary that a child is placed outside of his/her own home. In these cases, the SWB has the right to contact any person who can contribute information, even if the custodians do not consent to this (see 11 chap 2 § SoL). The SWB also is allowed to talk with the child without the consent of the custodians and without the custodians being present. The reason for this is that the SWB shall then get the best picture of the situation (see Leviner 2011).

If the investigation shows that a placement outside the home of the child is the best action, but the custodians (and the child, if he/she is older than fifteen years) do not give their consent, an application for removal by coercion has to be made by SWB to the local administrative court. Before this happens, however, the social workers have to present the case to the SWC. The custodians and the child (if he/she is older than fifteen years) have the right to be present at this meeting. A public counsel also shall be appointed for the custodians and the child. If the child is younger than fifteen years, the public counsel is the legal representative for the child instead of the parents. This is the case because of the likelihood that the parents and the child have different interests in these situations.

Argumentation from the custodians or the child (or the public counsel of the child) may result in the SWC *not* making an application to the county administrative court. The social workers then have to go on trying to find a voluntary solution. In most cases, however, the SWC agrees with the social workers and consents to an application to the county administrative court.

According to the Care of Young Persons Act, LVU (1990), the decision about coercive care is made by the county administrative court. Before the decision by the court there is an oral session. All parties, including their public counsels, are invited to this oral session. At the oral session the parties have the opportunity to add arguments and views on the investigation in written form. In addition, the judge often questions the parties. The court process is an inquisitorial model rather than an adversarial one. At the end of the oral session, the court declares when there will be a decision in the case. If the child is taken into immediate care the decision often will be given the same day at the oral session, otherwise the decision is announced within a couple of weeks.

According to the LVU Act, removal by coercion can be done in two different cases; the environmental case and the behavioral case. The *environmental case* is described in 2 § of the LVU:

> A care order is to be issued if, due to physical or mental abuse, exploitation, neglect or some other circumstance in the home, there is a palpable risk of detriment to the young person's health or development.

The applications for care removals in environmental cases focus on the child's family circumstances. A care order in these cases can be given up until the child is eighteen years old (see the second section of the 1 § LVU). The *behavioral cases* are described in the 3 § of LVU, and the first section of this provision is worded as follows:

> A care order is also to be made if the young person exposes his health or development to a palpable risk of injury through the abuse of addictive substances, criminal activity or some other socially degrading behaviour.

As can be seen in this section, the causative factors in behavioral cases are bound to the young person him/herself. A care order can be given up until the young person is twenty years old (see the third section of the 1§ of LVU). If the young person is older than eighteen years, a prerequisite is that care according to LVU is better than any other care (e.g., the treatment of offenders).

In both environmental and behavioral cases, however, it is not enough that one can identify the causative factors; the crucial point is that there is *a palpable risk* for the health or development of the child. The assessment of what constitutes a palpable risk is one of several difficult questions that arise when the provisions of LVU are put into practice; more about this in the discussion, section 'the rule of law'. section 5

The county administrative court only answers yes or no to the question of whether coercive care shall be allowed. If the court says yes, the child is removed from his/her home and placed in either a family home (earlier described as "foster home") or in an institution. Care in an institution can be given as residential care (HVB) or in special supervisory homes ("§ 12-homes"). In special supervisory homes there are certain departments where a child can be placed in a secure (i.e., locked) placement. Less than 3 percent of all children in care in Sweden are placed in special supervisiory homes. After a period of time where parents have demonstrated progress and the home situation has improved, the child also can be placed in his/her own home, but care shall always start outside his/her own home (11§ LVU). When children are placed in their own homes, it is mostly done as a test to establish whether coercive care can come to an end.

Where the care shall be provided is a question for the SWB to decide upon (11 § LVU). Through a "treatment-plan," which the SWB shall attach to its application to the court, the court shall, however, be informed where the SWB intends to place the child. If the first placement does not work, the SWB has the right to decide upon a new placement. This decision can be appealed to the county administrative court by the custodians or by the young person if he/she is older than fifteen years (see 41 § LVU).

If the county administrative court assents to the application of the SWB the custodians and the child have the right to appeal this decision to the regional administrative court. In these cases, the regional administrative court consists of three professional judges and two laypersons. If the child is younger than fifteen years the appeal is made by the public counsel, usually a lawyer, who, instead of the custodians, is the public deputy for the child in matters related to the case. On the other hand, should the county administrative court reject the SWB's application, the SWB has the right to appeal this decision. This right also can be exercised by the child him/herself or by the public counsel for the child, if the child is younger than fifteen years. The child or the public counsel can argue that it is in the best interest of the child to be placed outside her/his own home, even if the custodians do not agree. The verdict of the regional administrative court can be appealed to the Supreme Administrative court. A precondition for this is a "trial permission," which is given very seldom and only in obvious matters of principle.

As has been described above, the decision about coercive care is rendered by a court after an application from the SWB. This is sometimes quite a long process and if a delay is combined with a risk for the child, he or she can be placed in care immediately (6 § LVU). Such a decision should be taken by the SWC, but in urgent cases, it can be taken by the chairman or some other member of the SWC who has been delegated this responsibility. In these cases the police can be asked to execute the decision. In all cases the decision shall be submitted to the county administrative court within one week (7 § LVU).

If the county administrative court has decided about coercive care the SWB every sixth month has to *consider*, in environmental cases, whether care shall continue and, in behavioral cases, *examine* whether the care can be terminated. When the SWB *examines* a case a new decision is rendered no matter whether the care is terminated, a decision against which an appeal can be made. This is not the case when the SWB only has *considered* whether the care shall continue. The state's aim with coercive care, in the same way as with voluntary care, is that it shall promote a reunion with the biological family where possible. In coercive care (as with voluntary care) the SWB shall consider, when the child has lived for three years in the same family home, whether the custody of the child could be transferred to the foster parents (see, for example, Leviner 2014). If the SWB does not succeed with this transfer of custody, the coercive care under all circumstances must come to an end when—in the environmental case—the young person is eighteen years old, and—in the behavioral case—the young person is twenty-one years old (see 21 § LVU).

STATISTICS ABOUT CHILDREN IN CARE IN SWEDEN

In 2013, Sweden had slightly fewer than 10 million inhabitants, with a relatively high influx of immigrants.[8] In fact, around 17 percent of this total population of 10 million was not born in Sweden. One-fifth of the population is between zero and seventeen years of age—slightly fewer than 2 million children (see Table 4.1).

The number of children placed in care in Sweden at the end of 2013 was 22,668 (see Table 4.2). This represents a little less than 1 percent of the population in the respective age group, or 0.98 percent to be precise. As described above, Swedish law allows children and young persons to be placed in care up to age twenty years, providing certain preconditions are met. When compared with other European countries, where the age group normally is children younger than eighteen years of age, the number in care in Sweden was

Table 4.1. Number of children in Sweden zero to seventeen years of age and percentage of population in 2013

Age Groups	Numbers	Percentage of Population in 2013
0–12	1,448,317	15.0%
13–17	504,148	5.2%
Total	**1,953,265**	**20.2%**

just above 16,600. This represents 0.85 percent (8.5 per 1,000) of the population, more than England and Ireland, but less than Finland and Norway (see other chapters). More boys than girls are placed in care, especially among teenagers.

Teenagers are on the whole placed in care much more often than are children between zero and twelve years of age. In relative terms it is four times as common to be placed in care as a teenager compared with younger age groups (1.85 vs. 0.47 in relation to the age group). If a close-up picture is given, the most prevalent age for children being placed in care in Sweden is between fifteen and seventeen years of age (see Table 4.3). There are differences in relation to placement patterns between boys and girls. Overall, boys' placements represent 60 percent of the total and girls 40 percent, accordingly. The difference is smaller, however, for younger children placed in care, but it increases with age (see Table 4.2 and 4.3). Especially for teenagers older than fifteen years, more boys than girls are placed in care.

In November 2013, 17,000 Swedish children (0–20 years of age) were placed in care on voluntary grounds (SoL) and 5,400 through involuntary processes (LVU). Additionally, about 250 children were immediately and involuntarily placed in care by the board, according to 6 § LVU (for the legal foundations of this, see previous sections). This means that almost three out of four placements are voluntary under the SoL, which is even higher than the ratio of children placed in voluntary care in Ireland (see Chapter 7). In relative terms, just over

Table 4.2. Number and percentage of children looked after in care, end of year 2013.[i] Percentages refer to the share of children in same age group

Age Group	Total Numbers	Percentage	Boys	Percentage	Girls	Percentage
0–12	6,388	0.47	3,376		3,012	
13–17	10,215	1.85	6,645		3,570	
Total 0–17	*16,603*	*0.85*	*10,021*	*1.02*	*6,582*	*0.67*
18–20	6,065	1.52	3,980		2,085	
Total 0–20	*22,668*	*0.98*	*14,001*		*8,667*	

[i] According to Swedish statistics the figure describes the situation on November 1 each year.

Table 4.3. Age of children in care at the end of the year 2013. Numbers, presented with age and sex of children

Age Placed in Care	0–3	4–6	7–9	10–12	13–14	15–17	18–20	0–20
Boys	622	725	918	1,111	1,240	5,405	3,980	**14,001**
Girls	632	668	755	957	950	2,620	2,085	**8,667**
Total	**1,254**	**1,393**	**1,673**	**2,068**	**2,190**	**8,025**	**6,065**	**22,668**

7.3 children per 1,000 are placed in care voluntarily and 2.4 per 1,000 involuntarily (see Table 4.4).

When examining the reasons to be placed in care, it is more commonly due to environmental causes than behavioral ones. Environmental causes include various forms of neglect and abuse. Previous research has shown that among the reasons for placing young people in care in Sweden, neglect dominates over different forms of abuse (Sundell et al. 2007). The older the child, however, the more commonly was care based on the child's own behavior. When it comes to care orders for young people over eighteen years of age, the law restricts these to orders based on the child's own behavior. Because boys are overrepresented in care orders due to their own behavior, placement patterns and causes for the placement intersect.

Between 2008 and 2013 the number of children on involuntary care orders increased from 2.13 to 2.43 per 1,000 children in the total population, an increase of 14 percent (see Table 4.4). Voluntary care orders during the same period have increased from 4.45 to 7.35 per 1,000 children, an increase of 65 percent. These

Table 4.4. Children 0–20[i] years of age placed in care according to SoL (voluntary) or LVU (involuntary) placement from 2008 to 2013, as a result of environment/family, behavior, or both. Figures end of each year, per 1,000 children in the total population

Year	SoL Total	LVU[ii] Total	Total Children in care (SoL and LVU)	There of LVU Only Environment	There of LVU Only Behavior	There of LVU both Environment and Behavior
2008	4.45	2.13	6.58	1.45	0.53	0.05
2009	4.61	2.13	6.74	1.47	0.49	0.06
2010	4.98	2.16	7.14	1.48	0.49	0.06
2011	5.66	2.26	7.92	1.56	0.49	0.07
2012	6.56	2.36	8.92	1.67	0.49	0.08
2013	7.35	2.43	9.78	1.76	0.47	0.10

[i] Note, this table shows placements in care 0–20 years, not 0–18.

[ii] LVU here contains both children in care because of decisions of immediate custody from the board (signifies between 0.10 and 0.12 the various years) and children placed in care by care orders of the administrative court.

increases occurred despite the fact that during this period many municipalities were trying to develop open-care interventions in order to decrease the number of children placed in care.

The increase in care placements in the group over thirteen years of age is especially to be noted. A possible explanation often mentioned for this is the increase of unaccompanied refugee children; however, this is only a tentative explanation given that the evidence-base is limited at present. National statistics do not record how many children in care are unaccompanied (minor) refugees. We do know, however, how many unaccompanied children arrive in Sweden each year and these numbers have increased during the last decade. During 2013, 3,000 unaccompanied children arrived in Sweden, with many of these children being looked after through the care system (Socialstyrelsen 2014b). The number has increased further during the last two years.

Foster care is the dominant form of care in Sweden. As described above, we differentiate among three main forms: foster care, residential care (HVB), and special supervisory homes (so-called §12 homes). The latter are state owned and have a right to, among other things, incarcerate children against their will, and use other kinds of restraint such as detention. Residential care can be owned by various types of public or private providers. There are two other forms presented in the table, one is called "own home" and involves cases where the child under certain conditions can be placed in care in his/her own home (see Table 4.5).

Young children zero to twelve years of age are almost always, close to nine times out of ten, placed in foster care with no significant difference between boys and girls. When it comes to older children, however, the teenage boys are more often placed in residential care, whereas almost three out of four of the teenage girls are placed in foster care. This pattern has been quite stable over time and was more or less the same fifteen years ago (Höjer 2001). The special supervisory homes represent 3 percent of the placement of boys and 2 percent of the placement of girls. During 2013, 364 girls and 926 boys were placed. The average number of days in this form of placement was 140 (SiS 2014).

Table 4.5. Gender and age differences in form of placement. Share of different forms of placement for children placed in care, November 1, 2013

Form of Placement	0–12 Years Boys/Girls	13–17 Years Boys/Girls	18–20 Years Boys/Girls	Total 0–20 Boys/Girls
Total number Part of in percentage:	3,376/3,018	6,645/3,570	3,980/2,085	14,001/8,667
Foster care	86/86	42/72	36/62	51/74
Residential care	11/11	51/22	55/31	43/21
Special supervisory homes	0/0	4/3	4/3	3/2
Own home	2/2	1/2	1/1	1/2
Other	1/1	2/1	4/4	2/2

DISCUSSION AND CHALLENGES

Rights for the parents or for the child?

When discussing the legal situation for children in Sweden, international conventions are, of course, of great importance. Two that should be mentioned especially are the European Convention on Human Rights (ECHR) and the United Nations Convention on the Rights of the Child (UNCRC). Concerning the situation for children and families, the two conventions to a certain extent have different foci, which makes the situation somewhat complicated.

ECHR was for a long time just a part of Swedish international law, but when Sweden entered into the European Union in 1995, ECHR was transformed into Swedish internal law. In Article 8 of the ECHR "family" is an important concept. During the late 1980s and early 1990s Sweden was convicted several times by the European Court in Strasbourg.[9] The reason was that Swedish social legislation, especially the provisions in the LVU from 1980 and the application of them, was considered not to be in accordance with the ECHR. The judgments from the European Court in Strasbourg can be interpreted as stressing the importance of the family.

The UNCRC, on the other hand, declares that when there is an action concerning children the best interest of the child shall be a primary consideration. To meet the demands of the UNCRC, the Swedish legislation concerning child protection has, at least formally, a very distinctive child-orientated perspective.[10] Since 1998, it was stated in the SoL that when actions concerned children, the best interest of the child should be considered especially important. From the same year, 1 § of the LVU states that, when it comes to decisions, the best interest of the child shall be decisive. There are ongoing reforms to reinforce legal protections for children. Since January 1, 2013, an amendment in SoL has stated that the best interest of the child shall be the decisive factor when decisions are taken about care and treatment of children.

But despite this reinforcement of the law to protect children, the legislation still might be criticized in some ways. The provisions concerning the investigations that the board shall make are not coherent. During recent years, legislature has emphasized that the investigations should cover situations where the SWB can give not just protection, but also *support* to the families involved.[11] Thus 11 chap 2 § SoL speaks about investigations on "protection and support" of the child. But the 1 § of the same chapter still states that the SWB shall open an investigation when it has knowledge about something that might lead to an action from the board. A consequence of this is that if the custodians refuse to cooperate, an investigation cannot be opened if it is not a serious situation. In fact, the situation must be so serious that the SWB, as an utmost action, has to intervene with coercion, according to LVU. A situation where the SWB realizes from the beginning that it will only be able to offer support is not sufficient (Svensson 2012b; Östberg 2010).

Another part of the legislation that is questioned is the principle that the work of the social services, after a child is removed from his/her own home, shall aim at the reunion of the child with the rest of the family. The principle could be interpreted as meaning that the interest of the parents and the family supersedes the well-being of the child. The official view, however, is that a reunion, if it is done early, is always in the best interest of the child (and in the best interest of the family).[12] The biological parents are considered to have something unique for the child, something that other adult persons cannot recreate, whatever sense of responsibility they may have. A separation will thus cause negative effects, above all a disturbance of the child's process of connection and attachment to his/her parents, even if it brings about benefits (and risks) in other respects. Thus the official view is that *if* a separation has become unavoidable, it is natural that the work of social services should aim for a reunion. But according to the law it is also (nowadays) regarded natural that after three years in the same care placement the SWB shall consider whether the custody of the child shall be transferred to the foster parents. After such a long separation, the child's safety is regarded as a higher priority than maintaining the idea that perhaps, in the future, a reunion with the biological parents might be possible.

A third point where the Swedish legislation has been questioned is the fact that cases concerning children are handled by the common administrative courts. The question has been raised whether it would be better to let such cases be handled by special juvenile courts (see, for example, Leviner 2012b). This question is complicated by many factors and there are both advantages and disadvantages to such a change, but these are not enumerated here. When it comes to practicing the legislation, research reports have indicated the law is not always applied in the way that the legislature expects (see Leviner 2011).

Up until the end of 2012 professionals working with children had an obligation to report to the SWB if they learned of something that could mean that the SWB had to intervene in a child protection matter. Research has shown, however, that there was an "under-reporting" of child cases to the SWB from professionals (e.g., reports from hospitals) (Svärd 2014). The professionals conducted investigations of their own before, or sometimes instead of, reporting to the SWB and that meant, many claimed, that the children did not get the protection to which they were entitled. Therefore, the provisions for reporting to the SWB have been changed and from the start of 2013 professionals are obliged to report to the SWB if in the course of their work they suspect that a child is at risk. Perhaps this change will improve the identification of children at risk.

If on the other hand an investigation is opened, research has shown that the investigation, despite the provisions in the legislation, has a parent-focused perspective rather than a child-centric one. Social workers include and talk with children in the assessment process, but the view of the child appears to have had little importance in social workers' decisions. Social workers act only when harm has occurred and not when there is a risk for harm (Ponnert 2007).

As has been described in section 3, children also can request to be placed in an out-of-home placement. There are many obstacles, however, for a child in this situation. Firstly, the child has to be older than fifteen years. Secondly, the child has to convince the social workers that a placement is necessary for the child to obtain a "reasonable level of living." Thirdly, even if the child succeeds with this, the consent of the custodians is mandatory. If the custodians do not consent, the child's situation must represent, and must be assessed as, a palpable risk before the SWB can act.

Children younger than fifteen years have no right to plead their own cause in front of the SWB. They can, of course, contact the social services even if they have not reached that age, but that very seldom happens. So, according to Swedish legislation, it is obvious that these children to a very large extent are depending on someone else to report their situation and family to the SWB.

The rule of law

When it comes to the removal of children from their own homes the "rule of law" is an important concept, but it can be given many different meanings (Gustavsson 2002). One central meaning is that it should be possible to foresee the outcome of the decisions of authorities and courts. What can, from this perspective, be said about the decisions on removal of children from their own homes in Sweden?

The possibility for the custodians to obtain a *voluntary placement* of their child depends on an assessment of the need for such a placement. This assessment, which in the first instance is made by the SWB, is, of course, a difficult assessment where no objective measures are available. However, if the SWB rejects the application from the parents, the parents can appeal that decision to the county administrative court. In court, the parents get a new, independent judgment and perhaps with that second opinion the reasonable demands on rule of law must be considered fulfilled.

When it comes to the removal of children *by coercion* the rule of law gives rise to many questions. One is the question of when and how an investigation is started. As discussed earlier, many children are reported to social services, but a lot of those reports do not result in an investigation. The assessment of when an investigation shall be opened will differ from municipality to municipality, and sometimes from one social worker to another. Some children may not be given the help that the legislation makes possible. The decision not to open an investigation cannot be appealed and this is open to criticism from a rule-of-law perspective (Cocozza and Hort 2011). In June 2015 a public commission published a final report concerning children's rights in connection with coercive care.[13] The main aim of the report is to strengthen the child's perspective when coercive care is about to be decided and also to improve the rule of law. The commission proposed that it should be possible to place a child outside his/

her home solely on the child's own request, even if the parents do not consent to this and even if it is not a situation where LVU is applicable. Another proposal is that the judges in administrative courts who work with placement cases should be offered education concerning children and children's needs. The commission proposes that the new provisions come into force in July 2017.

When it comes to the question of whether coercive care shall be called upon, the prerequisites are prescribed in the LVU. The first version of LVU came into force in 1982. Looking back on these three decades it is quite obvious that the prerequisites have been made clearer and more pertinent over time. However, one difficult judgment remains (and perhaps always will remain); namely, what shall be considered a "palpable risk" for the child. This concept, which is used in the legislation, is, of course, commented upon in the preparatory works of the law. The concept also has been interpreted in verdicts from the Supreme Administrative court. The comments in the preparatory works are quite short, however, and research has shown that the verdicts from the Supreme Administrative court, when it comes to this crucial point, add little to the understanding of the concept (Svensson 2012a).

The fact that what is meant by a "palpable risk" is still "open to interpretation," has, of course, important consequences from the perspective of the rule of law. It entails that the parents, in the first instance, are depending on the assessment of the social workers and that social workers, on the other hand, have great power over individual lives. Room for professional discretion is substantial. Of course the parents, if they disagree with the assessment of the social workers, can appeal to the county administrative court, but the general evaluation must be that it is a quite uncertain situation for the parents whether their child shall be removed.

In one way the situation resembles voluntary removals. Thus, if we accept open assessments concerning voluntary removals, there are also reasons to accept open assessments concerning coercive actions. The difference is that the actions that result from coercion mean an obvious infringement of the personal integrity, and that they, therefore, shall be surrounded by clear and distinct guarantees of the rule of law. It can be questioned, however, whether Swedish legislation fulfills these demands for the moment.

One way to solve this problem is to introduce and allow social workers to use some kind of objective instruments for measuring palpable risk (Lundström 2011). The argument against this is that reality is so complex as to make it difficult, some might argue impossible, to capture reality in a way that such an instrument will be of value. Another suggestion, which to a certain extent could contribute to a solution, is that verdicts from the Supreme Administrative court could contain more explanation of what is and what is not a palpable risk for the child (Svensson 2012a). This is a potentially helpful tool for social workers as they are undertake their assessments. The Supreme Administrative court could underpin such statements from contemporary psychological and social research on so-called risk and safety factors for children.

Voluntariness versus coercion

This chapter has shown that child protection work in Sweden can be carried out in voluntary forms as well as by coercion. It also has been made clear that (almost) the same measures can be used in voluntary as well as coercive care.[14] Problems can be equally great in either form of care, so the big difference is that sometimes one misses the necessary consents when it is about coercive care. If we just look at the number of children removed from their own homes the statistics indicate that most of the work done takes voluntary forms (see section 4); one can, of course, wonder why this is. There are many possible explanations as to why voluntary care is the most used pathway. One is that the Swedish legislation exhorts social workers to, as far as possible, find solutions that build on voluntariness. Another is that almost all experiences suggest that voluntary solutions give the best result. On the other hand, one must consider that actions that are executed voluntarily may be actions that the parents, and perhaps also the child, have felt themselves "forced" to accept, even if they disagree. The reason is, of course, that social workers will have explained that if they do not accept the proposed measures, the SWB make seek to utilize the coercive measures available through the LVU. The element of hidden coercion is, therefore, probably quite great. The risk with this is that the parents and the child are "forced" to accept measures where there may be no, or insufficient, legal and evidence base to support a care placement. As has been shown in the previous section 'Removals from children outside their home' section 3, the child's situation has to be very difficult and risky before LVU allows society and social services to use coercion against the family.

Transparency

Transparency is a measure of how much of the work of child protection is visible and accessible to public scrutiny. Starting with the actions of the *courts*, it is important that the verdicts of the courts in these cases are public. The problem with the verdicts is rather that the judge has to be careful and not mention more private circumstances in the verdict than are necessary to make the outcome understandable for the common man. If the judge fails with this, the verdict itself will be a violation of the integrity of the persons involved.

At the level of the *SWB* the main rule is the opposite; that is, there exists a high degree of secrecy. One exception is decisions about coercion through the SWB-level, which are made public. This is probably an exception that few people know about, and it is also not always clear how it should be practiced. For example, the SWB has the right to restrict the information in the decision to just the most basic facts, otherwise this exception would lead to a breach of a child's and family's right to anonymity. At the SWB-level, the possibilities for insight are quite limited for the public. The parties involved, however, shall be guaranteed full insight in the case, both to documents, but also through the right to appear personally in front of the investigating social worker and the SWB. This "openness" can be restricted only in small details; for example, the reporting person is not entitled to know who has made the report to the SWB if the reporting person has pronounced some kind of threat.

Layperson system's effects for the social work profession

Decision-making in child welfare in general, and in child protection cases in particular, is done within a system where laypersons play an important part. Laypersons participate as decision-makers both in voluntary care in the social welfare committees and in compulsory care in the committees, and also later within the administrative court system (see also Liljegren et al. 2014 for a comparison along these lines among Sweden, the United Kingdom, and the United States). Despite the fact that the actual decisions very seldom differ from the proposals of the professional social workers, the system has been criticized. In a recent study it was hard to find examples where laypersons actually decided against the proposals from the social workers, even if they did influence the investigations, mostly by the way they asked questions and commented to the social workers (Höjer et al. 2014). Further commentary on the role of laypersons as decision-makers concerns their participation in such fora, and argues that decisions are not being made according to the rule of law or are leading to a de-professionalizing of social work. It has, for instance, been argued that this system is a major reason social workers in Sweden are not certified, as for instance health workers are, and that social work practice is not a protected area wherein only social workers with a social work degree are allowed to function (Wingfors 2004). Arguments for changing the system have come from professional organizations and some politicians who think that individual issues in child protection should be handled by professionals instead of by politically appointed persons whose focus should be on policy issues (Newsmill 2010). However, the main argument for keeping laypersons in these decision-making positions is that it seems to work fairly well and that it contributes to the legitimacy of decisions that involve the state placing onerous restrictions on parents' rights to decide matters for their own children. And given that child protection is a complex, value-based, risky business with sensitive decisions wherein many moral aspects need to be taken into consideration, it requires legitimacy. So although the Swedish system a guarantees that social workers will not be solely responsible if something goes wrong, it also hampers the social work profession in its ability to strive for status and independence.

CONCLUSIONS

When comparing the Swedish system, as described in this chapter, with child protection systems in other countries and the decision-making systems in the others chapters, some things stand out. One is the use of laypersons in decision-making bodies. As described above, this can on the one hand increase the legitimacy and responsibility of child protection in society as a whole. On the other hand, it can threaten the idea of having decisions handled in a professional way, with consequential effects for the social work profession. The use of local social welfare committees with responsibilities for decisions also on the individual level is another distinctive trait of the Swedish model. Other Nordic countries, such as Norway and Finland, have changed this model, while Sweden has kept it. The third factor in the Swedish system we have tried to describe is the role of children over fifteen years of age in the decision-making process. The law prescribes that their voices and opinions must be taken into consideration before some decisions are made.

In the introduction to this chapter we mentioned that Sweden generally is described as a country with a family-service-oriented system as opposed to a more child-protection-oriented system. What can be said about that characterization? It is true that many conditions in the Swedish system make such a description correct. The fact that the social authorities always aim for a voluntary solution is a condition, which in a very clear way, contributes to a family-service-orientation. A voluntary solution builds upon consents from the involved parties, and if the consent of the child is important, especially when he/she is older than fifteen years, it is even more important to obtain the consent of the parents. Moreover, the problems of the children are often regarded as the problems of the parents. That is why, in reality, the investigations often focus on the parents despite the significance based on the best interest of the child. Also, the fact that when a child is placed outside his/her own home, the work of the social services shall aim at a reunion can in reality be considered a family-oriented factor, even if the official explanation is that a reunion initially always is in the best interest of the child. Another family-oriented condition is the fact that the right to plead their own cause is restricted to young people who are older than fifteen years. This age restriction may result in increased risk for younger children seeking a placement outside of the family home, given that their request may not be accorded the same weight as young people aged fifteen years or older. Instead, the social authorities, together with the parents almost by routine, will search for a solution wherein the child remains at home.

In recent years, however, many changes have occurred—not only in legislation, but also in daily social work practice—that have reinforced elements of child protection. Starting with the legislation, since July 1, 2003 new provisions have specified that after three years in the same family home the SWB shall consider whether the custody of a child in care should be transferred from the biological parents to the foster parents. That is the duty of the SWB in both voluntary and involuntary cases. Since January 1, 2013, it is also stated in SoL that when the SWB is to decide about an action of care or treatment for a child, the best interest of the child shall be decisive. Moreover, since the same date, new provisions have strengthened the position of the child during both the investigation of SWB and the time when the child gets care in a family home or a HVB. In a recent state inquiry, many suggestions were proposed in order to strengthen the child protection system (SOU 2009, 68); however, we have yet to see many of the recommendations implemented in practice. Thus, a summarizing opinion might be this: Social work in Sweden with children still has a family-service-orientation, but during recent years the child-protection elements of the system have become more pronounced.

NOTES

1   SFS 2012:776. For the preparatory works, see prop 2012/13:10 Stärkt skydd för barn och unga [Strengthened protection for children and young persons].

2   The SWB has great freedom to decide on what level the decisions on behalf of the board shall be taken, to the SWC, to the first-line manager, or to the social worker (see 6 chap 33 § of the Act of Municipalities [1991:900]). However, some of the decisions can only be delegated to the SWC; see 10 chap 4 § SoL.

3   See Svensson (2014) for more details on the Swedish administrative court system and the use of coercive care in child welfare.

4   Since January 2016 there is a third option. From this date there are provisions in SoL about *supported residence* (Swedish: *stödboende*). Supported residence should be a placement-option for the SWB concerning young people between 16–20 years whose situation is *not* so severe that they have to stay in an HVB. However, if the child is just 16 or 17 years old special reasons are required to place him/her in a supported residence. For those children the custodians also have to consent to the placement.

5   In Cocozza and Hort (2011, p. 93 ff) this is described as the first "gate-keeping point" (see also, Östbergs 2010, p. 179 ff).

6   If the parents are married both of them are automatically custodians. If the parents are not married the father has to report to the authorities that he wants to be a custodian.

7   About the participation of children in the investigation, see Hollander (1998), Mattsson (2002), and Leviner (2012a).

8   Figures in this section build on the statistics from Socialstyrelsen (2013) if nothing else is noted.

9   See, for example, Olsson ./. Sweden(No 1) (10465/83), Eriksson ./. Sweden (11/1988/144/209), Andersson ./. Sweden (61/1990/252/323) and Olsson ./. Sweden (No2) (74/1991/326/398).

10 Even though Sweden was one of the first nations to ratify the UNCRC, this convention up until now was not in Swedish law. Sweden has been criticized for this by the United Nations Commission for the rights of children. The

counterargument has been that the Swedish legislation fulfills the rights mentioned in the convention even though the convention is not Swedish law. Due to all the criticism, work is going on at the moment to transform the UNCRC into Swedish law.

11 See prop 1996.
12 See prop 1989/90:28, p 23.
13 SOU 2015:71. Barns och ungas rätt vid tvångsvård. Förslag till ny LVU [Rights for children and young people in connection with coercive care. Proposal to a new LVU] (Stockholm 2015).
14 The main difference is that it is only children subject to coercive care who can be locked up in the special supervisory homes.

REFERENCES

Cameron, G. and Freymond, N. (2006) "Understanding International Comparisons of Child Protection, Family Service, and Community Systems of Child and Family Welfare." In Fraymond, N. and Cameron, G. (Eds.), *Towards Positive Systems of Child and Family Welfare*, pp. 3–26. Toronto: Toronto University Press Inc.

Cocozza, M. and Hort, S. (2011) "The Dark Side of the Universal Welfare State?: Child Abuse and Protection in Sweden." In Gilbert, N., Parton, N., and Skivenes, M. (Eds.), *Child Protection Systems: International Trends and Orientations*, pp. 89–111. New York: Oxford University Press.

Esping-Andersen, G. (1996) *Welfare States in Transition: National Adaptations in Global Economies*. London: Sage.

Forkby, T., Höjer, S., and Liljegren, A. (2014) "Making Sense of Common Sense. Examining the Decision-making of Politically Appointed Representatives in Swedish Child Protection." *Child and Family Social Work* 21 (1) 14–25. doi: 10.1111cfs.12100.

Gilbert, N., Parton, N., and Skivenes, M. (Eds.) (2011) *Child Protection Systems. International Trends and Orientations*. New York: Oxford University Press.

Gilbert, N. (1997) *Combating Child Abuse: International Perspectives and Trends*. New York: Oxford University Press.

Gustafsson, H. (2002) *Rättens polyvalens. En rättsvetenskaplig studie av sociala rättig-heter och rättssäkerhet* [The polyvalence of the law. A legal study of social rights and the rule of law]. Lund: Lunds universitet, Sociologiska institutionen.

Hollander, A. (1998) "Barns rätt att komma till tals. En väg till ökat inflytande för barn eller för vuxna?" [The rights of children to be heard. A way to increased influence for children or for adults? *Nordiskt Socialt Arbeid* 4, 194–200.

Höjer, I. (2001) *Fosterfamiljens inre liv* [The inner life of the foster family]. Doktorsavhandling. Göteborg: Göteborgs universitet.

Höjer, S., Forkby, T., and Liljegren, A. (2014) "Lekmän inom den sociala barnavården. En studie av förtroendevalda i sociala utskott i 99 kommuner" [Laypersons within the child protection. A study of politically appointed members of child protection committees]. *Socionomens forskningssupplement* 35, 42–54.

Leviner, P. (2011) *Rättsliga dilemman i socialtjänstens barnskyddsarbete* [Legal dilemmas in the child protection work of the social services]. Stockholm: Jure.

Leviner, P. (2012a) "Barnperspektiv I socialtjänstens barnskyddsarbete – samtal med barn och bedömningar av barns bästa" [Child perspective in the child protection work in the social services – talks with children and assessments of the best of the child]. In *Rätt, social utsatthet och samhälleligt ansvar [Justice, social marginalisation and social responsibility]*, pp. 273–287. Festskrift till Anna Hollnader. Stockholm: Norstedts.

Leviner, P. (2012b) "Domstolens funktion I LVU-ärenden—behov av specialiserade barndomstolar?" [The function of the court in LVU—cases—a need for specialized child courts?]. *Nordisk Socialrättslig Tidskrift* 5–6.

Leviner, P. (2014) "När kan och bör barn flytta hem – en oklar balansering mellan återförening och stabilitet i tre olika processer"[When children can and should move home – an unclear balance between reunification and stability in three different processes]. In Cederborg, Warnling-Nerep (Eds), *Barnrätt. En antologi [Childlren's rights. An anthology.]*. Stockholm: Norstedts Juridik.

Liljegren, A; Höjer, S., and Forkby, T. (2014) "Laypersons, professions and governance in the welfare state: The Swedish child protection system." *Journal of Professions and Organization.* 1 (2) 161–175. doi:10.1093/jpo/jou005.

Lundström, T. (2011) "Om senmodernitet, riskbedömningar och social barnavård [On late modernity, risk assessments and social care of children]" In Höjer, I. and Höjer S. (Eds.), *Familj vardagsliv och modernitet. En festskrift till Margareta Bäck-Wiklund* [Family, every day life and modernity. A festschrift to Margareta Bäck-Wiklund]. Göteborg: Göteborg University. Department of Social Work.

Mattsson, T. (2002) *Barnet och rättsprocessen. Rättssäkerhet, integritetsskydd och autonomi i samband med beslut om tvångsvård*[The child and the legal process. Rule of law, protection of integrity and autonomy in relation to decision-making in compulsory care]. Lund: Juristförlaget.

Mattson, T. (2008) *Ungas delaktighet. Exemplet institutionsvård* [The participation of young people. Examples from institutional care]. SiS Forskningrapport 2. Stockholm: Statens institutionsstyrelse.

Östberg, F. (2010) *Bedömningar och beslut. Från anmälan till insats i den sociala barnavården* [Assessments and decisions. From report to intervention within child protection]. Rapport i socialarbete nr 134. Stockholm: Stockholms universitet.

Ponnert, L. (2007) *Mellan klient och rättssystem. Tvångsvård av barn och unga ur socialsekreterares perspektiv* [Between the client and the legal system. Coercive care of children and young people from a social work perspective]. Lund: Lund University.

Prop 1989/90:28 Vård i vissa fall av barn och ungdomar [Care in some cases of children and young people].

Prop 2012/13:10 Stärkt skydd för barn och unga [Enhanced protection for children and young people].

SiS 2014. SiS i korthet 2013. En samling statistiska uppgifter om SiS [A collection of statistical information about SiS]. Stockholm: Statens institutionsstyrlse.

Socialstyrelsen 2013. Barn och unga insatser 2012. Sveriges officiella statistik [Children and young persons—measures 2012. Official statistics of Sweden].

Socialstyrelsen 2014a. Nationella adoptioner av barn i familjehem [National adoptions of children in foster care]. Socialstyrelsen/National Board of Health and Welfare. Retrieved June 22, 2015 from http://www.social-styrelsen.se/publikationer2014/2014-3-11.

Socialstyrelsen 2014b. Barns och ungas hälsa, vård och omsorg 2013 [Health, care and support to children and young people 2013]. Retrieved June 22, 2015 from http://www.socialstyrelsen.se/lists/artikelkatalog/attach-ments/19016/2013-3-15.pdf.

SOU 2009:68. Lag om stöd och skydd för unga [Law concerning the support and protection of children and young persons]. Socialdepartementet.

Sundell, K., Egelund, T., Andée Löfholm, C., and Kaunitz, C. (2007) *Barnavårdsutredningar En Kunskapsöversikt* [Child protection investigations. A literature review]. Stockholm: Gothia, Centrum för utvärdering av socialt arbete (CUS), Socialstyrelsen.

Svensson, G. (2012a) *Högsta förvaltningsdomstolen och tvångsvården. Om betydelsen i rättssäkerhetshänseende av domstolens domar angående LVU och LVM* [The Supreme Administrative Court and the coercive care]. Stockholm: Norstedts Juridik.

Svensson, G. (2012b) "När anmäla barn till socialtjänsten?" [When to report children to the social services?]. In *Rätt, social utsatthet och samhälleligt ansvar* [Justice, social marginalisation, and social responsibility]. Festskrift till Anna Hollander. Stockholm: Norstedts Juridik.

Svensson, G. (2014) "Tvång i socialtjänsten. Förutsättningarna för tvångs-vård i barn- och missbruksärenden" [The preconditions for compulsory care in child protection and drug-abuse cases]. *Institutionsvård i fokus* (2) 6–37.

Svärd, V. (2014) "Hospital social workers' assessment processes for children at risk: positions in and contributions to inter-professional teams." *European Journal of Social Work*, 17(4), 508–522.

Wiklund, S. (2006) *Den kommunala barnavården—om anmälningar, organisa-tion och utfall* [Municipal child welfare—child protection reports, organization, and outcomes]. Rapport i social arbete 117. Stockholm: Stockholms universitet, Institutionen för social arbete.

Wingfors, S. (2004) *Socionomyrkets professionalisering* [The professionalization of social work]. Akademisk avhandling. Göteborg Studies in Sociology No 20. Göteborg: Göteborg University.

5

REMOVING CHILDREN FROM THEIR FAMILIES DUE TO CHILD PROTECTION IN GERMANY

Monika Haug and Theresia Höynck

INTRODUCTION

In Germany, child protection has been the subject of intensive public debate and legislative activity in the last decade. Triggered by individual fatality cases extensively covered by the media, there has been some shift as to how much state intervention is perceived as acceptable (see also Wolff et al. 2011). One of the key issues of the 1990 reform of the child and youth welfare act was to make clear what had been discussed since the 1970s; namely, that removals of children should not be the standard reaction to difficulties in families, and as far as possible should be replaced by family support measures.[1] Whereas the primacy of supportive measures within the family is, in principle, still accepted, there seems to be increasing support for the idea of favoring removals when in doubt.[2] In public debates the removal of children from problematic homes is sometimes presented as an instant solution to a complex problem. In legislation and application of the law, however, changes are much more subtle but can nonetheless be observed.

The German child and family welfare system today can be described as a family-service-oriented system, which offers a wide array of family support services ranging from regular day-care facilities to special forms of residential care (Kindler 2010; Cameron 2007; for more detailed information about the German child welfare system, see Wolff et al. 2011). In terms of child protection the system promotes early state action through supportive services while upholding a high barrier for interference with parental rights (e.g., removing children from families). Interventions usually are closely intertwined with supportive measures (Meysen 2014), and the professionals involved are usually social workers. Child welfare and protective services generally are organized and financed by the local authorities. Only recently the federal government has gotten involved in creating and funding early preventive services to detect risk factors and to foster collaboration between the child welfare healthcare systems (for details, see Wolff et al. 2011).

If the term "care order" in the context of child protection is understood, in a strict sense, as a direct court order by which a child is placed somewhere other than with his or her family, Germany does not have care orders. Nevertheless, of course, children in need of protection are removed from their families by public agencies. There are various legal routes, which can be taken by the youth office[3] (*Jugendamt*) or the family court, and can lead to the separation of children from their families and to placements in out-of-home care.[4]

This chapter will focus on the state's response to severe external risk situations for children, mainly caused by parents. Therefore, after mapping the legal and political context, it will describe the various public actions in child protection cases that can lead to a removal of children from their families based on social law and family law. Given that it is the only way to remove children from their families for longer periods or permanently, special focus will be given to family court proceedings by considering the participation rights in light of the severe consequences connected to these decisions. Finally, the number of measures as reflected by official statistics will be presented.

LEGAL CONTEXT AND POLICY ISSUES

The decision-making processes underlying children's removal from home by the child protection system are strongly influenced by the constitutional framing of the relationship among children, their parents, and the state (Art. 6 of the German Constitution). From a fundamental rights perspective, the parents' right to care for and educate their children is understood as a right of defense against state interventions (decision of German Constitutional Court 24, 119, 138). This parental right, however, has to be exercised in consideration of the child's rights and his or her interests and will (decision of German Constitutional Court 59, 360, 376). One key assumption is that children are generally best cared for by their parents (decision of German Constitutional Court 59, 360, 376). If parents fail to care for their children's basic needs, there are a range of options for public action deriving from the context of social law and family law, including voluntary placement by the youth office and involuntary placement by the family courts. For voluntary options, the child welfare system offers a wide range of supportive services (*Hilfen zur Erziehung*), ranging from (low-threshold) educational counseling to in-home services, as well as foster family placements or residential care. Because formally these measures are entirely voluntary, there is no issue of proportionality; decisions are based on a need-principle (Höynck and Haug 2012; see further Wiesner 2007). Interventions involving involuntary measures such as the separation of the child from his or her parents are only permitted on the grounds of a formal law, and if there is a serious risk to the child. The key term "serious risk to the child" (*Kindeswohlgefährdung*) originates from civil law, has existed since the year 1900, and has been interpreted differently throughout various epochs, while adapting to changing concepts and realities in the lives of children.[5] The question of where the threshold of state action needs to be set always has been influenced by political and public debate (Marthaler 2009). Only at the level of a serious risk and under strict adherence to the principle of proportionality are state authorities allowed and required to act due to their responsibility as "watchman" (*Staatliches Wächteramt*); and, where necessary, they must interfere with parental rights. The existence of a "serious risk to the child," however, does not necessarily end in a separation of children from their families. Even in cases where the threshold of a serious risk to the child is passed, the youth office is obligated first to assess whether supportive measures would suffice to reduce the risk. Only if that cannot be ensured, must the court be informed. The court then, too, is bound by the principle of proportionality: convincing parents to accept supportive services takes priority over intervening actions. Only if that is not possible, is the court allowed and obligated to intervene, which may range from orders to make use of supportive services to removing children from their families. The wording of the Constitution allowing the separation of children from their families is outdated ("Versagen der Erziehungberechtigten," "Verwahrlosung") but the unanimous interpretation of the Article is very clear with regard to the requirement of serious parental failure resulting in severe risk to the child's welfare (decision of German Constitutional Court 60, 79, 91). In situations of imminent risk, the youth office is obligated to place children into emergency out-of-home care. State interventions in this regard may not be applied in order to enforce certain educational ideals. Unless the threshold of "serious risk to the child" is passed, parents are free to determine what is good for their children according to their personal opinion and own moral concepts (decision of German Constitutional Court 24, 119, 143 f.; 31, 194, 204 f.; 59, 360, 376). And even in cases of state actions, the public authorities are obliged to respect the parents' educational ideals.

The child protection system also has undergone some major changes in recent times. Whereas child welfare services during the 1950s and 1960s aimed at securing public order and protecting society from difficult children, new forms of programs, emphasizing preventive and supportive services through nongovernmental services, have emerged since the 1970s (for details, see Wolff et al. 2011). This development eventually led to the passage of the Child and Youth Welfare Law in 1990.[6] This Act placed child and youth welfare within the realm of social law and thus reconceptualized the youth office as a supportive institution, aimed at preventing harmful developments at an early stage. Since then, there has been a strong emphasis and identification of youth welfare with the ideas of social law and a clear distance sought from the former understanding of it as a repressive institution. Since the early 1990s, a number of highly publicized child protective cases have ended with the death of the child and resulted in a criminal investigation of the social workers involved. These cases have posed a significant challenge to the German child protection system (see also Wolff et al. 2011) and have caused a high level of anxiety among child protection workers dealing with these cases. Being able to prove that legally prescribed procedures had been followed became an important issue in fatality cases. The following legal developments thus aimed at establishing more certainty among practitioners (see parliamentary documents 15/3676; 17/6256; 16/6815) through more precise procedural regulations and distribution of responsibility.

One of these legal amendments was the Child and Youth Welfare Development Act of 2005,[7] which delineated the various steps that have to be taken by the youth office in situations of possible risk. Even though this amendment only had a clarifying function rather than introducing substantial change, it had high symbolic relevance and received a lot of attention. The amendment made very explicit that the youth office is the first and primary entity to assess risk in potential child protective cases.[8] It determines whether there is any further action needed in the case and if so, whether this action is of a supportive or a controlling nature. Whatever decision is taken by the youth office in a case is, therefore, of key importance for further proceedings.

The once clear distinction between the responsibilities of the youth office and those of the family courts has become increasingly blurred by legal amendments to the child and youth welfare law and the family law (including its procedural law) during the last decade, amendments which closely intertwined the tasks of both institutions in this field. The aim was to establish "joint responsibility" (*Verantwortungsgemeinschaft*) between the youth office and the family courts in child protective cases to guarantee early referral to court as well as low-threshold interventions (parliamentary document 16/6815). To achieve the early involvement of family courts, the Child and Youth Welfare Development Act of 2005 also clarified that the youth office is not only obliged to refer a case to family court in cases of serious risk, but also in cases where parents do not cooperate with child protective services to assess a risk situation. In procedural family law, steps have been taken toward early involvement of the family courts in order to foster early preventive actions by the courts. One feature of early involvement is a meeting between family courts and parents (including, if possible, the children) prior to formal courtroom proceedings in cases of (possible) risk to talk about the situation and possible supportive measures (BGBl. I 1188 [2008]). This dialogue is aimed at strengthening and appealing to parental responsibility and at finding an appropriate solution to avert the risk situation through mutual agreement between the involved participants (parliamentary documents 16/6815; 16/6308). Preliminary and short-term proceedings were another feature introduced (BGBl. I 1188 [2008]; parliamentary document 16/6815) and recommend an early meeting within one month after the proceedings have started.

In family law, amendments removed obstacles for family court actions by reducing legal requirements, which are typically subject to evidentiary problems[9] (e.g., the proof that shortcomings in parenting are causal for the risk situation [parliamentary document 16/6815]). Along with lowering the threshold for family court action, an explicit list of various actions, including the order to make use of family services, was integrated into the relevant article. This underscored the availability of options other than ruling on parental custodial rights[10] and further clarified that the removal of children ought to be regarded as *ultima ratio*.

TYPES OF REMOVAL

The options in child protection cases deriving from family law and social law and covering the range from support to control can have the same factual outcome, namely the removal of children from their families and subsequent out-of-home placement. However, specific legal routes relate to different legal requirements, which are associated with different consequences for parental rights. There are two primary out-of-home placement options: family foster care and residential child care. In both forms the duration of care varies based on the individual situation. By law, the primary goal of any type of removal is to improve the situation of the family of origin sufficiently for reunification to occur. Only if this seems impossible, does a different permanent living situation for the child have to be found. Given that foster families and residential child care are typical settings for this, children usually stay in their previous care model. Adoption is not a permanency option because there is neither a legal base nor a culture to work toward a release for adoption. In Germany only parents can release children for adoption. The parental declaration toward a release for adoption cannot be replaced by a court order due to reasons of child protection.

If placed in a foster family children live in a private household outside the parental family. This aims at offering emotional proximity and constancy to the child within a family-like relationship (Rüting 2012). In these cases, family is conceptualized broadly and may include unmarried couples and single persons (Struck in: FK-SGB VIII § 33 Rn.7; Schmid-Obkirchner in: Wiesner-SGB VIII § 33 Rn.21). Generally, foster parents are not understood as professionals. Only some foster families have a more professional character and provide special forms of therapeutic care (Rüting 2012). Residential child care comprises various models of congregate living under professional care. Institutions vary in size and character: some are organized in family-like group home settings; others have a more therapeutic orientation. For older adolescents there are group homes aimed at independent living with pedagogical support (see Struck/Trenczek in: FK-SGB VIII § 34 Rn. 2). Both family foster care and residential care include considerable state involvement: Residential child care institutions are monitored by the child welfare system and fall under licensing and regulatory guidelines. Foster parents need to be licensed; they have a right to professional counseling and support. In any out-of-home care situation the persons providing care are authorized under the law to make decisions for the child in everyday matters (§ 1688 BGB). Following is a description of various legal routes leading to out-of-home care and their consequences for parental rights.

Out-of-home supportive services ("voluntary" services)

Under social law, out-of-home care—like other forms of supportive services—is framed as a service to parents and a way of supporting them in parenting in cases of crisis or deficiencies in parenting. These services relate to situations where the child's development is impaired by problems, which given the parents' and children's resources cannot be overcome without public support (Schmid-Obkirchner in: Wiesner-SGB VIII/§ 27 Rn.21). This implies that whenever possible parents should be the ones solving the situation. The decision to provide supportive services has to be made by a team of qualified social workers in the youth office. Because parents are requesting to receive supportive services, the administrative process involved to approve them cannot be qualified as an order. The notion that parents voluntarily request and accept support has to be understood, however, within the context of the legal powers the youth offices have to enforce interventions they assume to be suitable. The youth office has various options to "induce" parents to make use of child welfare services (Tammen/Trenczek in: FK-SGB VIII § 27 Rn. 44). In these cases, it is realistic to assume that the consequences of a refusal to cooperate are pointed out. This may include referring the case to court with the goal of intervening in parental rights if necessary.

Because these are "voluntary" services, parents keep full parental rights. Care-givers may only decide everyday matters. Parents may limit this right at any time. In these cases, however, as well as in cases where parents disagree with single decisions by the caregivers, the youth office will arbitrate between the parties (§ 38 SGB VIII, see also Meysen in: FK-SGB VIII § 38 Rn.12 ff.) and report to the court if it is deemed necessary to limit parental rights.

Short-term placements (emergency orders)

Child protective services are authorized to implement emergency placements (*Inobhutnahmen*) but only under strictly defined conditions. In cases of imminent and serious risk to the child, in which a family court's decision cannot be awaited, the youth offices (after evaluating all relevant aspects of the individual case) are mandated to take children into care, directly from their parents if necessary, and place them outside the family home as a measure of professional crisis intervention. For that, the youth office cannot apply direct coercion. Where this becomes necessary, authorized institutions like the police must be called for support.

This model represents only a temporary intervention in order to further appraise the situation and install appropriate support. Parents must be informed immediately about the intervention. If there is a possibility to attain parental agreement and cooperation at this stage, that route has to be taken (Wiesner in: Wiesner-SGB VIII/§ 42 Rn. 36; Trenczek in: FK-SGB VIII § 42 Rn. 41). If the parents disagree with the intervention in cases of persistent imminent risk, youth offices must contact the family court, which then must make a decision about the case. In cases without continuing risk the child must be handed back to the parents. This illustrates that in such cases the youth office does not have its own powers to limit parental rights; it is providing practical short-term protection in cases where courts cannot be reached in time. One of the key elements of this intervention is the placement of children outside the parental home. The wording of the law emphasizes consideration of the specific needs of children in acute risk situations. It lists various possible placement settings, including temporary foster family care by professionals or suitable persons from the child's family or circle of acquaintances, as well as residential child care and other forms of housing. The emergency placement not only provides immediate protection, but is also meant to organize future support with regard to the child (Wiesner in: Wiesner-SGB VIII/§ 42 Rn.26; Trenczek 2008; Meysen 2014). The aim is to resolve the problem or crisis and identify strategies, especially in the area of family support services, to avoid a return of the situation. Working with parents cooperatively after a heavy-handed state intervention obviously poses a professional challenge. The crisis out-of-home placement usually ends when follow-up support services have been installed successfully. Because the development and implementation of supportive services can take some time, especially in complex risk situations, the duration of the initial placement varies quite remarkably (according to official statistical data about 10 percent of emergency out-of-home placements last one day or less, one-third of the placements last for fifteen days or longer; see Haug and Höynck 2012; Pothmann 2009 states that a considerable number of short-term placements last longer than six months).

During the time of the emergency placement, the parents' rights are (partially) superseded by the rights of child protective services (Wiesner in: Wiesner-SGB VIII § 42 Rn. 31; Trenzcek in: FK-SGB VIII § 42 Rn.35; Trenczek 2008). Parents do not, however, (fully) lose their custodial rights; the law clarifies that the parents' presumptive will must be considered in the decision made by child protective services. Given the principle of proportionality and the short time during which decisions have to be made, it can, however, be difficult to ascertain the parents' will (Wiesner in: Wiesner-SGB VIII § 42 Rn.32).

Family court measures (involuntary orders)

The central legal norm regarding child protection cases is § 1666 of the German civil code (BGB), which is part of the book of family law. It empowers the family courts to intervene into parental rights in cases of serious risk to children (*Kindeswohlgefährdung*) if parents are either unwilling or unable[11] to avert the risk situation. The law aims at comprehensive protection for children and young people by addressing (in the law's wording) the physical, mental, and emotional dimensions of possible harm (Coester 2009; Götz in: Palandt § 1666 Rn.7).

Any decision to interfere with parental rights requires substantiating a serious risk to a protected interest (a "serious risk to the child"). Therefore, the court has to state which interest is at stake. The interpretation of interests meriting protection through the limiting of parental rights has always been subject to contemporary values, the existing legal framework, and empirical findings (mainly from social sciences and psychology). During recent years, the spectrum of interests meant to be protected has increased to cases beyond the typical forms of physical or sexual abuse and neglect. Cases resulting in removals usually include dangers for children's lives or their physical integrity as well as severe forms of impending emotional damage. The risk must be grave and palpable ("erhebliche Schädigung mit ziemlicher Sicherheit" [BGHFamRZ 1956, 350]). This means that, without raising the question of blame, family courts have to take a prognostic stance on the basis of available facts of an individual case. At this point it should be obvious that the mandatory report by the youth office in family court proceedings is of utmost importance because it is the entity in closest contact with the family and the one best able to gather facts that are relevant for the court's decision.

Decisions, which include a removal of children from their parents, are generally achieved by either a partial withdrawal of parental rights (e.g., suspending parents from their right to determine the place of residence for the child [Coester in: Staudinger-BGB § 1666 Rn. 226, Olzen in: MüKo-BGB § 1666 Rn. 194, 196]), or by full termination of parental rights (Olzen in: MüKo-BGB § 1666 Rn. 194, 195). From a constitutional and systematic point of view, the latter must be regarded as a last resort (see also Olzen in: MüKo-BGB § 1666a Rn. 25). If the court believes that placement in out-of-home care is necessary to protect the child, it first has to assess whether a court order stating that the parents have to apply for this kind of support will suffice. In cases where this option is available, it must be evaluated critically whether it makes sense to order supportive services when there usually has been a failed process of cooperation between the youth office and the family (Coester in: Staudinger-BGB § 1666 Rn. 219).

FAMILY COURT PROCEEDINGS ON REMOVALS

Given that they are the only way to enforce long-term or permanent removals by heavily interfering with parental rights, family court proceedings deserve a more detailed consideration. The main goal of all family court proceedings is to make a decision that is in the child's best interest (§ 1697a BGB). The family court usually is represented by a single judge at a district court. There are 661 district courts in Germany, which are mandated to establish departments for family law. The departments are staffed with judges who according to the law must not be in their first year of practice. There are twenty-four higher district courts, which deal with appeals. Decisions at the higher district courts are taken by senates of three judges, one of whom presides. The judges tend to be specialized through experience and training, although specialization among the judiciary is not generally common. Child protection constitutes only one of their tasks; the courts' main business consists of divorces and related matters.

The recent procedural changes in family law have improved the legal situation of the participants[12] by extending their procedural rights. To what extent these rights are actually implemented is difficult to know. There are only a few studies on this topic (see, for example, Simitis et al. 1979; Münder et al. 2000; Rosenboom 2006; Hannemann and Stötzel 2009; Karle et al. 2010), varying considerably in their empirical designs and representativeness. Many of them are older studies that do not address legal amendments that occurred afterward. A new project on this topic is currently being conducted by scholars of OTH Regensburg, TU Berlin and FH Münster (2015), specifically aiming at providing comparable data to the study by Münder et al. (2000) and Simitis et al. (1979). The following describes the legal foundation and the process of family court orders, which lead to a (partial) withdrawal of parental custodial rights. This will be, where possible, contrasted with findings from research about the implementation of this law.

Initiation of family court actions

In child protection cases, family courts have to take actions ex officio as soon as a relevant case is noticed by the court (§ 26 FamFG). The fact that the youth office has a legal duty to involve the family courts in cases of serious risk to children (see p. 92) suggests that many court cases can be traced back to a referral by this system.[13] The officiating judge subsequently needs to clarify the facts of the case; this can comprise actions like consultation review of records, hearings of witnesses, and obtaining expert opinions. In child protection cases, expert reports play an important role, because they provide specialized knowledge in fields where judges typically do not have much expertise, such as with psychological or medical issues. The law requires no specific order for the investigation. The appropriate scope of investigation must be assessed and conducted by the family judges, who must consider higher standards for the extent and the formality of the investigation in cases that might lead to severe consequences (Olzen in: MüKo BGB § 1666 Rn. 214, 219). At any time during the proceedings, it must further be examined whether interim measures are necessary.

Parties involved and participation rights

Child protection cases might lead to severe consequences for families. Therefore, it is necessary to involve the concerned persons and institutions and provide participation rights. The inclusion of various participants is established on different bases: There are participants whose rights are directly affected (parents and children), participants who by law have to be included (youth office and the guardian ad litem), and those who can participate on an optional basis after a family court admission (foster parents who have cared for the child for a long time). The participants must be heard or consulted. Participation encompasses further rights such as the right to procedural requests (§ 25 FamFG) or access to files (§ 13 FamFG). All oral proceedings of the family court processes are closed to the public (§ 170 GVG).

A personal hearing of the parents provides for the parents' right to a fair hearing and is obligatory in child protection cases unless there are serious reasons rendering this impossible. The same applies to foster parents in cases where children have been living with them for quite some time and they have been admitted as party by the family court. In cases where the hearing is cancelled due to extenuating circumstances, it must take place as soon as possible afterward.

Children aged older than fourteen years must be heard personally; younger children must be heard if their will, preferences, or emotional bonds are relevant for the court's decision, or if the hearing is indicated for other reasons (§ 159 I, II FamFG).[14] Besides establishing facts, the special aim of the hearing is to get a personal impression of the child (parliamentary document 7/2060). The mandatory hearing, which has to be conducted for all procedures that concern children's rights, is meant to strengthen the position of children as subjects rather than objects of proceedings (see also Schumann in: MüKo-FamFG § 159 Rn. 1). This is in line with the leading principle in family court proceedings, which aims to ensure the best interests of the child and is strongly influenced by the children's will. As a rule, children three years and older are regarded as being able to provide relevant information about the facts in question (see Schumann in: MüKo-FamFG § 159 Rn. 5). Exceptions are (only) discussed for infants (see Schumann in: MüKo-FamFG § 159 Rn. 5). But a personal impression also can be important in getting a picture of how children interact with their parents. A nationwide study examining the implementation of all hearings concerning children in cases of family law[15] showed that only one-third of the judges hear children from the age of three whereas children aged seven years and older are heard in almost every case, with an average of 4.1 years of age (Karle et al. 2010). It must be taken into consideration, however, that the study included all kinds of proceedings concerning children and not only child protection cases. The majority of these proceedings deal with questions of parental custody in cases of separation and divorce. An actual proportion of hearings in child protection cases was described by Münder et al. (2000), who stated that most judges reported hearing all children in such cases in order to gain a personal impression. This is based on dated findings, however, and no conclusions can be drawn regarding the current situation.

The hearings have to be conducted in consideration of the age and the individual needs of the child. Whether and how a hearing of younger children can be executed, depends essentially on individual factors such as previous strain by the parents (Eschweiler 2005). A professional and sensitive hearing, however, is considered to help avoid or diminish any adverse impact on children (Eschweiler 2005). Quite a few recommendations for the implementation of hearings have been developed (see e.g., Stötzel and Prenzlow 2011; Schweppe and Bussian 2012). The previously mentioned study by Karle et al. (2010) revealed that one-fifth of the hearings take place in the courtroom[16] whereas nearly half of the hearings take place during separate appointments. It is further described that one-third of the hearings are conducted solely with the child, in 30 percent, a guardian ad litem is present, and in 10 percent a social worker from the youth office is present (Karle et al. 2010).

In child protection cases the interests of the children may conflict with the interests of the parents and the consequences might have a huge impact on the children. A state-paid guardian ad litem (*Verfahrensbeistand*) usually needs to be appointed to secure the procedural rights for the children (parliamentary document 13/4899). The aim is to balance deficits in representing the children's interests through their parents (Vogel 2010). One of the tasks of the guardian ad litem is to find out the interests of the child and present them to the court. He or she is—other than a lawyer would be—not bound by the declared will of the child; he or she may consider points contrary to the child's volition in his or her best interest (see also Schumann in: MüKo-FamFG § 158 Rn.27; Sommer 2012). The law is fairly open regarding qualification requirements for the guardian ad litem. A nationwide but nonrepresentative study examining the practical implementation of the guardian ad litem counselling children in family court proceedings has shown that the majority are social workers (44%), followed by lawyers (35%) and psychologists (8%) (Hannemann and Stötzel 2009). The study further showed that two-thirds of the appointments have taken place in cases dealing with parental care (Hannemann and Stötzel 2009); Prenzlow (2012) points out that the number of appointments vary considerably among regions. Cases dealing with parental care can include the withdrawal and the transfer of parental rights in child protection cases, but given that the main business of the court is the arrangement of parental care due to divorce, it is, as mentioned before, not possible to distinguish these from child protection cases.

The youth office is required by law to be heard[17] in child protection cases. This regulation ensures the court's reliance on the youth office's expertise (Schumann in: MüKo-FamFG § 162 Rn.6; Katzenstein 2011; Oberloskamp et al. 2009). The youth office informs the court about family support services offered and rendered, as well as about the psychosocial development of the young person, and points out further options for support (§ 50 II S.1 SGB VIII, § 162 I FamFG). As such, the youth office plays a central role in family court proceedings: judges who deal with a particular family for just a short period of time strongly rely on the reports from social workers who have been familiar with a case for a long time and have expert knowledge. The aim of the report is to contribute autonomously to a successful solution for the child and the family based on their expertise and impressions from family contacts (Katzenstein 2011). The statement before the court often requires extensive preparation (see Trenczek in: FK-SGB VIII Vor §§ 50-52 Rn. 26) and, therefore, can lead to difficulties in cases of short-term proceedings, which should take place within one month. There is anecdotal evidence that the youth office is not always able to produce the report in time. Whether this is a general problem or whether this relates to a lack of resources, difficulties with getting access to families, or to other reasons has not been evaluated systematically. There are no rules for the format and structure of the consultation. Generally, a written statement is provided, but in some cases, oral reporting (in imminent cases via telephone) is permitted (Engelhardt in: Keidel-FamFG § 162 Rn. 5; Schumann in: MüKo-FamFG § 162 Rn. 8).

Decision

The judge is free in his or her decision and decides according to his or her conviction based on the content of the entire proceeding. This requires a reasonable degree of certainty but does not need to exclude any doubt (Ulrici in: MüKo-FamFG § 37 Rn.14). In child protection cases the courts' decisions frequently rely heavily on expert reports. Considering the possible consequences for families, expert reports are of major importance. However, the quality of expert reports and the manner in which courts relied upon them also have been criticized (Lüblinghoff 2015; Stürmer and Salewski 2014). Therefore, the German Constitutional Court ruling that courts are required to evaluate expert reports very critically in terms of plausibility and objectivity received a great deal of attention (Decision of the German Constitutional Court, 19.11.2014, 1 BvR 1178/14). Decisions including a withdrawal order usually also include further actions like supportive services for the family of origin (in realization of the guiding principle of the reunification of the family, Coester in: Staudinger-BGB § 1666 Rn.225 and 209) as well as supportive services in cases of children's special needs (e.g., after traumatic experiences of abuse). In cases of deficiencies in parental care, a legal representative (*Ergänzungspfleger*) must be appointed to carry out decisions in deficient areas. In cases where parental rights are fully withdrawn, the court must appoint a guardian (*Vormund*) who carries out full rights in terms of care for the child and legal representation. When parental rights are legally terminated, the court must decide what will happen to the child and cannot transfer this responsibility to the child's guardian.

In cases where the courts decide to take no protective measures, the decision needs to be reviewed after three months.[18] This regulation aims at reducing the number of cases where the situation of the child worsens without the recognition of the authorities. Decisions that lead to longer-term interventions (i.e., more than three months, see Heilmann in: MüKo FamFG § 166 Rn.18) must also be reviewed at reasonable intervals. The interpretation of the reasonable interval is strongly influenced by the type of intervention and the age of the child (Heilmann in: MüKo-FamFG § 166 Rn.20).

Court decisions are enforced by administrative fines, by arrest in case of contempt of court, or by direct force in cases where administrative measures do not help. Appeals are admissible to the appellate court, which is the higher regional court (*Oberlandesgericht*). The appellate court conducts its own evaluation of the facts and the legal classification of the case, thus replacing the family court decision (Olzen in: MüKo-BGB § 1666 Rn. 252). Appeals that deal with the infringement of fundamental rights (e.g., parental rights) by the family courts can be made to the Federal Constitutional Court (*Bundesverfassungsgericht*). The cost of the out-of-home placement is primarily assumed by the child welfare system, which has to demand reimbursement (contributions) by the parents if their income is sufficiently high (which frequently is not the case).

STATISTICS

Due to the different pathways leading to the removal of children from their families and the interconnectedness of the youth office and the courts, statistics related to child protection cases also can come from different sources and offer views through different lenses. In Germany, relevant information can be drawn from official statistics on child and youth welfare as well as from the official statistics of the family courts. Both, however, vary considerably in their content, and different years are not fully comparable because there have been numerous changes in the respective laws. The main focus of the statistics is documentation regarding the activity of the institutions involved; they are not primarily statistics about child protection. In fact, child protection cases make up a comparatively small proportion of family court cases (compared with divorce cases, for instance) and family support services are only one type of service provided through the youth office. Thus only limited information is available about the areas discussed here, but changes toward more detailed case information can be observed. For example, since 2012, information about the type of family court decisions as well as the age and sex of the children concerned can be obtained. Another shortcoming of the available data is that they are only cross-sectional and do not allow one to follow the course of various cases. Despite all of these problems, data from official statistics plays an important role in the professional and political debate.

Children in care

Germany has about 80.5 million inhabitants; 13 million of them (16%) are children younger than eighteen years of age[19]. When comparing the number of children receiving various child welfare measures, the vast majority received supportive services (see Figure 5.1). Out-of-home care placements amount to

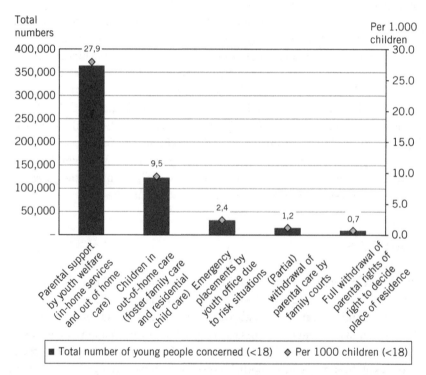

Figure 5.1. Number of children (< 18) concerned by measure/decision in 2013 (end-of-year figure).
Source: Statistisches Bundesamt, Kinder- und Jugendhilfestatistik 2013: Erzieherische Hilfe, Eingliederungshilfe für seelisch behinderte junge Menschen, Hilfen für junge Volljährige—Vollzeitpflege/Heimerziehung, sonstige betreute Wohnform, Tab. 6; Vorläufige Schutzmaßnahmen, Tab. 1; Pflegschaften, Vormundschaften, Beistandschaften, Pflegeerlaubnis, Sorgerechtsentzug, Sorgeerklärungen, Tab.4; Statistisches Bundesamt: Bevölkerungsfortschreibung auf Grundlage des Zensus 2011, Tab. 4.1, (Bevölkerungsstand vom 31.12.2012); own calculations.

30 percent of all measures at the end of the year, consisting of almost equal parts foster family care and residential care. Looking at the end-of-year figure, however, offers a distorted picture. As residential care and foster family care are both generally longer lasting interventions (e.g., the length of a residential care placement had been on average between fifteen and sixteen months between 2008 and 2013; length of stay in foster care had been between twenty-six and twenty-nine months on average for minors during that period) and most of the other family support services last less than one year using reference day measurement, the proportion of out-of-home care is overestimated. This also is confirmed by looking at the measures, which are begun each year: The percentage of foster family care placements initiated per year compared with other measures of family support amounted to about 3.5 percent during the period 2008 to 2013; the corresponding percentage of residential care amounted to about 8 percent. The general development during the past two decades has been characterized by a decline of out-of-home family care compared with in-home family care, which is congruent with the aims and priorities of the Child and Youth Welfare Law of 1990 (Kolvenbach 2008; Rauschenbach and Pothmann 2010; Lotte and Pothmann 2010).

During the years 2008 to 2013 there had been a moderate but continuous rise of all measures in the context of removals of children in total numbers (for numbers per 1.000 children see Table 5.1), whereas the proportions among them—as pointed out in Table 5.1—remained mostly stable. It is important to remember that the various measures concern different institutions and legal issues. Children are, for example, in out-of-home care due to different legal reasons: by parental consent, as an emergency placement by the youth office, or due to decisions by the family courts related to § 1666 BGB (for details, see p. 93 et seq.). At the end of the year 2013, 64,055 children were in family foster care and 59,331 children were in residential child care, which means that 123,386

Table 5.1. Development of measures and decisions in the context of removing children due to child protection issues between 2008 and 2013 per 1,000 children

	2008	2009	2010	2011	2012	2013
All services	21.7	23.4	24.9	25.8	26.4	27.9
Foster family care	3.7	4.0	4.2	4.4	4.6	4.9
Residential child care	3.6	3.8	4.0	4.2	4.3	4.5
Emergency placements	1.7	1.8	1.9	2.1	2.3	2.4
(Partial) Withdrawal of parental care	0.9	0.9	0.9	1.0	1.1	1.2

Source: Statistisches Bundesamt, Kinder- und Jugendhilfestatistik: Erzieherische Hilfe, Eingliederungshilfe für seelisch behinderte junge Menschen, Hilfen für junge Volljährige—Einzelhilfen/Vollzeitpflege/ Heimerziehung, sonstige betreute Wohnform, Tab. 6; Vorläufige Schutzmaßnahmen, Tab. 1; Pflegschaften, Vormundschaften, Beistandschaften, Pflegeerlaubnis, Sorgerechtsentzug, Sorgeerklärungen, Tab.3 (since 2012 Tab.4); Statistisches Bundesamt: Bevölkerungsfortschreibung auf Grundlage der Volkszählung 1987 (Westen) bzw. 1990 (Osten), Tab 2.1; Bevölkerungsfortschreibung auf Grundlage des Zensus 2011, Tab. 4.1; considered period: 2008 – 2013, own calculations.

children were in these types of placements (see Figure 5.1). Available child and youth welfare data offer more in-depth information on the type of placements and family court decisions: 46 percent of the cases of foster family care involved a (partial) withdrawal of parental custodial rights (the percentage remained stable during the period 2008–2013). In the context of residential child care, 23 percent to 27 percent of the cases between 2008 and 2013 involved a (partial) withdrawal of parental rights. This means that in situations of out-of-home care, cases based on court decisions are not exceptional. In foster care placements especially, they clearly play more than a marginal role.

Ages of children in care

Descriptive data on the age groups of children in out-of-home care between 2008 and 2013 show a moderate but continuous rise for all age groups across the two examined placement types. The increase varies between age groups (see Table 5.2 for numbers per 1,000 children of each age group).

Figure 5.2 shows that while children of all ages are in foster family care to rather equal proportions, placement in residential care is mainly associated with being older and/or being an adolescent. These results must be viewed in

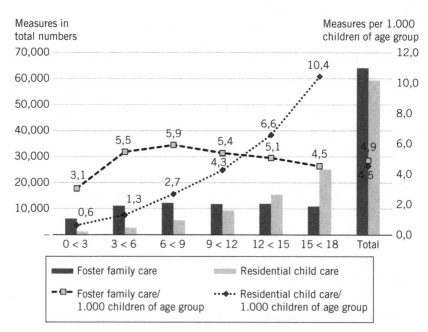

Figure 5.2. Ages of children in foster family care and residential child care 2013 (end-of-year figure).
Source: Statistisches Bundesamt 2013, Erzieherische Hilfe, Eingliederungshilfe für seelisch behinderte junge Menschen, Hilfen für junge Volljährige—Vollzeitpflege/Heimerziehung, sonstige betreute Wohnform, Tab.5; Statistisches Bundesamt: Bevölkerungsfortschreibung auf Grundlage des Zensus 2011, Tab. 4.1, (Bevölkerungsstand vom 31.12.2012); own calculations.

Table 5.2. Development of numbers per 1,000 children of each age group in foster family care and residential child care between 2008 and 2013

Age group (foster family care)	2008	2009	2010	2011	2012	2013
0 < 3	2.5	2.7	2.8	2.8	3.0	3.1
3 < 6	3.7	4.2	4.6	5.0	5.2	5.5
6 < 9	4.0	4.3	4.6	4.9	5.3	5.9
9 < 12	4.0	4.3	4.6	4.8	5.1	5.4
12 < 15	4.0	4.2	4.4	4.5	4.8	5.1
15 < 18	3.6	3.9	4.1	4.1	4.3	4.5
Total	3.7	4.0	4.2	4.4	4.6	4.9
Age group (residential child care)						
0 < 3	0.5	0.5	0.5	0.5	0.5	0.6
3 < 6	0.9	1.0	1.1	1.2	1.2	1.3
6 < 9	1.7	1.9	2.1	2.3	2.5	2.7
9 < 12	3.1	3.4	3.6	3.9	4.0	4.3
12 < 15	5.5	5.8	6.1	6.2	6.4	6.6
15 < 18	8.2	8.8	9.4	9.9	10.1	10.4
Total	3.6	3.8	4.0	4.2	4.3	4.5

Source: Statistisches Bundesamt, Kinder- und Jugendhilfestatistik: Erzieherische Hilfe, Eingliederungshilfe für seelisch behinderte junge Menschen, Hilfen für junge Volljährige –Vollzeitpflege/Heimerziehung, sonstige betreute Wohnform, Tab. 6; Statistisches Bundesamt: Bevölkerungsfortschreibung auf Grundlage der Volkszählung 1987 (Westen) bzw. 1990 (Osten), Tab 2.1; Bevölkerungsfortschreibung auf Grundlage des Zensus 2011, Tab. 4.1; considered period: 2008 – 2013, own calculations.

the context of the aims of the two forms of out-of-home care. The aim of family foster care is to offer parental proximity within a family context (see above) and serves the needs of young children being removed from their families. Older children and adolescents, who are typically faced with other problems and sometimes have complex attachment histories requiring a more professional setting, are more likely to be placed in residential care.

Numbers of cases presented to and decided by the family courts

Child welfare statistics offer data on family court decisions that have been taken due to reasons of child protection (decisions based on § 1666 BGB, see p. 96 et seq.). Being the only legal way to remove children from their families permanently against the parents' will, the data on family court decisions in this field deserve a deeper analysis. Up to 2011, the available data had offered some information on the consequences of the family court decisions (whether there had been a [partial] withdrawal of parental rights or not). Since a change in the data collection method in 2012, there is more detailed information available on family court decisions due to child protection. The statistics offer information about the type of decision; for example, whether the court has ruled a separation of children from their families (by a full withdrawal of parental rights or a termination of the right to decide on the child's place of residence [*Aufenthaltsbestimmungsrecht*]) or whether the court has taken decisions not involving a separation. Further, there is information about the age and sex of the children concerned. There is, however, no information obtainable about the concrete reason (risk situation) for the decision or the duration of the intervention. Long-term comparisons are interesting but only possible at some points due to the changes in statistical items. Statistics show that the absolute number of referrals by the youth office has increased by more than 80 percent between the years 2004 and 2011 (from about 9,000 to more than 16,000 referrals; see Figure 5.3). Family court decisions (partially) terminating parental custodial rights have increased by about 60 percent (from about 8,000 decisions per year in 2004 to about 12,700 per year in 2011). Before that remarkable rise, the numbers had remained quite stable since 1995. The developments during the last decade lead to interpretations that have to be viewed in the context of legal amendments and public discourses during that period.

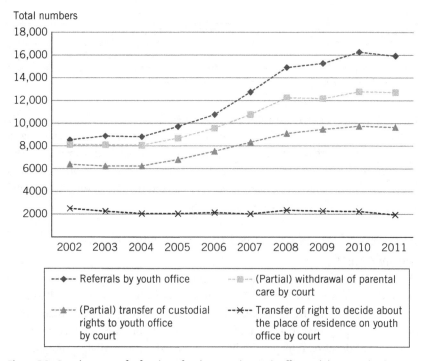

Figure 5.3. Development of referrals to family courts by youth office and decisions by the family courts 2002–2011.
Source: Statistisches Bundesamt, Kinder- und Jugendhilfestatistik: Pflegschaften, Vormundschaften, Beistandschaften, Pflegeerlaubnis, Sorgerechtsentzug, Sorgeerklärungen, Tab.3; considered period: 2002–2011 (numbers for 2012 and onward are not fully comparable).

Table 5.3 Referrals to court by youth office between 2008 and 2011 and decisions by family courts on § 1666 BGB between 2008 and 2013 per 1,000 children. Due to a different method of data collection, the data for 2012 onward is not fully comparable to the previous data

	2008	2009	2010	2011	2012	2013
References in total	1.1	1.1	1.2	1.2	x	x
(Partial) Withdrawal of parental custody in total	0.9	0.9	0.9	1.0	1.1	1.2
(Partial) Transfer of custodial rights to youth welfare office	0.7	0.7	0.7	0.7	0.3	0.4
Transfer of right to decide about place of residence to youth welfare office	0.2	0.2	0.2	0.1	0.1	0.2

Source: Statistisches Bundesamt, Kinder- und Jugendhilfestatistik: Pflegschaften, Vormundschaften, Beistandschaften, Pflegeerlaubnis, Sorgerechtsentzug, Sorgeerklärungen 2011, Tab.3 (since 2012 Tab.4); Statistisches Bundesamt: Bevölkerungsfortschreibung auf Grundlage der Volkszählung 1987 (Westen) bzw. 1990 (Osten), Tab 2.1; Bevölkerungsfortschreibung auf Grundlage des Zensus 2011, Tab. 4.1; considered period: 2008–2013, own calculations.

Therefore, it is worth at this point to present the data for a longer period. Table 5.3 shows the development of referrals to family courts by the youth office when seeking a decision according to § 1666 BGB, and the type of decision by family courts, per 1,000 children between 2008 and 2011. Data on family court decisions is also available for 2012 and 2013 as shown in Table 5.3; it must be noted, however, that the data is largely but not fully comparable due to the change in the statistical items. These methodical changes may be, for example, responsible for the break in the series on (partial) transfers of custodial rights to the youth welfare office.

The rise of referrals to court can be explained by legal amendments, which were aimed at encouraging early referrals to court. In addition, the debate about criminal liability of child welfare workers is likely to have increased the inclination to involve the court earlier. As Figure 5.3 shows, while there has been an increase in court-involved cases, the number of cases not leading to interventions with parental rights also has increased. This may be indicative of increased pressure on parents, who subsequently agree to interventions recommended by the youth office. It may also indicate higher numbers of cases where courts do not see the necessity of measures proposed by the youth office. Overall, there still is a clear rise in (partial) termination of parental rights, which is contrary to lawmakers' objectives to keep interventions related to parental rights to a minimum (see p. 93). It cannot be clarified how many cases where (partial) termination of parental rights occurred ended in the removal of the children from their families, given that family courts can rule on other domains of parental care, such as medical care, without affecting custodial rights. Given the stable number of decisions ruling on the right to decide about the place of residence, it is quite probable that in a considerable number of cases the child was left in the family.

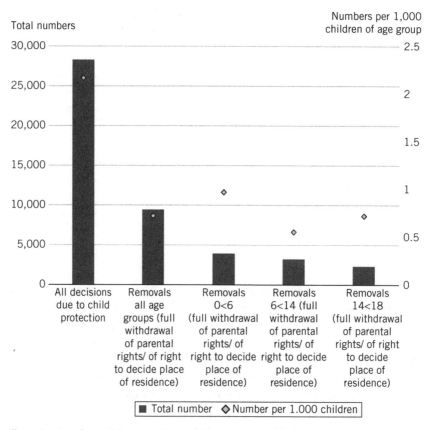

Figure 5.4. Family court decisions due to child protection and family court decisions including a removal according to different age groups 2013.
Source: Statistisches Bundesamt, Kinder- und Jugendhilfestatistik: Pflegschaften, Vormundschaften, Beistandschaften, Pflegeerlaubnis, Sorgerechtsentzug, orgeerklärungen 2013, Tab.4; Statistisches Bundesamt: Bevölkerungsfortschreibung auf Grundlage des Zensus 2011, Tab. 4.1, (Bevölkerungsstand vom 31.12.2012); own calculations.

Figure 5.4 indicates that today about one in one thousand children are affected by family court decisions that necessarily lead to a separation of children from their family (withdrawal of parental rights or the right to decide the place of residence). These decisions make up about 30 percent of all family court decisions based on § 1666 BGB. Considering the numbers per 1,000 children of the age group, it can be seen that, in relative terms, younger children especially are affected by removals. Across all age groups and years such decisions affect slightly more boys.

MAJOR TENDENCIES AND BLIND SPOTS

Child protection actions leading to the removal of children from their families have been subject to a great deal of debate and reform efforts in recent years.

Two major tendencies appear particularly interesting from a systemic-legal point of view: shifts in the way the relationships among the state, parents, and children is seen and the focus on procedural regulations.

In Germany the decision-making process involved in the removal of children by child protective services is significantly shaped by the constitutional framework, which protects parental rights against undue state influence. This strong rule-of-law perspective that regards the family as an area free of state influence can partly be understood in the historical context of Nazi-Germany, which was a period of systematic and strategic interference of the state into family life. The constitutional framework is based on the assumption that balancing the right of parents and their children is not entirely possible, because both rights are so closely intertwined. This, in turn, implies that it is difficult to support children if their parents do not cooperate and that any removal of a child from his or her parents may solve one problem but create a great number of new ones. Removals have thus for quite some time been conceived as *ultima ratio*. Raising children is considered a right of parents, and any state intervention needs to be based on compelling reasons.

Nevertheless, the last several years have seen a tendency to lower the threshold of state intervention into parental rights, including removals. This has not so much been achieved by lowering the requirements for removing children from their parents (see also parliamentary document 16/6815; Meysen 2008; Seier 2008) but rather by supporting less severe interventions and by lowering the threshold for the obligation to initiate formal risk assessment procedures (see also Coester 2008).

The recent debate on child protection has been triggered and dominated by prominent and highly publicized fatality cases and the related question of responsibility of professionals for these cases. Even though there also has been a considerable debate about the United Nations Convention on the Rights of the Child (UNCRC) and European regulations regarding children's rights and the situation of disadvantaged children, they have had limited influence on the field of child protection. They may have subtly contributed, however, to placing greater responsibility on the state for providing optimal living conditions for children and thus changed perceptions of state interventions.

The new procedural framework aimed at facilitating earlier and more continuous state involvement is not quite in line with the formal framing of parents as autonomous recipients of support and procedural subjects. Given the fact that there usually is a clear imbalance of power in child protection cases, which implies a potential for overreach, the interventionist character of state action seems to be somewhat masked. Interestingly transparency of proceedings has not been an issue. The fact that court proceedings are not public is widely accepted in Germany. The issues at stake are considered as private matters deserving of privacy protection. Public court proceedings generally are associated with criminal cases. The public acceptance of the system also may have to do with the fact that state interventions in child protection tend primarily to involve citizens from disadvantaged groups with weak lobbies, and thus fit with a perspective that emphasizes the need for getting tough with members of society who are not performing according to general expectations. Only a few cases concerning excessive intervention through child removals have resulted in public scandal.

As for the professional actors involved, the legal reforms have led to much more detailed legal regulation of individual procedural steps, especially at the level of the youth office, where social workers are the main actors. Together with the general discussion on more standardized methods in professional social work this has produced considerable anxiety about "good" professional practice in the field and the degree to which law can and should provide detailed rules.

The new procedural regulations also have produced an interlacing of areas of responsibility, which is contrary to traditional disciplinary understanding. The court's role has changed from an institution purely making decisions to one of continuous involvement; the youth office has to some degree become an integral part of court proceedings by involving the family courts early and playing a decisive role in the court's risk assessment (Höynck and Haug 2012). This requires new professional and interdisciplinary skills on both sides (see also Arbeitsgruppe "Familiengerichtliche Maßnahmen" 2009; Coester 2009; Wiesner 2008). There still seems to be considerable uncertainty about adequate ways to fulfill the respective roles, especially those of social workers, judges, and guardians ad litem.

Although there is quite a bit of research on the questions of risk assessment and decision-making by the child welfare system in cases of possible risk situations for children (see, e.g., Urban-Stahl 2004; Bode and Turba 2014; Ackermann 2014), empirical knowledge about the current system of child removals by family courts, especially with regard to recent developments, remains sparse. Interestingly, the question whether the reforms in family law and family procedural law really have improved child protection (including the question of what exactly this means) is as much a blind spot as the implementation of suggested procedures in everyday practice. This is especially true in cases involving a permanent removal of the child. At this point, however, it does not seem clear (and probably is quite heterogeneous throughout the country) who the leading agents in the cases are, under which circumstances the court or the youth office favor removals, and what factors determine these dynamics. The law aims to ensure the safety of all children while at the same time respecting and supporting parental rights. Given the involvement of multiple actors, the youth office, parents, children, guardian ad litem, and a complex mix of negotiated and at the same time authoritative procedures, the balance of power in the cases might warrant closer attention. One important aspect would seem to be verifying the impression that removals occur mainly in families of low socioeconomic status—a fact that would increase the structural imbalance of power inherent in these cases.

Focusing the discussion on removals runs the risk of losing sight of the long-term perspective for the children concerned. There still is not sufficient follow-up research about what exactly happens to the children removed from their families. For instance, under which circumstances do they return to their parent(s); what are the effects of reunification; and, under which circumstances do they develop positively, away from their parents? If removing children from their parents is meant to ensure their protection, there is more to "success" that relieving an acute risk. Currently, the pace of reform seems to have slowed down. Local practices will need more time to implement the legal framework developed in recent years. Research can then start looking at a system that has had some time to mature.

NOTES

1   The term "measure"—not common in the English literature on child protection—is oriented toward a literal translation of the term "Maßnahme," which can be used in the German legal context to describe different forms of state action in child protection cases. In this sense it represents a collective term for services aimed at supporting parents in parenting as well as for actions interfering with parental rights.

2   For example, the number of child protection cases, which were referred to court by the youth office with the aim of withdrawing parental custodial rights, has increased more than 80 percent during the last decade.

3   The term "youth office" is a literal translation of the German term "Jugendamt." The youth office is based on the community level and performs as the central institution in child and youth welfare, taking responsibility for offers and measures ranging from child day care and services supporting parents in parenting to child protection.

4   The consideration of out-of-home care as a whole also would include placements of children into closed institutions outside the criminal justice system. Being a deprivation of liberty, these cases need to be approved by family courts. Closed accommodation is mainly used in cases of mental illness in psychiatric health care institutions. There are also, however, some closed institutions in the youth welfare system. There is considerable overlap regarding the problems addressed by the different systems. The difference from the cases discussed in this chapter is that these cases concern dangers originating from the children themselves (children being a danger to themselves or others), and not typical child protection cases concerning external risk situations mainly caused by parents.

5   As in many European countries, the view on children in Germany has changed remarkably during the last century. An examination of the development of parental care under German family law throughout the last

one hundred years indicates that the focus in parental care changed from a parental (until the 1950s a paternal) approach toward a child-centered approach.

6   "Gesetz zur Neuordnung des Kinder- und Jugendhilferechts", BGBl. I (1990) p. 1163, effective from 1.1.1991 (resp. 3.10.1990 in the new area of the former GDR).

7   "Kinder- und Jugendhilfeweiterentwicklungsgesetz," BGBl. I p. 2729 (2005), effective from 1.10.2005.

8   Most cases start with uncertain facts and are, therefore, difficult to classify. In decisions where it is difficult to clarify whether the outcome is right, legitimation can be reached by due process (Luhmann 2008).

9   By the Act on Facilitating Family Court Measures in Cases of Serious Risk for Children ("Gesetz zur Erleichterung familiengerichtlicher Maßnahmen bei Gefährdung des Kindeswohls"), BGBl. I p. 1188 (2008), effective from 12.7.2008.

10   Dealing with the cases at a very late point in time (where situations had reached a distracted level), it was observed that family judges made significant use of withdrawing parents' custodial rights, instead of ruling other options (parliamentary document 16/6815; Arbeitsgruppe "Familiengerichtliche Maßnahmen" 2006).

11   This interpretation can, for example, result from former supporting measures without effect (Götz in: Palandt § 1666 Rn.28).

12   One of the achievements of the legal reform in 2009 (Act on the reform of procedural family law "Gesetz über das Verfahren in Familiensachen und in den Angelegenheiten der freiwilligen Gerichtsbarkeit," BGBl. I p.2586 [2008], effective from 1.9.2009) was that the parties are not regarded anymore as parties in a classical sense, but as involved persons with their own subjective interests and rights. Therefore, the term "party" was replaced by "participants" ("Beteiligte") in § 113 V FamFG. This, however, has not been comprehensively implemented by the courts (see Fest 2011).

13   No exact numbers, however, can be derived from official statistics.

14   Cases of exigent circumstance might cause an omission of the hearing. In these cases the hearing must be caught up immediately. Only for important reasons is it possible to desist fully from the hearing; for example, in cases where the hearing would produce an enormous strain on the children (Olzen in: MüKo-BGB, § 1666 Rn.225).

15   The study refers to data that had been collected under the former legal situation (before 2009). The legal amendments at this point were mainly of formal nature, therefore, the results are still considered to be effective.

16   Other places for hearings are, for example, the judge's room or specially arranged children's rooms.

17   The obligatory involvement was implemented in 2012 after it was found that the involvement of the youth office in child protection cases was necessary,

but there has not been much use made of this possibility (parliamentary document 17/10590).

18 The principle was introduced with Act on Facilitating Family Court Measures in Cases of Serious Risk for Children (see footnote 9).

19 Child protection in Germany addresses all children and adolescents up to seventeen years old. For reasons of legibility this text refers to the term "children", meaning both age groups.

REFERENCES

Ackermann, T. (2014). Entscheiden über Fremdunterbringungen. Praktiken der Fallerzeugung. In Bütow, B., Pomey, M., Rutschmann, M., Schär, C., and Studer, T. (Eds.), *Sozialpädagogik zwischen Staat und Familie*, pp. 153–173. Wiesbaden: Springer VS.

Arbeitsgruppe "Familiengerichtliche Maßnahmen bei Gefährdung des Kindeswohls – § 1666 BGB." (2006). Abschlussbericht vom 14. Juli 2006. BMJ.

Arbeitsgruppe "Familiengerichtliche Maßnahmen bei Gefährdung des Kindeswohls – § 1666 BGB." (2009). Abschlussbericht vom 17. November 2009. BMJ.

Bode, I. and Turba, H. (2014). *Organisierter Kinderschutz in Deutschland. Strukturdynamiken und Modernisierungsparadoxien.* Wiesbaden: Springer VS.

Cameron, G. (2007). Grundsätzliche Methoden in der Kinder- und Jugendhilfe: Erfahrungen aus kinderschutz-, familien- und gemeinwesenorientierten Hilfesystemen. In *Kinderschutz gemeinsam gestalten: § 8a SGB VIII— Schutzauftrag der Kinder- und Jugendhilfe. Dokumentation der Fachtagung am 22. und 23. Juni 2006 in Berlin*, edited by Verein für Kommunalwissenschaften e.V., 13–39. Berlin: Verein für Kommunalwissenschaften e.V.

Coester, M. (2008). Inhalt und Funktion des Begriffs Kindeswohlgefährdung— Erfordernis einer Neudefinition? *JAmt*: 1–9.

Coester, M. (2009). Kinderschutz. Übersicht zu den typischen Gefährdungslagen und aktuellen Problemen. *Familie, Partnerschaft, Recht*: 549–52.

Eschweiler, P. (2005). Kindesanhörung—Chancen und Risiken. *Neue Juristische Wochenschrift*: 1681–1686.

Fest, T. (2011). Zwei Jahre Reform des familiengerichtlichen Verfahrens: Eine Zwischenbilanz. *Neue Juristische Wochenschrift*: 2611–2616.

Hannemann, A. and Stötzel, M. (2009). Die Verfahrenspflegschaft im deutschen Rechtssystem. *Zeitschrift für Kindschaftsrecht und Jugendhilfe* (2): 59–67.

Haug, M. and Höynck, T. (2012). Kindeswohlgefährdung—staatliche Handlungsmöglichkeiten im Spiegel amtlicher Daten. In Marthaler, M., Bastian, P., Ingo Bode, I., and Schrödter, M. (Eds.), *Rationalitäten des Kinderschutzes. Kindeswohl und soziale Interventionen aus pluraler Perspektive*, pp. 133–174. Wiesbaden: VS-Verlag.

Höynck, T. and Haug, M. (2012). Kindeswohlgefährdung—Rechtliche Konturen eines schillernden Begriffs. In Marthaler, M., Bastian, P., Ingo Bode, I., and Schrödter, M. (Eds.), *Rationalitäten des Kinderschutzes. Kindeswohl und soziale Interventionen aus pluraler Perspektive*, pp. 19-45. Wiesbaden: VS-Verlag.

Karle, M., Gathmann, S., and Klosinski, G. (2010). Zur Praxis der Kindesanhörung in Deutschland. Ein Abschlussbericht. *Zeitschrift für Kindschaftsrecht und Jugendhilfe* (12): 432-434.

Katzenstein, H. (2011). Formelle Beteiligung des Jugendamts im familiengerichtlichen Verfahren: Fach- oder Machtfrage? *Familie Partnerschaft Recht*: 20-23.

Keidel, T., Engelhardt, H., Sternal, W., et al. (2014). *Kommentar zum Gesetz über das Verfahren in Familiensachen und in den Angelegenheiten der freiwilligen Gerichtsbarkeit* (18th ed.). München: C. H. Beck. (cit.: "author in: Keidel-FamFG § . . . Rn. . . .")

Kindler, H. (2010). Kinderschutz in Europa. Philosophien, Strategien und Perspektiven nationaler und transnationaler Initiativen zum Kinderschutz. In Müller, R. and Nüsken, D. (Eds.), *Child Protection in Europe. Von den Nachbarn lernen—Kinderschutz qualifizieren*, pp. 11-29. Münster: Waxmann Verlag.

Kolvenbach, F.-J. (2008). 16 Jahre Kinder- und Jugendhilfegesetz in Deutschland—Ergebnisse der Kinder- und Jugendhilfestatistiken—Erzierhische Hilfen 1991 bis 2006. "Von der Erziehungsberatung bis zur Heimerziehung." *Statistisches Bundesamt*: 1-24.

Lotte, J., and Pothmann, J. (2010). Bedarf an Hilfen für Familien ungebrochen—Inanspruchnahme steigt auf über 1 Million junge Menschen—Hilfen zur Erziehung und Eingliederungshilfen für seelisch behinderte junge Menschen 2009. *KOMDAT Jugendhilfe* (2/2010): 2-4.

Lüblinghoff, J. (2015). Fingerzeig aus Karlsruhe zur Qualität von Gerichtsgutachten. *Deutsche Richterzeitung*: 52-53.

Luhmann, N. (2008). *Legitimation durch Verfahren*. Vol. 8. Frankfurt am Main: Suhrkamp.

Marthaler, T. (2009). *Erziehungsrecht und Familie—Der Wandel familialer Leitbilder im privaten und öffentlichen Recht seit 1900*. Weinheim/München: Juventa Verlag.

Meysen, T. (2008). Familiengerichtliche Maßnahmen bei Gefährdung des Kindeswohls—Geändertes Recht ab Sommer 2008. *JAmt/Zeitschrift für Kindschaftsrecht und Jugendhilfe* (5): 233-242.

Meysen, T. (2014). Schutz oder Hilfe? Schutz als Hilfe! *RdJB* 4/2014: 502-512.

Münder, J., Meysen, T., and Trenczek, T. (Eds.) (2013). *Frankfurter Kommentar zum SGB VIII. Kinder- und Jugendhilfe* (7th ed.). Baden-Baden: Nomos. (cit.: "author in: FK-SGB VIII/ §... Rn. ...")

Münder, J., Mutke, B., and Schone, R. (2000). *Kindeswohl zwischen Jugendhilfe und Justiz—Professionelles Handeln in Kindeswohlverfahren.* Münster: Votum Verlag.

Oberloskamp, H., Borg-Laufs, M., and Mutke, B. (2009). *Gutachtliche Stellungnahmen in der sozialen Arbeit. Eine Anleitung mit Beispielen für die Mitwirkung in Familiengerichts- und Jugendstrafverfahren.* Köln: Luchterhand.

OTH Regensburg in Kooperation mit TU Berlin und FH Münster. (2015). Kindeswohl zwischen Jugendhilfe und Justiz—Forschungsprojekt zur Entwicklung von Entscheidungsgrundlagen und Verfahren zur Sicherung des Kindeswohls zwischen Jugendämtern und Familiengerichten, *JAmt*: 13–14.

Palandt, O. (Ed.) (2016). *Bürgerliches Gesetzbuch* (75th ed.). München: C. H. Beck. (cit.: "author in: Palandt-BGB § . . . Rn . . . .")

Pothmann, J. (2009). Zwischen Leistung und Eingriff—die vielen Gesichter der Inobhutnahme. Einsichten auf Basis der amtlichen Kinder- und Jugendhilfestatistik. In Lewis, G., Riehm, R., Neumann-Witt, A., Bohnstengel, L., Köstler, S., and Hensen, G. (Eds.), *Inobhutnahme konkret. Pädagogische Aspekte der Arbeit in der Inobhutnahme und im Kinder- und Jugendnotdienst*, pp. 103–121. Frankfurt am Main: IGfH-Eigenverlag.

Prenzlow, R. (2012). Gleiches Recht für alle Kinder!? Vom Verfahrenspfleger zum Verfahrensbeistand—Was hat sich geändert? *Zeitschrift für Kindschaftsrecht und Jugendhilfe* (3): 93–97.

Rauschenbach, T. and Pothmann, J. (2010). Frühe Hilfen als aktiver Kinderschutz—Rückgang der Kindstötungen—Zunahme der Hilfen. *KOMDAT Jugendhilfe* (2/2010): 1–2.

Rauscher, T., Coester-Waltjen, D., Fickmann, D., et al. (2013). *Münchener Kommentar zum FamFG. §§ 1-491 IZVR EuZVR* (2nd ed.). München: C. H. Beck. (cit.: "author in: MüKo-FamFG § . . . Rn. . . .")

Rosenboom, E. (2006). *Die familiengerichtliche Praxis in Hamburg bei Gefährdung des Kindeswohls durch Gewalt und Vernachlässigung nach §§ 1666, 1666a BGB.* Bielefeld: Gieseking.

Rüting, W. (2012). Pflegekinder, Rückführung in die Herkunftsfamilie, Umgang. *Familie Partnerschaft Recht*: 381–385.

Säcker, F. J., and Rixecker, R. (Eds.) (2012). *Münchener Kommentar zum Bürgerlichen Gesetzbuch: BGB. Band 8: Familienrecht II (§§ 1589-1921), SGB VIII* (6th ed.). München: C. H. Beck. (cit.: "author in: MüKo-BGB/ § . . . Rn. . . .")

Schweppe, K. and Bussian, J. (2012). Die Kindesanhörung aus familienrichterlicher Sicht. *Zeitschrift für Kindschaftsrecht und Jugendhilfe* (1): 13–20.

Seier, N. (2008). Reform des § 1666 BGB und Verfassungsschutz. *Familie Partnerschaft Recht*: 483–487.

Simitis, S., Rosenkötter, L., Vogel, R., Boost-Muss, B., Frommann, M., Hopp, J., Koch, H., and Zenz, G. (1979). *Kindeswohl. Eine interdisziplinäre*

Untersuchung über seine Verwirklichung in der vormundschaftsgerichtlichen Praxis. Frankfurt: Suhrkamp.

Sommer, A. (2012). Die Rechtsstellung des Kindes im familiengerichtlichen Verfahren. *Familie Partnerschaft Recht*: 374–377.

Staudinger, J. von (Ed.) (2016). *J. von Staudingers Kommentar zum Bürgerlichen Gesetzbuch: Staudinger BGB—Buch 4: Familienrecht.* Berlin: Sellier—de Gruyter. (cit.: "author in: Staudinger-BGB/ § . . . Rn. . . .")

Stötzel, M. and Prenzlow, R. (2011). Die Kindesanhörung im familieng-erichtlichen Verfahren. *Zeitschrift für Kindschaftsrecht und Jugendhilfe (6)*: 200–204.

Stürmer, S. and Salewski, C. (2014). Studie: Viele Fehler in Gutachten. *Deutsche Richterzeitung*: 282–283.

Trenczek, T. (2008). *Inobhutnahme—Krisenintervention und Schutzgewährung durch die Jugendhilfe—§§ 8a, 42 SGB VIII* (2nd ed.). Stuttgart: Richard Boorberg Verlag.

Urban-Stahl, U. (2004). *Professionelles Handeln zwischen Hilfe und Kontrolle: Sozialpädagogische Entscheidungsfindung in der Hilfeplanung.* Weinheim u.a.: Beltz Juventa.

Vogel, H. (2010). Der Verfahrensbeistand. *Familie Partnerschaft Recht*: 43–46.

Wiesner, R. (2007). Schutzauftrag des Jugendamtes bei Kindeswohlgefährdung. *Familie Partnerschaft Recht*: 6–12.

Wiesner, R. (2008). Leistungen der Kinder- und Jugendhilfe nach dem SGB VIII. *Familie Partnerschaft Recht*: 608–613.

Wiesner, R. (Ed.) (2015). *SGB VIII. Kinder- und Jugendhilfe. Kommentar* (5th ed.). München: C. H. Beck. (cit.: "author in: Wiesner-SGB VIII/ § . . . Rn. . . .")

Wolff, R., Biesel, K., and Heinitz, S. (2011). "Child protection in an age of un-certainty. Germany's response." In Gilbert, N., Parton, N., and Skivenes, M. (Eds.), *Child Protection Systems. International Trends and Orientations*, pp. 183–203. Oxford: Oxford University Press.

6

CHILD REMOVAL PROCEEDINGS IN SWITZERLAND

Stefan Schnurr

INTRODUCTION

This chapter[1] examines child removal proceedings in Switzerland, a country of 8.2 million inhabitants, 18 percent (1.48 million) of whom are children under the age of 18 years (as of December 2014, Swiss Statistics 2015). Switzerland—a multilingual country with four official national languages, which are German (64 percent), French (23 percent) Italian (8 percent) and Romansh (0.5 percent)—is a confederation of twenty-six cantons, divided into 2,249 municipalities (Federal Chancellery 2016). The size of the cantons ranges from ca. 16,000 to 1,500,000 inhabitants. In thirteen of the twenty-six cantons the population is under 200,000. The principle of federalism is implemented at all levels of policy-making. The responsibilities of the federal state are restricted to tasks "that the cantons are unable to perform or which require uniform regulation by the Confederation" (Art. 42, Federal Constitution of the Swiss Confederation). Accordingly, the twenty-six cantons each have their own constitution, parliament, government, legislation, jurisdiction, and so forth, and are important players in policy-making at the federal level. The core principles of federalism and subsidiarity are inscribed in the relations between the federal state and the cantons, between the cantons and the municipalities, and in the formulation and implementation of their politics and policies. The principle of subsidiarity ensures that the lower entity has considerable autonomy from the higher entity; decisions about organizational frameworks and procedures normally are located in the lower entity. Political decision-making incorporates extraparliamentary experts, the cantons, the two chambers of parliament, political parties, and citizens (via mandatory and optional referenda). Owing to these features of strong federalism and direct democracy the political decision-making process is characterized by "a strong vertical and horizontal fragmentation of power," and, therefore, policy-making in Switzerland is "slow and often incremental as well as incoherent" (Obinger et al. 2010, p. 191; et passim.). Switzerland's political system and its small-scale federalism have a significant impact on the institutionalization of children's services and child protection.

CONTEXTUALIZING THE SWISS REGIME(S) OF CHILDREN'S SERVICES AND CHILD PROTECTION

In cross-country analyses of children's services, it has become almost a convention to locate the country under consideration within the framework of the three worlds of welfare capitalism (Esping-Andersen 1990). In this regard, studies of the Swiss welfare state have argued that it underwent a significant shift from the 1970s to the late 2000s, from the liberal model toward the conservative welfare model (Obinger et al. 2010), and, as a consequence, it now represents a hybrid liberal–conservative regime (Bonoli and Häusermann 2011, p. 187; Mach and Trampusch 2011, p. 22). Reference is also typically made to the classificatory system that emerges from the distinction between a *child-protection-oriented* system, with an emphasis on legal interventions, and a *family-service-oriented* system, with an emphasis on family support (Gilbert 1997). Recently another set of coordinates for the mapping of child protection systems has been presented, proposing a distinction between *risk-oriented* and *service-oriented* systems (Gilbert et al. 2011). In order to incorporate the dynamic changes associated with the emphasis on children's rights and the "social investment state" (Giddens 1998), a third axis has been added to these bipolar frameworks, namely *a child-focused orientation* (Gilbert et al. 2011). This extension to the frameworks is particularly supported by developments in Finland and Norway, which have been analyzed as representing the emergence of a *child-centric perspective* (Skivenes 2011) or *child-centered orientation* (Pösö 2011).

With regard to these distinctions between models of child protection systems, it has been stated that "the Swiss child protection system might be labeled as 'family service-oriented'" (Jud and Gartenhauser 2014, p. 3). In contrast to this position, it is argued in this chapter that Switzerland has more in common with both *child-protection-oriented* systems, with an emphasis on legal interventions, and *risk-oriented* systems. These two classifications are suggested by two characteristics of the Swiss system of children's services and child protection. On the one hand, legal interventions aimed at child protection are set out in the federal civil law and applied by specialist authorities (Child and Adult

Protection Authorities [CAPAs]) throughout the country; on the other hand, a "universal" system of services for children and families is missing and the provision and availability of such services varies considerably across the cantons. Thus, legal interventions are a universal feature in a landscape of diverse and often low-level accessibility to services; these legal interventions can be understood as the backbone of the institutionalization of state responses to threats to the well-being of children. Nevertheless, Swiss federal legislation from 2013 onward has introduced features that have a *child-focused orientation*, such as strengthening the rights of children to be heard in CAPA proceedings and placement proceedings.[2] Given these countervailing tendencies, any classification of the Swiss system of children's services at the present time must remain preliminary and be put forward with caution, owing to the diversity of institutional arrangements and the paucity of data and research. Features of the Swiss system of children's services and child protection that are general (across the cantons) and distinctive are:

- The late implementation of a professionalized decision-making body in cases of compulsory removal of a child from his/her home (in 2013);
- The constitution of the decision-making body as an "interdisciplinary" or multiprofessional body[3];
- The substantial diversity in the structures set up by twenty-six cantonal regimes serving a population of only 8 million people;
- The reluctance to have legislation and formal regulation of voluntary and support-oriented services for children and families at all levels of policy-making;
- The lack of statistics and data on the supply, use, and costs of services.

TYPES OF REMOVAL

Switzerland has four routes to alternative (out-of-home) care (see Table 6.1). They can be differentiated with regard to whether the removal is voluntary or compulsory,[4] and distinguished further with respect to the decision-making body, its legal basis, and the professions involved.

Throughout the remainder of this chapter, the removal of a child from his or her home to alternative care is regarded as voluntary if the parent(s) consent to the removal. The removal of a child is regarded as compulsory if the decision to remove him or her is combined with an explicit and lawful limitation of the parental right to decide the place of residence of the child, including when parents disagree with a removal decision of an authority. Although decisions on *voluntary removals* of children are, generally speaking, located within the remit of social services, children's services, and (in some cantons)

Table 6.1. Switzerland: Types of Removals

Type No.	Type of Decision	Decision-making Body	Legal Basis	Professions Represented in the Decision-making Body	Type of Removal
1	Child Protection Authority decides that removal is necessary in order to ensure the well-being of the child. "Care order"/"Ordered Removal."	Child and Adult Protection Authority (CAPA).	Swiss Civil Code (SCC). *Federal Law.*	Law Professionals, Social Workers, Psychologists, Pedagogues and others in multiprofessional ("interdisciplinary") Bodies. The professional composition of the decision-making body varies.	Compulsory.
2	A service advises the removal of a child and the parents agree. "Agreed removal."	Social Services/ Children's Services/School Administration. Depending on cantonal law or regulation the final decision may lie with a specialist municipal committee or the mayor.	Cantonal Acts in a number of cantons. *Cantonal Law.*	Social Workers.	Voluntary.
3	The parents decide to place a child in out-of-home care.	Diverse and opaque.	Swiss Civil Code (SCC). *Federal Law.*	Diverse and opaque.	Voluntary.
4	Juvenile Justice Authority decides that a placement is necessary in order to ensure education and treatment of a child.	Juvenile Justice Authority.	Juvenile Justice Act (offenders aged 10–18 years). *Federal Law.*	Law Professionals (Judges).	Compulsory.

school administrations, decisions on *compulsory removal* (care orders) are the responsibility of specialist authorities, namely, the CAPAs, which since January 2013 have been constituted as multiprofessional ("interdisciplinary") bodies. Compulsory removals also can be instigated by Juvenile Justice Authorities.

This chapter examines compulsory removals through decisions of CAPAs (*Type 1*) and voluntary removals with parental consent following decisions made by social services and children's services (*Type 2*). The number of children placed through care orders made by the precursor authorities to CAPAs (*Type 1*) in the period 2008–2012 ranges from 2.4 to 2.6 per 1,000 children (KOKES 2014). Owing to a lack of statistics, the number of children placed with parental consent (*Type 2*) cannot be specified. Only two cantons have published relevant data, according to which voluntary removals range from 3.4 to 4.5 per 1,000 children in 2008–2013 (Kommission 2014).

Type 3 refers to placements decided by the parents through the exercise of their parental rights and duties, which are laid down in the *Swiss Civil Code*. This type of placement is not considered in this chapter, not least because of the scarcity of information about the number of such placements and the procedures followed in respect to them.

Type 4 refers to removals decided by a Juvenile Justice Authority through the exercise of the Swiss Juvenile Justice Act (JJA) (2003), which governs state responses to violations of the law by young persons aged 10–18 years. The Act generally allows two types of responses: penalties and protective measures. Penalties and protective measures can be decided upon as separate disposals or they can be used in combination. Protective measures are instigated if an assessment of a child referred to a Juvenile Justice Authority reveals the need for special education or therapy (Art. 10 JJA). These measures can be initiated regardless of whether the child is found guilty. The law defines four types of protective measures including placement with specific persons (e.g., foster parents) or in institutions (Art. 12-15 JJA). Because education and protection are key principles of the Juvenile Justice Act (Art. 2 JJA), the Juvenile Justice Authorities in Switzerland have wide discretion in responding to individual circumstances and needs and are able to choose from the entire spectrum of children's services, educative programs, therapies, and the like, if they decide on protective measures. A great number of Juvenile Justice Authorities have units of social workers and psychologists who conduct assessments and make recommendations with regard to protective measures. The authority to make decisions on penalties and/or protective measures lies with the judge. In the period 2008–2013, the number of placement decisions under the Juvenile Justice Act ranged from 0.12 to 0.34 per 1,000 inhabitants aged 10-18 years (average: 0.22) (Swiss Statistics 2014).[5] Given the focus of this volume on the removal of children through child protection systems in interventions that are not linked to delinquency, *Type 4* is not considered further in this chapter.

COMPULSORY REMOVALS

The legal basis of child protection in federal law:
The *Swiss Civil Code*

Legislation on child protection is part of the federal civil law, the *Swiss Civil Code* (SCC). The Code provides definitions of the child-parent relationship, including the rights and duties of parents, thresholds of state intervention into family autonomy, and child protection measures.[6] Furthermore, it defines the responsibilities and duties of the Child and Adult Protection Authorities (CAPAs), a number of core organizational characteristics of the CAPAs, and a set of rules and regulations concerning their proceedings, including arrangements for hearing the views of the child.

The SCC sets out a number of child protection measures, which together constitute a graded system of interventions with corresponding limitations on family autonomy:

1. *Appropriate Measures (Art. 307)*: These include: reminding parents, foster parents, or the child of their duties; instructions regarding care, upbringing or education; appointing a suitable person or agency with powers to investigate and monitor the situation.[7] The particular measures mentioned in the law are not regarded as a complete list, given that the law explicitly requires the Child Protection Authority to "take all appropriate measures to protect the child." In principle, decisions on the measures taken are linked to the condition that "the child's well-being is threatened and the parents are unwilling or unable to remedy the situation."

2. *Deputyship (Art. 308)*: The appointment of a child deputy is the most frequent response by far (see Table 6.2), presumably because the preconditions for such an appointment are vaguely defined ("where circumstances so require") and deputyship can be used in very flexible ways. The assignment of a child deputy can be linked to certain functions such as establishing a trusted contact person for the child or to "help the parents look after the child by providing advice and practical support" (Art. 308 SCC). Generally, the competences of a deputy include rights of access to and gaining information about the family (Cottier 2012, p. 793). Deputyship can be tailored to particular issues and involve (very specific) corresponding restrictions on parental rights. For example, a child deputy may be assigned to enforce medical examination or treatment of a child, to select a suitable out-of-home placement, or, if a child has been taken into care, a child deputy may function as an intermediary among the CAPA, the provider of out-of-home care, the parents, and the child. A child

Table 6.2. Child Protection Measures 2008–2012 in Switzerland in total numbers and per 1,000 Children (0–17) (end of year)

Year		2008		2009		2010		2011		2012	
Children (0–17)		1,451,144		1,449,021		1,453,981		1,457,151		1,461,568	
		Measures	Per 1,000 Children	Measures	Per 1,000 Children	Measures	Per 1,000 Children	Measures	Per 1,000 Children	Measures	Per 1,000 Children
Type of Measure	Appropriate Measures Art. 307 SCC	2,397	1.65	2,102	1.45	2,177	1.50	2,272	1.56	2,487	1.70
	Deputyship Art. 308 SCC	22,942	15.81	22,381	15.45	27,249	18.74	26,260	18.02	26,239	17.95
	Revocation of the right to decide on place of residence Art 310/308 SCC	3,436	2.37	3,537	2.44	3,609	2.48	3,546	2.43	3,853	2.64
	Withdrawal of parental responsibility Art. 311/312 SCC	233	0.16	417	0.29	245	0.17	204	0.14	285	0.19

Sources: Konferenz der Kantone für Kindes- und Erwachsenenschutz (KOKES) (2014), Swiss Statistics, calculations by the author.

deputy can be assigned in cases of voluntary and compulsory removal of children, that is, with or without a revocation of the parents' right to decide on a child's place of residence. In practice the appointment of a child deputy and the revocation of the parents' right to decide on a child's place of residence are often combined. Deputyship has become a standard response in cases when a parent's right to visit a child is controversial or legally restricted.

In legal terms deputyship is a public office assigned to an individual person in her/his own right, rather than to an organization. A deputy can be located, however, in various organizational contexts, such as local social services, children's services, units of canton or municipal administration, or specialized (cantonal) associations of individuals who are carrying out deputyships as an occupation. The legal institution of deputyship contributes to the complexity of the Swiss child protection system in several ways. It introduces an additional formal party into the family/state relationship by installing a unique specialized legal *and* social role into the complex web of family, social services/children's services, CAPAs, and service providers. Given that the organizational locations of deputyship are diverse, it increases incongruity in the system with regard to a key function of child protection systems: the location of the state responsibility for children in care, because this is most often delegated to the individual appointed as a deputy. Furthermore, it increases organizational complexity because a social services/children's services worker has the dual role of being both an individual person holding the public office of deputyship in her/his own right and a member of an organization. This generates the possibility of uncertainty, ambiguity, and conflict.

3. *Revocation of the right to decide on place of residence (Art. 310):* A decision to remove a child from her/his parents and place him or her in a "suitable location" is linked to the condition that "there is no other way to avert a threat to the child's well-being." It is stipulated that less intrusive measures have to have been tried and that they have proved insufficient. Furthermore, the law grants the authority to act "at the request of the parents or the child," if relations between them "have deteriorated to the extent that it is no longer conscionable for the child to remain in the family home and provided no other practical remedy is available in the circumstances." An aspect of Art. 310 SCC concerns decisions about what is regarded as the "suitable location" for the child.

4. *Withdrawal of parental responsibility (Art. 311):* A withdrawal of parental responsibility is linked to the precondition that "other child protection measures have failed or offer little prospect of proving adequate" in combination with two other (alternative) conditions, which are defined as follows:

1. If the parents are unable to exercise parental responsibility as required on account of inexperience, illness, disability, absence, violent behavior or other similar reasons;
2. If the parents have not cared for the child to any meaningful degree or have flagrantly violated their duties towards the child.

5. *Committal to a secure institution or psychiatric hospital (Art 314b):* The application of Art 314b is linked to the preconditions that a severe threat to the well-being of the child in accordance with Art. 310 is evident and that necessary treatment cannot be met otherwise. Restrictions on the freedom of movement of the child in the context of secure institutions is limited to that needed in order to prevent serious endangerment to the self and/or others or to "remedy serious disruption to life in and around the institution" (Art. 383 SCC). Such restrictions are not permissible as a means of discipline or education (Cottier 2012, p. 818; 820).

The SCC also provides the legal basis for emergency placements, because it gives the CAPA complete competence to enforce its decisions. A person who is assigned to enforce a decision of a CAPA is also entitled to enlist the help of the police, if necessary (Art 450g SCC).[8]

The decision-making of a CAPA is bound by three overarching legal principles: proportionality, complementarity (meshing with the care provided by the parents), and subsidiarity (in relation to voluntary services) (Biderbost 2012).

The decision-making body: the Child and Adult Protection Authority (CAPA)

Since 2013 child protection authorities have been multiprofessional bodies. The amendments to the legislation on child and adult protection that brought this about completed their passage through the legislative procedure in 2008, after a process of reform that had begun in 1999 (Bundesrat 2006). Although the key aspect of the 2008 reform of the SCC was adult protection, a number of the intentions of the reform process and major changes in the legislation concerned child protection. This was most evident in the shift from lay to professional decision-making bodies. Until 2013 in many cantons in the German-speaking parts of Switzerland the former Guardianship Authorities were located in the elected political bodies of the municipalities.[9] This lay-person-based system was increasingly regarded as inadequate for the following reasons: (1) the closeness of those who were responsible for decisions, which often concerned very personal and intimate matters, to those who were affected by the decisions; (2) the lack of specialized knowledge and experience in matters calling for interventions to protect vulnerable children and adults; (3) the lack of expertise with regard to the law and its application, which led to the decision-making bodies depending on external experts (often workers in social services or children's services and the like), a situation that was often criticized as a "reversal of hierarchy"(Konferenz 2008, p. 75). Owing to the often very small size of municipalities, opportunities to gain the experience required for adequate handling of child protection cases was limited (ibid.). One of the remarkable features of the 2013 reform was the reduction in the number of authorities from 1,420 to 148 (Wider 2014).

The decision-making bodies: common features

In the 2008 amendments to the SCC, the legislation defined a set of characteristics that all CAPAs have to meet and also set out what is left to the discretion of cantonal legislation. By legal definition, the CAPA is a "specialist authority," it has "a quorum of three members for taking decisions" and "it also carries out the tasks of the child protection authority" (Art. 440 SCC). The CAPA holds responsibility for the entire process from investigation to decision-making. It conducts the required inquiries and gathers the required evidence either by itself or it "may instruct a suitable person or agency to carry out investigations" (Art. 446 SCC). The federal government (Bundesrat 2006) and an organization for intercanton exchange on issues of child and adult protection[10] (Konferenz 2008, p. 76 ff.) have expressed their views on the professional expertise that should be represented in the decision-making bodies. The latter saw law, social work, pedagogy, and psychology as the core professions that were required, with medicine and trust administration[11] as of secondary relevance. The majority of cantons have established three-person decision-making bodies and law and social work are about to gain the status of being the professions that have to be represented. Thirteen out of the twenty-six cantons have legislated that the chair of the decision-making body has to be a law professional (Wider 2012).

The decision-making bodies: variations

In twenty cantons (the majority of the German-speaking cantons), the CAPAs are organized as court-like administrative bodies. In six cantons (the majority of the French-speaking cantons), CAPAs are organized as courts. The populations in the catchment areas of the CAPAs range from 2,000 to 470,000 inhabitants, with the majority of cantons having established CAPAs that are responsible for more than 50,000 inhabitants (Wider 2014). Although the integration of professional knowledge was an explicit intention of the 2008 reform, the government's recommendations made wide concessions regarding the formal qualifications required by members of the decision-making bodies. As a consequence, what counts as professional varies across the cantons and so does the composition of the decision-making bodies in terms of formal qualifications. Moreover, it is only recommended, but not a legal requirement, that members of a decision-making body exercise the function as their main occupation (Rosch 2011, p. 32). The integration of child and adult protection within the same authority has the potential to contradict the idea of utilizing specialist professional knowledge when seeking the best responses to individual cases. Drawing on anecdotal knowledge, however, only a very small number of CAPAs have established specialized decision-making bodies ("chambers") for child or adult protection cases. Some have established procedures to consider individuals' expertise with regard to child or adult protection issues when distributing responsibilities for individual cases among the members of a decision-making body, and some distribute responsibilities regardless of such criteria.

The process of care orders

The 2008 amendment of the SCC does not have a code of procedures that applies only to child protection and thus there is a general requirement to apply—and often translate—the code of procedures for adult protection to child protection (Cottier and Steck 2012).

Pre-proceedings: notifications and assessment

Generally any person has the right to pass information about a person in need to a CAPA (Art. 443 SCC). The CAPA is responsible for and required to receive notifications and to carry out investigations "ex officio." It "may instruct a suitable person or agency to carry out enquiries" (Art. 446 SCC). Thus, assessments of the circumstances when there appear to be threats to the well-being of a child can be carried out by: members of the decision-making body; an internal organizational unit of a CAPA (internal assessment department); and external agencies like public social services and/or children's services; nonpublic external agencies (nonprofit or for-profit). If necessary, expertise from professionals in the mental health system or other systems may be sought.

There is little knowledge about how the CAPAs make use of these different options but, drawing on published debates and anecdotal knowledge, it seems that the majority of assessments are carried out by either internal assessment departments or by public agencies, mainly social services or children's services (Vogel and Wider 2010). In both cases, the CAPA is responsible for deciding on the form, focus, and extent of an assessment.

Notifications may be received from individuals, relatives, school principals, and from parents or children seeking support. Federal civil law contains a legal requirement for those who learn about a person in need in the context of carrying out an official function to make a notification (Art. 443 SCC). In addition, over the last years a number of cantons have legislated for mandatory reporting, thereby extending reporting requirements to certain professions (Affolter 2013). An amendment to the federal civil law, intended to harmonize the diverse cantonal rules and substantially extend mandatory reporting to a wider group of professionals (in medicine, psychology, education, social services, religion, and sports), is about to be passed in 2016.

A great number of the CAPAs have internal rules concerning the reception and appraisal of notifications about endangered children. These rules are intended to assist in making decisions about whether immediate intervention is required, whether an initial assessment should be conducted, or whether the notification can be ignored. Dissemination and use of detailed guidelines and research- and knowledge-based instruments in child protection assessments is still quite rare (Biesel and Schnurr 2014; Lätsch 2012; Spratt et al. 2014). Current forms of assessment regarding the well-being of a child last an average of three months and include interviews with the parents and the child, often combined with a home visit, and the gathering of information from other professionals and agencies. Information obtained through this process is collated in a written report to the CAPA. The report includes recommendations with regard to what services and/or limitations on parental rights are needed, if the latter have been found necessary in order to ensure the well-being of the child. In a number of cantons it is a common feature of the assessment process to present the report (selectively) to the parents and the child, and to listen to their comments, before the report is sent to the CAPA.

Hearing the parents, hearing the child

In child care proceedings two independent legal obligations apply to those affected by decisions of a CAPA. According to Article 447 SCC, the CAPA is obliged to hear an affected person "in person." The purpose of the hearing is twofold: to aid the collection of information, and thereby add to the understanding of the case, and to recognize fundamental citizenship rights (Bundesrat 2006, p. 7079; Steck 2012, p. 1334). The right to be heard can be suspended "in cases of particular urgency"; under such conditions, an authority "may take precautionary measures immediately without hearing the persons participating in the proceedings." In doing so, the authority must provide opportunities for those persons to express their views subsequently and then review its decision (Art. 445 SCC). Articles 447 and 445 of the SCC apply to both child and adult protection cases. An obligation to hear the child is augmented, however, by a special article (placed in the child protection section of the SCC), which states that "the child is heard in person in an appropriate manner by the child protection authority or by a third party appointed for this purpose, unless this is inadvisable due to the child's age or other good cause" (Art. 314a SCC). According to a decision of the Federal Court, a hearing for a child is to be regarded as obligatory if he or she is six years of age or older (BGE 131 III 553). Usually this hearing is conducted by the CAPA in the absence of the parents. The presence of a person trusted by the child is permissible, a record of the hearing is made in which core aspects are mentioned, and the content is made available to the child (Biderbost 2012, p. 992; 994). The key focus of the hearing is to provide an opportunity for the child to express his or her views, wishes, and interests and thus contribute to the knowledge that is taken into account in the process of decision-making. It is often asserted that the hearing for the child is an expression of the fundamental rights to which children are entitled (cf Gerber Jenni 2013). A 2012 government report on the implementation of children's rights acknowledged, however, that it could not be guaranteed that persons conducting hearings for the child have adequate qualifications for doing so and expressed the hope that change would come with the professionalization of child protection authorities (Bundesrat 2012, p. 45). Little is known about how hearings for the child have been conducted in the day-to-day practice of the CAPAs since January 2013. A recent study conducted in three cantons showed differences with respect to the persons conducting the hearing, the practices, and the age of the children (Hitz Quenon et al. 2014). Earlier research on participation issues in the context of child removals revealed that authorities and social workers from the services involved often failed to comply with the law and often justified this by reference to the alleged best interests of the child (Arnold et al. 2008; Cottier 2006; Voll et al. 2008). A study of voluntary and compulsory removals of children showed that parents participated in decision-making in relation to out-of-home removals in only 47 percent of the cases considered and children participated in only 16 percent (Arnold et al. 2008).

Two recent developments in federal legislation reflect the intention at the federal level to strengthen children's rights, including in the context of care decisions. These developments are *independent representation of the child* and *the child's participation in the case of removal*. These developments are considered further below. They add more legal measures to the existing arrangements for providing a hearing for the child (see above). As with the hearing, the developments have been understood as translating Article 12 of the Convention on Children's Rights into federal legislation (Biderbost 2012, p. 996; Gerber Jenni 2013; Stössel and Jenni 2012).

Independent representation of the child

The 2013 reform introduced independent representation of the child (Article 314a^bisSCC), giving the CAPA power to appoint a person who is "experienced in welfare and legal matters." The law stipulates that consideration should be given to the appointment of such a representative, especially if the proceedings relate to the child's accommodation or if "the parties file differing applications in relation to regulating parental responsibility or important contact issues" (Art. 314a^bis SCC). It is at the discretion of the CAPA whether a representative is appointed. It has been argued that the expressed wish of a child capable of judgment should be interpreted as a strong indicator for the appointment of a representative (Cottier 2012, p. 815). A person who is appointed as a representative of the child under Art. 314a^bis has the right to file applications and appeals against the CAPA, which constitutes an important difference when compared with the role of a deputy (Art. 308 SCC [see above]), who is instructed by the CAPA and, therefore, lacks such independence. According to an exploratory study in three cantons, it is doubtful whether the appointment of an independent representation of the child is considered by CAPAs on a regular basis (Hitz Quenon et al. 2014, p. 92).

Participation of the child in the case of removal

A recent amendment to the Regulation on the Admission of Foster Children[12] has reinforced the normative status of the best interests of the child in the context of removals and strengthened the supervision of foster care services. Approval and supervision of foster parents is now treated in the same way as approval and supervision of residential care under the auspices of the CAPA. Furthermore, the amendment introduced a responsibility for the CAPA to ensure that a child in alternative care is informed about his or her rights, is given a person of trust whom he/she can approach if he/she has questions and problems and who is involved in all decisions that have a significant impact on his or her life (Art. 1a, Regulation on the Admission of Foster Children). Up to now there has been no information available on the implementation of these amendments.

Decision-making

With the 2013 reform, interdisciplinarity became the cornerstone of decision-making in child and adult protection (Bundesrat 2006, p. 7009; 7073). Interdisciplinarity is seen as the key to achieving adequate understanding of the often complex and multilayered problems and conflicts in child and adult protection and as central to the creation of adequate responses to them (Konferenz 2008, p. 76 f.). Thus it has been assumed that constructing the decision-making body in child protection as an interdisciplinary entity allows knowledge from various disciplines to be used in the process of deliberation so as to inform decisions. In what ways and to what extent the day-to-day practice of decision-making in the recently constructed interdisciplinary bodies corresponds to the ideal that shaped the legislation can only be the subject of speculation. Drawing on anecdotal knowledge, the practices and cultures within the 148 CAPAs can be located on a continuum between interprofessional deliberation, through predominance of the juridical perspective to models of consultation between the members of the decision-making body that rely on written material.

It can be assumed that a decision is generally made in the absence of the parents and children who are affected by the proceedings during a meeting of what is (most often) a three-member body. Furthermore, it seems that one of the three members presents the case and recommends a particular decision; the consultation and decision-making that follow are based on a number of documents, such as records from the hearings involving the parents and the child; a report of an assessment, often commissioned by the presenting member of the decision-making body and undertaken by social workers of an internal or external service, is considered and usually includes a recommendation for a decision. If a decision is made, it must be presented to the persons affected by it in a written form that includes information on the right to appeal. A child can consent or object to a care order if he/she is considered able to make such a judgment; according to decisions of the federal court, ability to make such a judgment has been assumed or attributed at the age of ten years (Cottier 2012, p. 814).

Supervising and appellate authorities of the CAPAs vary according to cantonal legislation. Supervising authorities are typically located in cantonal government departments, but appellate authorities must be courts, with the federal law allowing for a single appeal at cantonal level (Cottier and Steck 2012). Thus, most of the courts that hear appeals against decisions of the CAPAs are cantonal high courts or cantonal administrative courts.[13] Beyond this cantonal level of appeal lies the possibility of a final appeal to the federal court. A search of the federal court's database (Bundesgericht 2015) for decisions related to Art. 310 SCC (compulsory removal) in the period 1995–2015 revealed a total of fifty-one cases. Searching the European Court of Human Rights (2015) database for cases related to child removals and family rights issues in Switzerland produced a total of five cases brought to the court, but none of them is concerned with decisions on the removal of a child from his or her family into alternative care.[14]

VOLUNTARY REMOVALS

Generally a removal of a child from his or her parents to which the parents give their consent comes under cantonal law and is decided or facilitated (depending on how "voluntary" the child's removal is with regard to the distribution of power between the parents and the service) by a local agency, such as a social service, children's service, or school administration. Owing to the limited development of cantonal legislation on services for children and families and to the diversity of arrangements across the cantons, there is very little knowledge about the proceedings, preconditions, and requirements for voluntary removals.

Although every canton has developed its own legislation with regard to the constitution of the CAPAs, only eleven out of the twenty-six cantons have legislated for the provision of voluntary services for children and families. The degree to which the cantons have initiated legislation establishing which agencies may provide voluntary services, together with their features and responsibilities, and/or legislated on the provision of access to voluntary services varies considerably, even within the group of eleven cantons that have specific legislation on children and family affairs. As a consequence, the extent and pattern of voluntary service provision varies across the cantons, though overall it represents a low level of provision compared with other

European countries in terms of the various services available and the clarity of access arrangements to them. Accordingly, entitlements to voluntary services for children and families do not exist in Switzerland in the way that they do in countries such as Austria[15] and Germany[16] at either the federal or the cantonal levels. Where cantonal legislation on services for children and families exists, it is normally confined to delineations of service provision and respective financial responsibilities, while questions about individuals' access to services are largely left to the discretion of local agencies. The result is a patchwork of law on children's services across the country and a system in which, to varying degrees, many issues are sorted out between local actors, institutions, and agencies below the thresholds of legislation and formal regulation. The diversity and lack of clarity in cantons' local regimes impede being able to obtain a sense of "the complete picture," especially knowledge about pathways, preconditions, and use of children's and family services that are not accessed via decisions of the CAPAs, including voluntary removals to alternative care. As a consequence, voluntary removals are under-researched. Of the two studies examining the circumstances of removals in Switzerland (prior to the 2013 reform), one has a focus on compulsory removals (Voll et al. 2008), the other includes compulsory and voluntary removals but does not differentiate between the two types of removal in reporting its findings (Arnold et al. 2008).

Given the diversity of legislation and regulations and the lack of current research, statements about voluntary removals can only be (unsatisfactorily) general and superficial:

- The majority of decisions are made by service workers who are social workers by training; in many cantons local rules concerning decision-making on voluntary child removals stipulate that a written assessment by a child psychiatrist or school psychologist is required[17];
- There is little formal regulation of the decision-making process;
- Decisions are influenced to a great extent by local rules as well as the organizational and professional cultures of the agencies involved;
- Lacking legal regulations for access to services increases opportunities for financial criteria to influence decision-making;
- From the perspectives of children and families the proceedings lack transparency and (in a great number of cantons) clear rules for access to services do not exist.

These characteristics of voluntary removals underline the necessity of further research in this area. This is reinforced by the opinion of child protection experts in Switzerland that voluntary removals represent 60 percent or more of the total number of child removals (see Table 6.4).

STATISTICS

"Swiss Statistics," the Federal Department of Statistics, does not collect statistics on children's services and child protection. Published and accessible statistics on children's services and child protection in Switzerland are limited to two sources:

(1) The statistics on measures of child and adult protection collected by the Conference of the Cantons on Child and Adult Protection (KOKES) from 1996 onward. The "KOKES-Statistics" data provide information on the number and proportion of child protection measures in terms of the application of the respective articles of the SCC, which are prepared as end-of-year data and newly-established-measures-per-year data. At the time of writing, available data from "KOKES-Statistics" refer to the situation before the reform of 2013 was implemented. The authorities involved (n = 1,420) provided data for these statistics on a voluntary basis.

(2) The cantons of Basel-Landschaft and Basel-Stadt started to collect statistics on child care issues in 2004. The "Two-Basel-Statistics" are primarily designed to inform the planning of alternative (primarily residential) care, but also include data on those children who are in alternative care. A recent report covering 2008–2013 was published in 2014 (Kommission 2014). Other cantons like Zürich and Bern recently have intensified their efforts to collect statistics on children's services issues and child protection, but have not yet published data.

Relying on this limited amount of published statistical data, only a few aspects concerning the removal of children from their families can be examined quantitatively. Table 6.2 illustrates, *inter alia*, the relevance of Deputyship (Art. 308 SCC) among the responses to child protection set out in the SCC and the low prevalence of compulsory removals. In the years 2008–2012 between 15.45 and 18.2 per 1,000 children were under Deputyship. Within the same period between 2.37 and 2.6 per 1,000 children were removed into alternative care based on a care order in accordance with Art. 310 SCC (compulsory removal). Between 0.16 and 0.29 per 1,000 children were involved in decisions about the withdrawal of parental responsibility in accordance with Art. 311/312 SCC. There are substantial differences in the proportion of child protection measures across cantons (KOKES 2014) and cities (Jud 2014).

With regard to the numbers of children in care and their ages data have been provided from the cantons of Basel-Landschaft, Basel-Stadt, and Zürich[18]. The data from the canton of Zürich only cover the population outside the city of Zürich. Table 6.3 gives tentative and illustrative information on children in

Table 6.3. Children in alternative care in the Cantons Basel-Landschaft, Basel-Stadt and Zürich (without City of Zürich) at year end 2008–2013

Year	2008		2009		2010		2011		2012		2013	
	Children placed in alternative care	Children in care per 1'000	Children placed in alternative care	Children in care per 1'000	Children placed in alternative care	Children in care per 1'000	Children placed in alternative care	Children in care per 1'000	Children placed in alternative care	Children in care per 1'000	Children placed in alternative care	Children in care per 1'000
Age <3	96	2.30	96	2.24	105	2.28	106	2.34	93	2.03	90	1.95
3–6	214	3.87	228	4.08	254	4.43	281	4.08	253	4.25	231	3.78
7–12	646	7.48	689	8.03	738	8.57	712	8.26	730	8.45	715	8.25
13–17	976	12.87	1'122	14.8	1'166	15.4	1'196	15.79	1'220	16.11	1'300	17.13
Total 0–17	1'932	7.45	2'135	8.20	2'263	8.54	2'295	8.31	2'296	8.58	2'336	8.66

Data courtesy of Canton Basel-Stadt (Department for Education, Office for Children Family and Sport), Canton Basel-Landschaft (Department Education, Culture and Sport; Office for the Children, Young People and Services for the Disabled), Canton Zürich (Department for Education; Office for Youth and Vocational Counselling); calculations by the author.

care in Switzerland (end-of-year data), covering approximately 18 percent of the Swiss population aged 0–17 years. With regard to the cantons of Basel-Landschaft, Basel-Stadt, and Zürich (outside the city of Zürich), in the period 2008–2013, 7.45 to 8.66 per 1,000 children had been in alternative care. The proportion of children aged 13–17 years is continuously over half of the total of children in alternative care. Children placed in alternative care under the Juvenile Justice Act are not included in the data.

Table 6.4 illustrates the proportions of voluntary and compulsory care decisions. It uses entries-per-year data from the "Two-Basel-Statistics" as an example and thus covers only around 5 percent of the Swiss population 0–17 years old. During the five-year period from 2008 to 2013, an average of 64 percent of the entries into alternative care per year were voluntary removals; that is, they resulted from the requests of the parents (both cantons), were facilitated by the local children's service (Basel-Stadt), or social service or other authorized agency (Basel-Landschaft).

DISCUSSION

It is no exaggeration to state that Switzerland has not one but twenty-six systems of children's services and child protection, so that any concluding discussion is difficult. As such, the focus of the discussion is on features that appear to be widespread in Switzerland, as well as distinctive to the Swiss system.

Features of the 2013 reform in Child Protection
Given how recent the changes have been and the lack of research about them, statements concerning the practice of the newly established multiprofessional decision-making bodies in child protection can only be made cautiously. It can be argued, however, that the reconstitution of the decision-making body has had a considerable impact on proceedings in child protection. Drawing on information obtained from social workers and representatives of canton departments, it appears that the process of decision-making has become more formalized. Decisions are more likely to be based on a complex understanding of the case rooted in a multiprofessional perspective, and compliance with legislation, including the protection of the fundamental citizenship rights of the persons affected, has improved. With respect to the day-to-day decisions made by the CAPAs, including the practice of "interdisciplinarity," and, more importantly, the practice of the newly introduced articles intended to strengthen the rights of children in child care proceedings, further research is needed.

Among the many challenges of the newly established decision-making bodies in child protection in Switzerland only a few can be mentioned here.

Table 6.4. Voluntary versus compulsory removals in the cantons Basel-Landschaft and Basel-Stadt 2008–2013 (entries per year)

Year	2008			2009			2010			2011			2012			2013		
Children (0–17)	76,006			75,804			75,860			76,006			76,218			76,767		
	Children in care	Proportion of compulsory vs. voluntary removals	Per 1,000	Children in care	Proportion of compulsory vs. voluntary removals	Per 1,000	Children in care	Proportion of compulsory vs. voluntary removals	Per 1,000	Children in care	Proportion of compulsory vs. voluntary removals	Per 1,000	Children in care	Proportion of compulsory vs. voluntary removals	Per 1,000	Children in care	Proportion of compulsory vs. voluntary removals	Per 1,000
Compulsory Removals (SCC)	160	38%	2.1	162	39%	2.1	160	32%	2.1	199	38%	2.6	187	42%	2.5	164	32%	2.1
Voluntary Removals	264	62%	3.5	256	61%	3.4	336	68%	4.4	326	62%	4.3	262	58%	3.4	349	68%	4.5
Total	424	100%	5.6	418	100%	5.5	496	100%	6.5	525	100%	6.9	476	100%	5.9	513	100%	6.7

Kommission Gemeinsame Planung Jugend- und Behindertenhilfe Basel-Stadt und Basel-Landschaft (2014); calculations by the author.

As a consequence of the diversity of canton and municipality regimes, the pre-proceedings, in particular, remain diverse and opaque and, from the perspective of the children and families concerned, lack transparency. What contributes to the lack of transparency is, *inter alia*, the multiplicity of organizations and/or actors involved. This includes:

- The three members of the decision-making body;
- The single member of the decision-making body who commissions the assessment and presents the case;
- The member of the decision-making body (or external expert) who conducts the hearing of the parents and the hearing of the child;
- The social workers who conduct the assessment—seeking to build worker-client alliances, earn trust, and strengthen the willingness of the parents to cooperate with agencies—and later present their conclusions and recommendations to the CAPA;
- The member of the decision-making body who presents the decision to the parents and child;
- The social worker and/or deputy to whom the responsibility for a child is delegated by the CAPA when he or she is taken into alternative care;
- The social workers in service-provider organizations who work directly with parents and/or children following decisions by the CAPA.

This situation raises questions about the extent to which parents and children, usually in situations of emotionally disturbing multifaceted conflicts:

- Are able to understand the issues at stake in the situations in which they find themselves;
- Know how and to what extent they are able to influence proceedings and decisions;
- Are adequately informed by the representatives of the authorities and services involved about the various stages and the different roles of the actors involved;
- Are actively supported in making use of their rights to participate.

Further research is needed to uncover the ways in which these issues are fashioned and played out.

Increasing public attention to issues of child protection

The establishment of the new CAPAs has attracted more attention to issues of children's services and child protection, albeit not always in positive ways. The CAPAs have become the target of a media campaign bringing allegations, which are well-known internationally, into the public sphere in Switzerland, such as authorities intervening too late, too early, being too family-averse, and making costly decisions. The media, as well as representatives of right-wing parties, have called for the rolling back of reforms and the return of child protection decisions to the municipalities, because the CAPAs themselves and the consequences of their decision-making have been regarded as too costly.

Role of social work

The first years of the CAPAs' operation have witnessed complaints from social workers about the growing predominance of the juridical perspective and the corresponding loss of influence of the social work perspective. Though many social workers agree that the institutionalized cooperation of representatives from different professions within the decision-making body has the potential to integrate the various disciplinary perspectives to the benefit of vulnerable children and in ways that enrich professional practice, they perceive multiprofessional cooperation as a challenging enterprise. Social workers frequently report anecdotally that law is strengthening its position at the expense of social work. If that is the case, there may be a risk of social work becoming merely an auxiliary profession. To a considerable extent the status and prospects of social work after the 2013 reform depend on how social work itself is able to present its expertise within the context of child care proceedings. Increased attention has to be paid to the construction and presentation of cases, that is, the multifaceted needs of children and parents that are embedded in complex intergenerational relations and conflicts. The future of social work in Switzerland's child protection system depends on whether social work is able to develop and practice the expertise that is demanded by the need to provide forms of assessments that are research-based, incorporate user participation, support conclusions about adequate services and/or interventions, and guide appropriate documentation in ways that are both coherent and understandable from different perspectives, including the perspectives of the parents and children concerned (Biesel and Schnurr 2014).

The lack of institutionalized access to voluntary services and family support

As shown in the recent Statistic Social Report, for families with two or more children and especially for single-parent families the risk of poverty is increased; in 2013, 18.8 percent of single-parent households proved eligible for social assistance (Sozialhilfe), and the poverty rate for people living in single-parent families is 16.5 percent. The average divorce rate during 2008–2013 was 46.3 percent (Swiss Statistics 2014). Against this backdrop, the weak institutionalization of voluntary and preventive services for children and families appears not only to be exceptional in comparison to the majority of other European countries but also inadequate in relation to the target of securing thriving conditions for children's upbringing. The 2013 reform has strengthened the institutions of child protection, but not the access to voluntary support for children and families. Moreover, it can be argued that the reconstitution of the child protection authorities has contributed to reinforcement of the public understanding that it is the CAPAs that are responsible for all family and children issues. Thus, with the implementation of the reform, there is a risk that the CAPAswill take the central position in all kinds of public responses to threats to the well-being of children.

The estimate that over 60 percent of removals (see above) are voluntary does not counter this argument. First, because removals must be regarded as extreme interventions into families and children's lives, which in many cases might not have been necessary if the system had provided timely access to adequate services. Second, the circumstances of voluntary removals continue to lack transparency and user participation, even if these two aspects may have improved in the context of compulsory removals. Given that there seems to be little formalization of proceedings for voluntary removal, and given that it lacks a legislative framework, the participation of parents and children depends even more on local organizational cultures as well as on the professional perspectives of individual service workers. Participation of children—in the sense of influencing decisions—can be regarded as even more unlikely (Arnold et al. 2008). Moreover, information has been obtained from a number of cantons indicating tendencies to recategorize cases strategically as of higher severity in order to make them compatible with the (anticipated) requirements of the CAPA. In this context limitations on parental autonomy become the price that has to be paid for access to services. Miscategorization of this kind seems to have emerged particularly in cantons having a system of divided financial responsibility for voluntary (municipality) versus involuntary (canton) services.

In recent years the federal state has promoted progressive legislative projects intended to adopt norms laid out by the UNCRC. This has led to a situation in which children have increasingly been accorded formal participative rights in the context of removals, but neither children nor parents are entitled to access voluntary services. To some extent this discrepancy is connected with distinctive features of policy-making, especially the division of power between the federal state and the cantons. It could be argued that the proactive legislative projects of the federal state may reflect its "limited policy capacity" (Mach and Trampusch 2011, p. 18). The federal state is responsible for legislation on basic rights - legislation on services for children and families is reserved for the cantons. Moreover, different matters of legislation have different financial consequences: The extension of participative rights by the federal legislature does not generate direct costs neither for the federal state nor for the cantons, whereas an extension of service provision by a single canton would generate direct costs for the respective canton and it would have to bear it alone. The introduction of elements of child-centered orientations appears to be constrained by the policies and politics of the cantons, as well as by the organizational and professional cultures in the field of children's services and child protection. In summary, the most demanding challenges of the Swiss system of children's services and child protection are first, the growing discrepancy between legislated norms on the participation of children and parents on the one hand and the application of these norms in day-to-day practice on the other hand and, secondly, the weak institutionalization of voluntary support for children and families that responds to needs below severe manifestations of endangerment to children. In order to "transform children's rights into real freedom" it seems essential to complement rights-based strategies with policies and programs of capacity building and support for both children and parents/caregivers (Biggeri and Karkara 2014, p. 35 f.).

Among other distinctive features, Switzerland may deserve further attention in the comparative analysis of child protection systems because it represents a case of the introduction of elements of a child-centered orientation into a system that is characterized by the dominance of child-protection and risk orientations and weak institutionalization of a family-service orientation.

NOTES

1   I owe great thanks to: John Harris for the English language editing; Stefan Blülle (Children's Services Basel), Michael Marugg (CAPA Winterthur-Andelfingen), and the editors of this volume for sharing knowledge and helpful comments on earlier versions of this chapter.
2   Amendments in the *Swiss Civil Code* (Art.314a Hearing for the Child; Art. 314a[bis] Representation for the Child) and in the *Regulation on the Admission of Foster Children*, which have been in force since January 2013.
3   Within this article, it is assumed, that first, decision-making in child protection is a process that involves profession(al)s instead of disciplines (or scholars) and secondly, it remains unclear whether a deliberative culture indicated by the suffix "inter" is actually about to emerge in the authorities under focus. Therefore, the term "multiprofessional" is preferred apart from when direct reference is being made to official discourse.
4   Common terminology for voluntary removal of children in the German-speaking parts of Switzerland is *freiwillige* (voluntary) *Unterbringung*; common terminology for compulsory removal of children is *behördliche* (statutory) *Unterbringung*.
5   Datasets: JUSUS (2014.03.26); ESPOP; STATPOP; STAT-TAB; calculations by the author.

6   Initially issued in December 1907; important amendments with regard to child protection in 1976, 1998, 2008, and 2014. Throughout this chapter, the official translation of the most recent version of the SCC (dated July 1, 2014) in English is used, which is available online from the federal administration (www.admin.ch). The 2014 version includes a number of alterations in the translation: the translation of *elterliche Sorge* (cf Art. 311) has been changed from "parental care" to "parental responsibility." The translation of *Beistandschaft* (Art. 308) has been changed from "Welfare Advocate" to "Deputyship."

7   A further measure, which is explicitly mentioned in the SCC, is requesting the parents to participate in mediation (Art. 314 SCC).

8   The police are the responsibility of the cantons. Cooperation of the CAPAs and the police is the subject of regulations at cantonal and/or municipal level.

9   Though participation of lay-persons in child protection decisions is also a significant feature of the Swedish model, the responsibility of Sweden's *Social Welfare Boards* or *Social Welfare Councils*, which include lay-persons, is limited to voluntary removals, while the responsibility for decisions on compulsory removals lies with the county administrative courts (see Svensson and Höjer in this volume).

10 Konferenz der kantonalen Vormundschaftsbehörden (Conference of the Cantonal Guardianship Authorities) now: Konferenz für Kindes- und Erwachsenenschutz (Conference on Child and Adult Protection)

11 That is, asset management for vulnerable people like children and older people.

12 Verordnung über die Aufnahme von Pflegekindern (PAVO); http://www.admin.ch/opc/de/classified-compilation/19770243/index.html

13 For a complete list, see KOKES (2013).

14 Two cases are related to decisions on places of residence for several members of migrant families; two relate to decisions about conflicts between parents on the place of residence of their child; one relates to decisions on the place of burial of a child. Search terms: [child AND removal AND protect*] AND [Art. 8 Right to respect for private and family life] AND [1995–2015].

15 Bundes-Kinder- und Jugendhilfegesetz (2013).

16 Sozialgesetzbuch VIII/Kinder- und Jugendhilfegesetz (1990/1991; 2012/2013).

17 Almost all cantons have established specialist organizations for the provision of child psychiatric services and school psychological services, such as counselling (for parents, teachers, etc.), counselling or therapy (for children) and assessments (for administrative bodies and agencies).

18 I owe great thanks to R. Hafner, A. Schönhofer (BS), A. Tucconi (BL), and D. Ljubisavljevic-Stoll (ZH) for providing data.

REFERENCES

Affolter, K. (2013). "Anzeige- und Meldpflicht" (Art. 443 Abs. 2 ZGB) [Mandatory reporting and notification]. *Zeitschrift für Kindes- und Erwachsenenschutz* [Journal of Child and Adult Protection] 68(1): 47–53.

Arnold, C., Huwiler, K., Raulf, B., Tanner, H., and Wicki, T. (2008). *Pflegefamilien- und Heimplatzierungen. Eine empirische Studie über den Hilfeprozess und die Partizipation von Kindern* [Placing children in foster and residential care. An empirical study on procedures and children's participation]. Zürich: Rüegger.

Biderbost, Y. (2012). "[Artikel] 307–317." In Breitschmid, P. and Rumo-Jungo, A. (Eds.), *Handkommentar zum Schweizer Privatrecht. Personen- und Familienrecht inkl. Kindes- und Erwachsenenschutzrecht* [Commentary on Swiss private, personal and family law including child and adult protection law], pp. 950–1040. Zürich-Basel-Genf: Schulthess.

Biesel, K. and Schnurr, S. (2014). "Abklärung im Kindesschutz: Chancen und Risiken in der Anwendung von Verfahren und Instrumenten zur Erfassung von Kindeswohlgefährdung" [Child Protection Assessment: pitfalls and potentials in the use of programmes and instruments designed assess the endangerment of children]. *Zeitschrift für Kindes- und Erwachsenenschutz* [Journal of Child and Adult Protection] 1: 63–71.

Biggeri, M. and Karkara, R. (2014). "Transforming Children's Rights into Real Freedoms: A Dialogue between Children's Rights and the Capability Approach from a Life Cycle Perspective." In Stoecklin, D. and Jean-Michel Bonvin, J-M (Eds.), *Children's Rights and the Capability Approach. Challenges and Prospects*, pp. 19–41. Dordrecht et al.: Springer.

Bonoli, G. and Häusermann, S. (2011). "Swiss Welfare Reforms in a Comparative European Perspective. Between Retrenchment and Activation." In Trampusch, C. and Mach, A. (Eds.), *Switzerland in Europe. Continuity and Change in the Swiss Political Economy*, pp. 186–204. London—New York: Routledge.

Bundesgericht. (2015). Rechtssprechung—Publizierte Leitentscheide [Jurisdiction—published decisions]. Accessed May 28, from: http://www.bger.ch/index/juridiction/jurisdiction-inherit-template/jurisdiction-recht/jurisdiction-recht-leitentscheide1954.htm.

Bundesrat. (2006). Botschaft vom 28. Juni 2006 zur Änderung des Schweizerischen Zivilgesetzbuches (Erwachsenenschutz, Personenrecht und Kindesrecht) (BBl 2006 7001) [Governmental commentary on the amendments in Swiss Civil Code (Adult Law, Personal Law, Children's Law) from June 28th 2006]. 7001–7138.

Bundesrat. (2012). Zweiter, dritter und vierter Bericht der Schweizerischen Regierung zur Umsetzung des Übereinkommens über die Rechte des Kindes [Second, third, and fourth report of the Swiss government on the implementation of the Convention on the Rights of the Child]. Bern.

Cottier, M. (2012). "[Artikel] 307-317." In Büchler, A. and Jakob, D. (Eds.), *Kurzkommentar Schweizerisches Zivilgesetzbuch* [Short commentary on the Swiss civil code], pp. 786–846. Basel: Helbing Lichtenhahn.

Cottier, M. (2006). *Subjekt oder Objekt? Die Partizipation von Kindern in Jugendstraf- und zivilrechtlichen Kindesschutzverfahren* [Subject or object— children's participation in youth justice and child protection proceedings]. Bern: Stämpfli Verlag.

Cottier, M. and Steck, D. (2012). "Das Verfahren vor der Kindes- und Erwachsenenschutzbehörde" [Proceedings at the Child- and Adult Protection Authority]. *Praxis des Familienrechts* [Practice of Family Law] 13(4): 981–1000.

Esping-Andersen, G. (1990). *The Three Worlds of Welfare Capitalism*. Princeton, NJ: Princeton University Press.

European Court of Human Rights. (2015). HUDOC database. Accessed May 21, 2015 from: http://www.echr.coe.int/Pages/home.aspx?p=caselaw/HUDOC&c=.

Federal Chancellery. (2015). The Swiss Confederation. A Brief Guide. Accessed December 30, 2015 from: https://www.bk.admin.ch/dokumentation/02070/index.html?lang=en&download=NHzLpZeg7t,lnp6I0NTU042l2Z6ln1ad1I Zn4Z2qZpnO2Yuq2Z6gpJCId355gWym162epYbg2c_JjKbNoKSn6A--.

Gerber Jenni, R. (2013). "Platzierung von Kindern und Jugendlichen und Partizipation: Grundlagen und Überlegungen zur Umsetzung" [Placing children and participation: foundations and practical considerations]. *Zeitschrift für Kindes- und Erwachsenenschutz* [Journal of Child and Adult Protection] 68(3): 158–173.

Giddens, A. (1998). *The Third Way: The Renewal of Social Democracy*. Cambridge: Polity Press.

Gilbert, N. (1997). *Combatting Child Abuse: International Perspectives and Trends*. New York: Oxford University Press.

Gilbert, N., Parton, N., and Skivenes, M. (2011). *Child Protection Systems. International Trends and Orientations*. New York: Oxford University Press.

Hitz Quenon, N., Paulus, E., and Luchetta Myit, L. (2014). Le droit de protection de l'enfant. Les premiers effets de la mise en oeuvre dans les cantons de Genève, Vaud et Zurich [Child protection Law. First effects in the cantons Geneva, Vaud and Zurich]. Bern: Swiss Centre of Expertise in Human Rights (SCHR).

Jud, A. (2014). "Fallzahlen im Kindes und Erwachsenenschutz in den Jahren 2002–2011: Eine ständige Zunahme?" [Case figures in Child and Adult Protection 2002–2001: A continuous increase?]. *Zeitschrift für Kindes- und Erwachsenenschutz* [Journal of Child and Adult Protection] 69: 373–393.

Jud, A. and Gartenhauser, R. (2014). "The impact of socio-economic status and caregiver cooperation on school professionals' reports to child protection services in Switzerland." *European Journal of Social Work*: 1–14.

KOKES (Konferenz der Kantone für Kindes- und Erwachsenenschutz) [Intercantonal conference for child and adult protection] (2014). "Schweizerische Statistik der Massnahmen im Kindes- und Erwachsenenschutz 2012 (alle Kantone)" [Swiss Statistics on Child and Adult Protection Measures 2012, all cantons]. *Zeitschrift für Kindes- und Erwachsenenschutz* [Journal of Child and Adult Protection] 69(1): 83–90.

KOKES (Konferenz für Kindes- und Erwachsenenschutz) [Intercantonal conference for child and adult protection] (2013). "Zusammenstellung der kantonalen Behördenorganisation (KESB - Aufsichtsbehörden - Rechtsmittelinstanzen)." *Zeitschrift für Kindes- und Erwachsnenenschutz* [Journal of Child and Adult Protection] 68(1): 54–57.

Kommission Gemeinsame Planung Jugend- und Behindertenhilfe Basel-Stadt und Basel-Landschaft. (2014). Bedarfsplanung stationäre Jugendhilfe der Kantone Basel-Stadt und Basel-Landschaft. Bericht 2013. Anhang Statistik [Requirements planning for residential and foster care in the cantons Basel-Stadt and Basel-Landschaft. 2013 report. Statistics]. Accessed April 29, 2016 from: http://www.jfs.bs.ch/dms/jfs/download/ueber-uns/aufgaben-organisation/JFA_jugendhilfe/bedarfsplanung-BS-BL-2013-anhang-statistik.pdf.

Konferenz der kantonalen Vormundschaftsbehörden. (2008). "Kindes- und Erwachsenenschutzbehörde als Fachbehörde (Analyse und Modellvorschläge)" [The child and adult protection authority as specialist authority—examination, models, recommendations]. *Zeitschrift für Vormundschaftswesen* 63(2): 63–128.

Lätsch, D. (2012). "Wissenschaftlich fundierte Abklärungen im Kindesschutz: Überblick über den internationalen Entwicklungsstand—und ein Ausblick in die Schweiz" [Research-based assessments in child protection: an overview at the international state of the art with prospects for Switzerland]. *Zeitschrift für Kindes- und Erwachsenenschutz* [Journal of Child and Adult Protection] 67(1): 1–20.

Mach, A. and Trampusch, C. (Eds.). (2011). *Switzerland in Europe: Continuity and Change in the Swiss Political Economy.* London—New York: Routledge.

Obinger, H., Starke, P., Moser, J., Bogedan, C., Gindulis, E., and Leibfried, S. 2010. *Transformations of the Welfare State. Small Sates, Big Lessons,* New York: Oxford University Press.

Pösö, T. (2011). "Combatting Child Abuse in Finland: From Family to Child-Centered Orientation." In Gilbert, N., Parton, N., Skivenes, M. (Eds.), *Child Protection Systems. International Trends and Orientations,* pp. 112–130. New York: Oxford University Press.

Rosch, D. (2011). "Neue Aufgaben, Rollen, Disziplinen, Schnitt- und Nahtstellen: Herausforderungen des neuen Kindes- und Erwachsenenschutzrechts" [New responsibilities, roles, disciplines—interfaces and intersections: challenges of the new child and adult protection law]. *Zeitschrift für Kindes- und Erwachsenenschutz* [Journal of Child and Adult Protection] 66(1): 31–46.

Skivenes, M. (2011). "Norway: Toward a Child-Centric Perspective." In Gilbert, N., Parton, N., and Skivenes, M. (Eds.), *Child Protection Systems. International Trends and Orientations,* pp. 154–179. New York: Oxford University Press.

Spratt, T., Nett, J., Bromfield, L., Hietamäki, J., Kindler, H., and Ponnert, L. (2015). "Child Protection in Europe: Development of an International Cross-Comparison Model to Inform National Policies and Practices." *British Journal of Social Work* 45 (5):1508–1525.

Steck, D. (2012). "[Artikel] 443-450 f." In Breitschmid, P. and Rumo-Jungo, A. (Eds.), *Handkommentar zum Schweizer Privatrecht. Personen- und Familienrecht inkl. Kindes- und Erwachsenenschutzrecht* [Commentary on Swiss private, personal and family law including child and adult protection law], pp. 1303–1380. Zürich—Basel: Genf Schulthess.

Stössel, S. and Gerber Jenni, R. (2012). "Partizipation des Kindes als Voraussetzung für wirksamen Kindesschutz: das Beispiel der Familien- und Heimplatzierung" [Children's participation as a requirement for effective child protection: placements in foster and residential care]. *Praxis des Familienrechts* 13(2): 335–352.

Swiss Statistics. (2014). Jugendstrafurteile nach Kanton und Sanktion [Statistics on criminal judgements for young offenders by canton and sanction] Accessed December 29, 2015 from: http://www.bfs.admin.ch/bfs/portal/de/index/themen/19/03/04/key/sanktionen.Document.50683.xls.

Swiss Statistics. (2015). Statistischer Sozialbericht Schweiz 2015 [Statistic Social Report Switzerland 2015]. In Statistik der Schweiz: 132. Accessed December 30, 2015 from: http://www.bfs.admin.ch/bfs/portal/de/index/news/publikationen.html?publicationID=6592.

Vogel, U. and Wider, D. (2010). "Kindes- und Erwachsenenschutzbehörde als Fachbehörde—Personelle Ressourcen, Ausstattung und Trägerschaftsformen" [Child and adult protection authority as specialist authority—resources and organizational arrangements]. *Zeitschrift für Kindes- und Erwachsenenschutz* [Journal of Child and Adult Protection] 65(1): 5–20.

Voll, P., Jud, A., Mey, E., Häfeli, C., and Stettler, M. (2008). *Zivilrechtlicher Kindesschutz: Akteure, Prozesse, Strukturen. Eine empirische Studie mit Kommentaren aus der Praxis* [Child protection under civil law: actors, process, structures. An empirical study with comments from the practice field]. Luzern: interact.

Wider, D. (2014). Organisation der KESB per 1.1.2013—Umsetzung in den Kantonen [Organization of Child Protection Authorities per January 1, 2013—Implementation in the cantons]. (30.09.2014): 1. Accessed October 22, 2014 from: http://www.kokes.ch/assets/pdf/de/aktuell/Organisation_KESB__Umsetzung_Kantone__1.1.2013__aktual._30.9.2014.pdf.

Wider, D. (2012). Umsetzung der neuen Behördenorganisation in den Kantonen—ein Überblick. Referat an der Fachtagung "Neues Kindes- und Erwachsenenschutzrecht - konkrete Umsetzungsfragen" vom 11.-12. September 2012 in Freiburg [Implementation of the new authorities in the cantons—an overview. Presentation]. Accessed December 30, 2015 from: http://www.vbk-cat.ch/assets/pdf/de/aktuell/2012_Referat_3_Wider.pdf.

7

CHILD REMOVAL DECISION-MAKING SYSTEMS IN IRELAND

LAW, POLICY, AND PRACTICE

Kenneth Burns, Conor O'Mahony, Caroline Shore, and Aisling Parkes

INTRODUCTION

Interventions into the private domain of the family by the State, and the consequent restriction of the right to respect for private and family life, and the child's right to a family, are a potential cause of significant tension. This is particularly so when the State seeks to place a child in alternative care, whether by consent or through some form of inquisitorial or adversarial decision-making process. Ireland[1] has a long history of alternative care for children through foster care. In Brehon law, which was a legal system in operation in Ireland for 700 years up until the seventeenth century, foster care was a regular practice. Shannon (2011) describes how children from all classes were fostered, a practice that was not limited to abandoned or orphaned children. When this practice petered out in the eighteenth century, a more-repressive residential care systems replaced it. One such system, called the Industrial School system, was funded by the State but principally run by Catholic religious orders from the 1920s to the late 1960s. Some of the children who were abandoned, neglected, or who were "troublesome," were often further abused and neglected by the largely religious staff in the Industrial School system who were charged with their care and protection. Survivor accounts detail physical abuse, emotional abuse, sexual abuse, child labor, and starvation (see, for example, Ryan 2009). The children sent to these institutions were placed there by the Courts, whereby,

> committal took place without the "inquiry" demanded by the law ... proceedings were perfunctory, and the evidence provided by largely untrained staff from the Irish Society for the Prevention of Cruelty to Children was 'rarely questioned' (Arnold 2009 cited in Garrett 2013, pp. 28–29).

Such a situation could not be further divorced from the principles underpinning Article 8 of the European Convention on Human Rights (ECHR), which exhorts states to intervene in a proportionate manner and to ensure decisions are supported by "relevant and sufficient reasons." An entirely new regime was implemented following the enactment of the Child Care Act 1991, but until quite recently, little evidence was available regarding the operation of this system in practice.

This chapter will examine Ireland's current approach to decision-making for the reception of children into alternative care. By alternative care, we mean children who are in the care of the State, either under a court-granted care order, through voluntary care with the consent of a parent or parents, or a child who has been removed by An Garda Síochána (police) in an emergency situation. This chapter specifically focuses on the *exact decision-making point* at which children come into the care of the State. The chapter will set out the legal and constitutional system that facilitates the removal of children from their families and examines thresholds for intervention. It will illustrate the dominance of an adult- and family-centric model that has privileged parental rights, and it charts the nascent emergence of a children's rights ethos. The chapter also highlights the prevalence of voluntary care in Ireland and raises questions regarding the protection of children's and parents' rights in this administrative system. The chapter goes on to show how the heretofore opaque child care proceedings in the District Court are opening up toward greater transparency. Although it acknowledges current reforms and positive developments, the chapter identifies and critically examines reforms, challenges, and blind spots in Irish decision-making systems for the reception of children into State care. The chapter begins by briefly setting out the Irish child welfare and protection system before going on to present data on childhood and children in care in Ireland.

At various points this chapter refers to the findings of an empirical research project undertaken by the authors examining professional perspectives on District Court child care proceedings in Ireland. This is the first interdisciplinary qualitative project to be undertaken in Ireland on this topic. It examined three counties, involving a mixture of urban and rural areas, in which the views and experiences of judges, lawyers, social workers, barristers, and guardians *ad litem* were analyzed (see Parkes et al. 2015; O'Mahony, 2016a,b). Findings are included here to shed light on some important points that would otherwise remain opaque.

THE IRISH CHILD WELFARE AND PROTECTION SYSTEM

The Irish child protection system is currently undergoing fundamental reform. (For more comprehensive examination of the historical development of child protection in Ireland, we recommend the following sources: Buckley and Burns 2015; Skehill 2004.) At the end of January 2014, for the first time in the history of the State, Ireland created a dedicated agency to consolidate most (but not all) children's services. Children's advocates have long been critical of the peripheral location of children's services in a monolithic health service (Burns and Lynch 2012). The newly established Child and Family Agency seeks to address previous criticisms of children's services, which centered on a lack of emphasis on early intervention, prevention, and family support, and on high thresholds for intervention. The Agency seeks to underpin the new system with a differential response model that would divert welfare and lower-risk cases away from statutory child protection services and toward local, community, and nongovernmental agencies (see Tusla, Child and Family Agency 2013a).

Although this reorientation of child protection and welfare services is necessary and welcome, a critical interpretation highlights significant issues that may influence the effectiveness of these changes. First, the community sector lacks adequate resources to take on this work, a situation that is exacerbated by significant cuts to their funding due to the fiscal debt crisis. Second, the failure to bring together *all* children's services may not address the previous failure of services and professionals to work together effectively for children. Third, the welfare state in Ireland, which is a residual, means-tested model based on subsidiarity, was further eroded during the economic crisis, and retrenchment has impacted families through cuts in welfare payments, universal services, and increases in eligibility requirements (e.g., access to medical cards) (see Considine and Dukelow 2013). Finally, the "delegation" of welfare cases to the community may have negative consequences for social workers in child protection whose work may become dominated by tertiary level, high-risk, and high-stress child protection cases.

Ireland has significantly modernized its legislation and policies in the area of child protection over the last twenty years. Current developments in the child protection system focus on shifting toward mandatory reporting and placing child protection guidelines on a statutory footing (Children First Act 2015); consolidating the standardization of child protection processes and systems (Health Service Executive 2009a); removing the defense of "reasonable chastisement," which effectively will prohibit parents from slapping their children;

reorientating the system away from tertiary, crisis responses towards prevention and family support (Tusla, Child and Family Agency 2013b); pressuring policy-makers to resource child- and family-welfare social work teams to deal with very long waiting lists; and implementing Ireland's first overarching policy framework for children and young people from 2014 to 2020 (Department of Children and Youth Affairs 2014). The publication of this new policy framework is timely, given that the Ombudsman for Children (2012) has previously argued that a children's rights ethos is not evident in children's services and Irish society. The recent amendment of the Irish Constitution to insert a new Article 42A dedicated to recognizing the independent rights of children may be a catalyst for change in this regard.[2]

CHILD CARE LAW AND THE IRISH CONSTITUTION

The legal framework for District Court child care proceedings in Ireland rests on Article 42A.2.1° of the Constitution. Article 41 of the Irish Constitution recognizes the "Family" (defined as the marital family) as "the natural primary and fundamental unit group of Society, and as a moral institution possessing inalienable and imprescriptible rights, antecedent and superior to all positive law," and provides that "[t]he State, therefore, guarantees to protect the Family in its constitution and authority, as the necessary basis of social order and as indispensable to the welfare of the Nation and the State." Article 42 builds on this by granting strong rights to parents with respect to the education of their children. Article 42A.2.1° qualifies these rights, however, by stipulating:

> In exceptional cases, where the parents, regardless of their marital status, fail in their duty towards their children to such extent that the safety or welfare of any of their children is likely to be prejudicially affected, the State as guardian of the common good shall, by proportionate means as provided by law, endeavour to supply the place of the parents, but always with due regard for the natural and imprescriptible rights of the child.

This obligation of the State is discharged through the Child Care Act 1991, which makes it a proactive duty of the Child and Family Agency to identify and promote the welfare of children who are not receiving adequate care and protection. To this end, it gives the Child and Family Agency the power to apply to the District Court for a range of child protection measures, each of which is discussed below.

Although the primary aim of the Child Care Act 1991 is to protect children at risk, the constitutional framework requires that the Act must go to some length to take account of the rights of parents (O'Mahony et al. 2016a).

Thus, although the Act stipulates that the Child and Family Agency (s.3(2) (b)) and the District Court (s.24) must regard the child's welfare as the first and paramount consideration, it also stipulates that in the implementation of its duties, the Child and Family Agency must have regard for the rights and duties of parents, whether under the Constitution or otherwise, and for the principle that it is generally in the best interests of a child to be brought up in his own family (s.3(2)(b) and (c)). Although the latter obligation is not expressly placed on the District Court, the Supreme Court has held on numerous occasions that the statutory welfare principle must be interpreted and applied by the courts in light of a constitutional presumption that the child's welfare is to be found within the family under the care and protection of the child's parents.[3] The circumstances that must be proven to rebut this presumption are extremely serious, and the Child Care Act 1991 reflects this by stipulating demanding standards of proof that must be met before the District Court may issue orders.[4] The statistical data examined in the next section highlight the high proportion of orders granted in care order applications, which raises interesting questions as to the extent to which these principles are emphasized in practice. As discussed in other chapters, however, the high proportion of care order applications that are granted by courts is not unique to Ireland.

In addition to spelling out the importance of protecting the substantive rights of parents, the Act provides various safeguards for their procedural rights. For example, while the Act allows for an emergency care order to be made *ex parte* (should the judge be satisfied that the urgency of the matter requires it) (s.13(4)(c)), the duration of such an order is limited to a maximum of eight days; and, this period cannot be extended (s.13(2)). The eight-day period is intended to allow the Child and Family Agency to carry out an investigation into the child's circumstances and its limited duration is clearly influenced by constitutional concerns relating both to the parents' substantive right to custody of their children[5] and the parents' procedural rights (specifically, the principle of *audi alterem partem*, which requires that as a rule, both sides to a dispute be heard, particularly where serious consequences attach to any court order).[6] If parents are to be properly heard and able to present their case, legal representation is key: our research indicates unanimous opinion among professionals that the provision of legal representation for parents is of the utmost importance in child care proceedings, and both judges and the Legal Aid Board go to great lengths to ensure that it is provided. However, the under-resourcing of the Legal Aid Board, coupled with late exchange of documents between the parties and the often chaotic nature of the lives of the parents involved, frequently results in representation being provided in less than ideal circumstances, with minimal opportunity for advance consultation and preparation (O'Mahony et al. 2016a).

PATHWAYS TO ALTERNATIVE CARE FOR CHILDREN

Ireland has a total population of 4.59 million, of which 1.15 million are children under the age of eighteen years (Central Statistics Office 2012). The population of children living in Ireland increased 13 percent between 2002 and 2011. Key child well-being indicators and an examination of the experience of childhood in Ireland are detailed in the annual *State of the Nation's Children* reports (see Department of Children and Youth Affairs 2013), *Growing Up in Ireland: National Longitudinal Study of Children* publications[7] and UNICEF (2010, 2013, 2014, 2016) reports, and are not examined in this chapter. In compiling the following statistical data, the most recent available *full* dataset for child protection is for 2013; however, where newer data was available, the most up-to-date figure is included.

There has been a 137 percent increase in the number of referrals to the State of a child protection or child welfare issue from 18,438 in 2004 to 43,630 in 2014. In 2014, 43 percent of these referrals were for child protection (child sexual abuse, emotional abuse, neglect, or nonaccidental injury), and 57 percent of the referrals were related to welfare cases (Tusla, Child and Family Agency 2015a). Figure 7.1 charts the 23 percent increase in the numbers of children in care at the end of each year between 2006 and 2014, and Table 7.1 highlights the number of children in care per 1,000 children of the population under eighteen years of age:

Of children in alternative care in Ireland, 64 percent live in general foster care, with a further 29 percent in kinship (relative) foster care. At the end of 2014, there were 6,463 children in the care of the State, which represents a rate of 5.6 children per 1,000 (Tusla, Child and Family Agency 2014c). Of the children in care at the end of December 2012, 34 percent were zero to four years

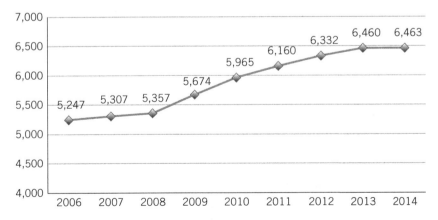

Figure 7.1. Total numbers of children in care at year end, 2006–2014.
Sources: Health Service Executive 2009b, 2013; Tusla, Child and Family Agency 2014a,b,c.

Table 7.1. Children in care per 1,000 at year end, 2008–2014

Year	Children in Care	Children per 1,000
2008	5,357	5.02 children per 1,000
2009	5,674	5.06 children per 1,000
2010	5,965	5.18 children per 1,000
2011	6,160	5.35 children per 1,000
2012	6,332	5.5 children per 1,000
2013	6,460	5.6 children per 1,000
2014	6,463	5.6 children per 1,000[i]

Sources: Health Service Executive 2009b, 2013; Tusla, Child and Family Agency 2014a,b,c.

[i] For 2010–2014 data, the rate was derived from the end-of-year figure divided by the 2011 child population census data. For the 2008–2009 date, the rate was derived from the end-of-year figure divided by the child population estimate in the *State of the Nations Children* report 2008.

old, 18 percent were from five to eight years old, 21 percent were between nine and twelve years of age, and 27 percent were between thirteen and seventeen years of age (Tusla, Child and Family Agency 2014b, p. 63). Overall, 73 percent of children in care are in the zero-to-twelve age bracket, which is in contrast to the profile of some Nordic countries, which tend to have more children in care who are thirteen to seventeen years of age (see Gilbert et al. 2011; see Chapters 2, 3, and 4). This is an interesting difference and may reflect a propensity in Nordic countries to intervene earlier and/or may be a symptom of the limited availability of universal, family-based [in-home] services in Ireland to maintain children at home. Although the number of children in care is increasing, the number of admissions of children to care has been decreasing since a peak in 2009:

In Figure 7.2 we can see a marked decrease of 21 percent in admissions between 2009 and 2013, despite the aforementioned significant increase in the number of new referrals during this period. It is unclear why the admissions to care are dropping in a climate of increased reports, whereby one might expect admissions to care to increase commensurately. Possible explanations for this situation are that: (a) entry thresholds for assessment and alternative care services are rising due to resource constraints; (b) a larger number of children and families are awaiting assessment; (c) the high figure in 2009 may have been the system's response to the publication of child abuse inquiries around this period; and/or (d) thresholds for children's entry into state care are becoming higher.

It is difficult to gather data on the complete costs of children in care (direct, indirect, capital, staff, therapeutic, education, mental health, Courts Service costs, and so forth). Data is available, however, on some of the court costs for child care cases and rates for alternative care placements. In 2012, the

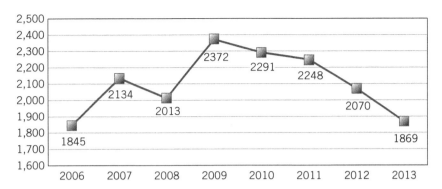

Figure 7.2. Admissions of children to care by year 2006–2013.
Source: Tusla, Child and Family Agency 2014b, p. 62; Tusla, Child and Family Agency 2015b, p. 47.

Department of Children and Youth Affairs paid out €31.1 million in legal fees for child care court cases, from which €13.1 million was paid to Health Service Executive (now the Child and Family Agency) solicitor contracts, €2.8 million on counsel fees, and €10.8 million on guardian ad litem costs (Kelly 2013). O'Brien and Ahonen (2015) reported that direct legal costs incurred by the Child and Family Agency in one region in Ireland for care order applications through the District Court are a minimum of €21,500, which excludes additional costs for a guardian ad litem, counsel fees, guardian ad litem legal fees, assessment fees, care placements costs, and so on. The allowance paid to foster carers is €352 a week per child (€18,304 a year), which covers the basic costs of caring for a child. The Child and Family Agency pay some private foster care companies €1,200 a week per child. Private residential care can cost between €5,000 and €7,000 a week, depending on staffing and additional services such as in-house education. According to reports, some private placements can cost up to €14,000 a week (O'Brien and Ahonen 2015). Estimates reveal that State-run residential care can cost between €5,000 and €12,000 a week per child, depending on the staff to young-person ratios, the provision of in-house education, and associated therapeutic services.

A care order in Ireland means that a court order under sections 13, 17, and 18 of the Child Care Act 1991 places a child into State care with the Child and Family Agency. A care order is, however, only one of three mechanisms and pathways through which a child can be placed in alternative care; namely, in an emergency situation through An Garda Síochána (police), through a voluntary process agreed between a parent or parents and the Child and Family Agency, and through an application to the District Court for a care order by the Child and Family Agency. There is an additional mechanism, not addressed in this chapter, whereby the Child and Family Agency can apply to the High Court for a detention order to place a child or young person in a Special Care (secure) unit, if that child is found by the court to pose a serious risk to him/herself or others. There were fourteen children resident in Special Care Units in Ireland in September 2015 (Tusla, Child and Family Agency 2015c). An amendment to the Child Care Act in 2011 codifies the power of the High Court to grant special care orders to detain children in rare circumstances; however, these provisions have yet to come into effect, and in the meantime, the High Court deals with the cases as part of its inherent jurisdiction.

Of the 1,896 admissions of children to the care of the State in 2013, 64 percent were voluntary admissions by parents under s.4 of the Child Care Act 1991, 13 percent involved emergency court orders under s.13, 15 percent were by interim care orders under s.17, 5 percent were by care orders under s.18, and 2 percent were under "other care order" (Tusla, Child and Family Agency 2015b, p. 45). Figure 7.3 provides a breakdown of the complete population of children in State care at the end of December 2012 (data unavailable for 2013), by care status:

Although 62 percent of *admissions* to care in 2012 were voluntary admissions, Figure 7.3 shows that only four in ten children in care at year-end were in care on a voluntary admission. Table 7.2 presents the primary reasons for admission to care between 2008 and 2013. Some caution should be exercised, however, when interpreting these statistics because the reasons for admission to care are often multifactorial. The category of "child welfare concern" is a "catch-all" category that includes issues such as parents unable to cope, parental abuse of substances, behavioral issues and so forth.

Data on the numbers of care orders made by the District Court is quite limited in official statistical publications. Figure 7.4 and Table 7.3 provide an overview of the available Courts Service data for these orders between 2005 and

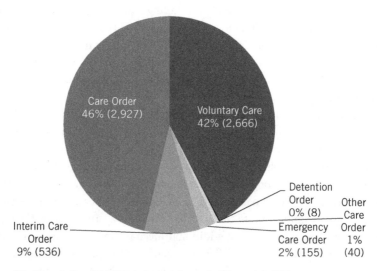

Figure 7.3. Care status of children in care at the end of December 2012.
Source: Tusla, Child and Family Agency 2014b, p. 55.

Table 7.2. Primary reason for admission to care 2010–2013

Primary reason for admission to care	2010	2011	2012	2013
Physical abuse	160	169	173	121
Emotional abuse	66	87	154	100
Sexual abuse	63	33	35	48
Neglect	398	483	593	608
Child welfare concern	1,604	1,446	1,115	1,019
Totals	**2,291**	**2,218**	**2,070**	**1,896**

Sources: Health Service Executive 2013; Tusla, Child and Family Agency 2014b, 2015b.

2013. When interpreting this data, the reader should bear in mind that "the number of applications does not necessarily reflect the number of children in respect of whom orders are made, as several orders may be made in respect of an individual child" (Courts Service 2013, p. 26).

Figure 7.4 charts the mostly steady rate of full care order applications between 2005 and 2013. The large spike in the numbers of care orders granted in 2011 and 2012 appears to be an anomaly and is not commented upon in the Courts Service statistics, nor is it corroborated in the Health Service Executive data. Therefore, it should be treated as an outlier or artefact of a change in processes or recording during these two years. Surprisingly, given that there was more than a doubling in the rate of referrals to the Health Service Executive/ Child and Family Agency during this period, the numbers of full care order applications were actually *fewer* in 2013 than in 2005. It was not possible due to the absence of data on care order applications for these years to comment on trends regarding care order applications versus orders granted, but a limited analysis was possible for 2011–2013:

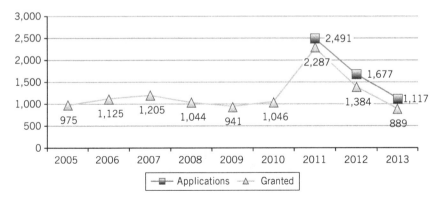

Figure 7.4. Full care orders applications vs. granted 2005–2013.
Sources: Courts Service 2014, 2013, 2012, 2011, 2010, 2009, 2008, 2007; Child Care Law Reporting Project 2014.

Table 7.3. Analysis of Courts Orders by Care Type 2008–2013

Type of order	2013	2012	2011	2010	2009	2008
Care order applications	1,117	1,677	2,491	Unavailable	Unavailable	Unavailable
Care orders made	**889** (80% granted)	**1,384** (83% granted)	**2,287** (92% granted)	1,046	941	1,044
Interim care order applications*	6,023	5,773	4,365	Unavailable	Unavailable	Unavailable
Interim care orders made*	**4,993** (83% granted)	**4,862** (84% granted)	**4,138** (95% granted)	**Unavailable**	**Unavailable**	**Unavailable**
Emergency care order applications	520	519	Unavailable	Unavailable	Unavailable	Unavailable
Emergency care orders made	**414** (80% granted)	**424** (82% granted)	**Unavailable**	**Unavailable**	**Unavailable**	**Unavailable**

Sources: Courts Service 2014, 2013, 2012, 2011, 2010, 2009; Child Care Law Reporting Project 2014.

* includes extensions of interim care orders.

Of particular note in Table 7.3 is the high rate of care orders granted. A closer examination of the orders applied for and granted by each District Court area (see Child Care Law Reporting Project 2014; Coulter 2014, Coulter et al. 2015) highlights inconsistencies among District Court areas, with orders being much more likely to be granted in some areas than in others. In some District Court areas, judges granted one hundred percent of orders applied for, and it is not uncommon for over 95 percent of applications to be granted. Social workers in our research suggested that such high rates of orders granted reflected the high levels of preparation before an order is applied for and an acute awareness of the very high threshold in the Constitution and the Child Care Act 1991 for the removal of a child. As a result, only the most serious cases are brought to the attention of the District Court (O'Mahony et al. 2016a). Contrary to the design of the Child Care Act 1991, however, it is arguable that the system may sometimes be weighted against parents—for two reasons. Firstly, the high rate of care orders granted may reflect a practice on the part of some judges to err on the side of caution, for fear of making a decision to leave children at home where their welfare may continue to be at risk. Secondly, an assumption may develop on the part of some judges that the Child and Family Agency only applies for orders where there are very strong grounds for doing so. A judge interviewed in our research raised both of these points (O'Mahony et al. 2016a). Ireland, however, is not unique in granting a high proportion of applications for care orders; other countries in this volume (see, for example, Finland and Norway chapters) also recorded a high percentage of orders granted (see also Coulter et al. 2015).

Subsequent sections in this chapter describe how the relevant provisions of the Child Care Act 1991 are utilized where there is a serious risk to the health or welfare of a child. The next section describes Ireland's social-work-led, voluntary care system, which is the most utilized pathway for children to come into State care.

VOLUNTARY CARE

Section 4 of the Child Care Act 1991 permits the Child and Family Agency to care for the child until the parent(s) or any such person wishes to resume care of the child. As noted above, in 2013, two-thirds (64 percent) of admissions to care were voluntary admissions by parents under s.4 of the Child Care Act 1991. To initiate voluntary care, a parent or guardian must sign a voluntary reception into care form with a social worker indicating a clear start and end date for the care placement. Parents can place their children in voluntary care anytime from the day the children are born up until their eighteenth birthday. Children received into care under s.4 are not brought to the attention of the Court, nor are they under the supervision of the District Court, because voluntary care does not require a care order from the Court. Parents have a right to cancel their consent for voluntary care at any time; however, if there is an ongoing risk and the child needs to remain in State care for his/her continued protection, the Child and Family Agency would apply to the District Court for an interim care order. Unlike in Norway, Finland, and England, children have no right to consent to voluntary care, irrespective of their age (see Chapters 2, 3, and 8).

Due to a lack of empirical research in this area, it is not possible to say why such a high proportion of the children received into care in Ireland are placed via the voluntary care route. Given the highly charged nature of the reception of a child into care, it would be interesting to know whether parents "choose" to sign voluntary consent to avoid court proceedings and preserve a modicum of control. To what extent voluntary care is initiated by parents, who may, for example, require short-term care while they undertake an addiction treatment program, or to what extent it is initiated by the Child and Family Agency, is also unknown. There is no published data regarding how long a parent typically agrees to voluntary care and whether voluntary care is more likely to be utilized in particular circumstances. It is also unclear to what extent parents make an informed, "voluntary" choice without recourse to an independent advocate or solicitor. Whether voluntary care is a more likely option for a child's *first* entry into care and whether subsequent entries to care are more likely to be through court orders is another unknown. Nevertheless, a recent study of care patterns in two areas in Ireland over ten years (O'Leary and Christie 2014), found that the use of voluntary care had declined from 67 percent to 43 percent for *first-time* admissions to care in the period from 2008 to 2012, with a corresponding rise in the use of care orders from 33 percent to 57 percent.

Consultations with child protection social workers in three practice locations during the preparation of this chapter suggested that practice in some teams is moving toward a diminution in the use of voluntary care in favor of seeking care orders through the District Court. These participants also advised that where a child comes into care voluntarily and where care is likely to extend beyond the short-term, social workers would then seek a care order in the District Court to "stabilize" the placement. They also confirmed that not all children in long-term care have been brought to the attention of the District Court; some remain in long-term care by voluntary consent, even until their eighteenth birthday. National statistics do not, however, evidence this claimed reduction in the use of voluntary care, with the percentage of children admitted to care on a voluntary basis virtually unchanged at 62–64 percent between 2011 and 2013 (Health Service Executive 2013; Tusla, Child and Family Agency 2014b, 2015b).

PROTECTION OF CHILDREN IN EMERGENCIES

Under Section 12 of the Child Care Act 1991, in exceptional circumstances, An Garda Síochána (police) are empowered to enter the family home, or any other place, without a warrant to remove a child to safety. The very high standard for intervention is where:

a. there is an immediate and serious risk to the health or welfare of a child, and
b. it would not be sufficient for the protection of the child from such immediate and serious risk to await the making of an application for an emergency care order by a health board [Child and Family Agency] under section 13.

Upon taking a child into care, An Garda Síochána shall as soon as possible deliver the child to the Child and Family Agency, who have three days to decide whether to return the child back to the parents or apply to the District Court for an emergency care order (section 13, see below). An Garda Síochána is the only State agency with the power to remove a child without a care order. Shannon (2011) notes that where s.12 applies, children should only be in the custody of the Gardaí for the shortest possible period, so as to avoid the children gaining the misconception that they have done something wrong. This section of the Act is only intended to be used in exceptional circumstances, whereby in normal circumstances, the Child and Family Agency would work with parents to receive children into care by voluntary consent or through the District Court under a care order (s.13, s.17 or s.18—see below). It is significant to note, however, that the Child and Family Agency in the final quarter of 2015 launched, for the first time ever in Ireland, a national emergency out-of-hours social work service; it will be interesting to see how this new service will influence the use of s.12 by An Garda Síochána.

There are no published statistics by An Garda Síochána or the Child and Family Agency on the numbers of children placed in care under s.12, but the Child and Family Agency provided the chapter authors with an unpublished report on this area (Tusla, Child and Family Agency 2014d). There were 365 s.12 interventions notified by An Garda Síochána to the Child and Family Agency in 2012 and 402 in 2013. This data may not provide a full and accurate picture, however; the report authors qualified their findings due to issues regarding the completeness of the dataset provided by some areas, because this type of data is not always routinely recorded. The primary reasons stated for An Garda Síochána to invoke s.12 over this two-year period were "neglect" (44%) and "welfare" (15%). Once the three-day period had elapsed after an s.12 removal, two-thirds of children were admitted to care and one-third "were returned home without further intervention/order" (p. 5). When a child is removed under s.12 and is not returned to the parent(s), the Child and Family Agency "shall . . . make an application for an emergency care order at the next sitting of the District Court" (s.12(4)).

CHILD CARE PROCEEDINGS IN THE DISTRICT COURT

Child care proceedings in Ireland are heard in the District Court, which is a court of limited and local jurisdiction. In the twenty-three District Courts, judges hear a mixture of family law (domestic violence, child care, maintenance, custody, and access), licensing, civil, and criminal cases. Ireland does not have a dedicated family court system (O'Mahony et al. 2016b). This means that, except for the Dublin Metropolitan District, judges hearing child care cases in these District Courts are not fully dedicated "specialist" judges. In some urban areas with a high volume of cases, however, particular judges have developed considerable expertise in child care cases. Some District Courts have dedicated family law rooms within the court building that are less like formal courts, but other courts hear child care cases in the regular courtroom. Child care hearings are held *in camera*, whereby only the key participants to a case are permitted to be present. There are, however, some limited exceptions now permitted by law to allow journalists (s.5 of the Courts and Civil Law [Miscellaneous Provisions] Act 2013) and researchers (s.3 of the Child Care [Amendment] Act 2007) to attend these proceedings, thus leading to greater transparency.

Child care cases in the District Court are heard by a single judge. Judges appointed to the District Court who hear child care cases may not have had previous child care and family law experience. Child care cases are brought by the State through the Child and Family Agency child protection and welfare social work teams. State-funded Legal Aid Board solicitors normally represent parents, but parents are occasionally represented by private solicitors. Among witnesses in child care cases, 49.5 percent are social workers, 37.4 percent are solicitors updating the courts on a case, 2.3 percent are psychiatrists/counsellors, 1.6 percent are Gardaí, 0.6 percent are teachers, 0.5 percent are public health nurses, 0.2 percent are doctors, and 7.9 percent are "others" (Coulter et al. 2015). There is little evidence in these courts of a culture of routinely employing independent specialist witnesses as happens in some other countries, nor does the judge have an expert and/or lay citizen(s) on the bench like in Sweden, Norway, and Northern Ireland. Research by our team has found that *direct* participation (e.g., attending proceedings) by children and young people in these proceedings is infrequent (Parkes et al. 2015). Participants in our research provided a range of reasons for this, including inappropriate court facilities, inconsistent judicial skills and training, the frequently adversarial nature of the proceedings, and the legal and constitutional frameworks, under which judges are not obliged to hear directly from children. Indirect participation by children and young people is more likely, wherein the voice of the child is represented by the social worker in the court report, by the child's parents, or in some cases through a guardian ad litem. In a small number of cases—mostly involving older children, and even then only in certain areas—an independent solicitor may be appointed for the child. The appointment of guardians and solicitors for children who are subject to care proceedings is a matter of discretion for the court, and a wide variety of practices exist across the country (see Daly 2010). For example, courts in areas such as Dublin are more likely to appoint a guardian ad litem for a child than are courts in other areas (Coulter 2013). In the sample of cases examined by the Child Care Law Reporting Project, guardians ad litem were appointed for children in 53 percent of cases (Coulter et al. 2015).

The Supreme Court in *Southern Health Board vs. CH* ruled that child care proceedings are "in essence an *inquiry* as to what is best to be done for the child,"[8] whereby proceedings should have a more inquisitorial format that other proceedings. Qualitative research undertaken by our team with professional participants in these proceedings suggests that notwithstanding this ruling, proceedings, in fact, are run in a predominantly adversarial format (Burns et al. 2013; O'Mahony 2016b). Social workers were more likely to perceive the proceedings as unnecessarily adversarial. Solicitors were largely of the view that an adversarial approach was appropriate to protect the rights of parents and to ensure that evidence is rigorously tested, given that parents could be denied the right to the custody of their child. Judges were more nuanced in their views and more likely to describe the system as a hybrid form that was neither purely inquisitorial nor purely adversarial. Parties can appeal the outcome of a case to the Circuit Court, or the judge (on his or her own motion or if requested by a party) can refer a point of law to the High Court (Nestor 2007).

The District Court hears applications by the Child and Family Agency under the Child Care Act 1991 to have a child placed in care under an emergency care order (s.13), an interim care order (s.17), or a [full] care order (s.18). The following sections are intended as a summary overview of these orders and powers. (For more comprehensive examinations of the Child Care Acts and associated case law, the following texts are recommended: Kilkelly 2008; Nestor 2007; Shannon 2011.)

Emergency care order
Section 13 of the Act allows for the Child and Family Agency to apply to the District Court to remove a child from his or her parents where "there is reasonable cause to believe that—

a. there is an immediate and serious risk to the health or welfare of a child which necessitates his being placed in the care of a health board [Child and Family Agency], or
b. there is likely to be such risk if the child is removed from the place where he is for the time being".

An emergency care order can be granted for up to eight days, and if neces-sary, the Court can grant this order on an *ex parte* basis, that is, without the parent(s) being present or being notified. The court also may, upon the granting of an emergency care order, issue a warrant to a member of An Garda Síochána to "enter (if need be by force) any house or other place specified in the war-rant to deliver the child into the custody of the health board [Child and Family Agency]." In 2013, 13 percent of admissions to care (246 out of 1,896) were through an emergency court order (Tusla, Child and Family Agency 2015b). The limited timeframe for this order is an attempt to ensure that parents' con-stitutional rights are protected. In practice, however, a social work assessment of the child's welfare normally would take longer than eight days, which means that if the Agency is not satisfied that the child can return home safely, it would then apply to the District Court for an interim care order to allow further time to complete the assessment.

Interim care order

The Child and Family Agency can apply to the District Court for an interim care order (ICO) under section 17 of the Child Care Act 1991. ICOs can be granted for a period not exceeding twenty-nine days. A judge can extend this period, however, on the application of a party where there are ongoing concerns and the "grounds for the making of an interim care order continue to exist with respect to the child" (s.17(2)). The period also can be extended with the consent of the Child and Family Agency and the parent(s). Unlike the emergency care order, which can be made on an ex parte basis, the Child and Family Agency must give parents notice of the intended application. The intention of this order is to allow the State, through the Child and Family Agency, time to under-take their assessment and to determine whether the child can return home or whether an application should be made for a [full] care order to keep the child in care. An application for an ICO also may be made by the Child and Family Agency when it is felt that the child could be "removed from voluntary care [see below] in circumstances where this would not be in the interests of the child" (Shannon 2011, p. 23). The grounds that the judge needs to be satisfied of before granting the ICO are:

(a) the child has been or is being assaulted, ill-treated, neglected or sex-ually abused, or
(b) the child's health, development or welfare has been or is being avoid-ably impaired or neglected, or
(c) the child's health, development or welfare is likely to be avoidably impaired or neglected,

and that it is necessary for the protection of the child's health or welfare that he be placed or maintained in the care of the Child and Family Agency pending the determination of the application for the care order (s. 17(1)). In practice, some ICOs may not be renewed and a child returns home to the care of his/her parent, whereas if the State feels that the child needs to stay in care for the medium- to long-term, it then applies to the court for a full care order.

Care order

If the Child and Family Agency and relevant professionals and agencies conclude their assessment, and they determine that a child's welfare requires that she or he stay in care on a medium- to long-term basis, the Child and Family Agency can apply to the District Court for a care order under section 18 of the Child Care Act 1991. Only the Child and Family Agency can bring an application for a care order. In any democracy, applying to remove a child from his/her parents is of the utmost seriousness and only should be pursued as a measure of last resort. The threshold in the Irish Constitution for the removal of a child from his/her birth family is that of exceptional circumstances. A District Court judge may make a care order, for any length of time up to the child's eighteenth birthday, if they are satisfied that:

(a) the child has been or is being assaulted, ill-treated, neglected or sexually abused, or
(b) the child's health, development or welfare has been or is being avoidably impaired or neglected, or
(c) the child's health, development or welfare is likely to be avoidably impaired or neglected,

and that the child requires care or protection which he is unlikely to receive unless the court makes an order under this section, the court may make an order (in this Act referred to as a "care order") in respect of the child (s.18).

In the sample of care order cases observed by the Child Care Law Reporting project in the District Court, the respondents (parent or parents) consented to the order in 37 percent of cases. Their sample reported,

81.7% of cases taking less than an hour, and a further 11.6 per cent taking less than three hours. More than 96 per cent are over in a day or less. The remaining four per cent are those complex and contested cases that can take several days (Coulter et al. 2015, p. 14).

Irish social policy clearly states that the removal of a child into State care is not a termination of the relationship between a child and his/her parent(s) and family; reunification of the child and the birth family must be a constant consideration, and appropriate contact with family must be maintained (Department of Children and Youth Affairs 2011). This is in line with the jurisprudence of the

European Court of Human Rights as well as the UN Convention on the Rights of the Child 1989, to which Ireland is a party, and has been confirmed by the Irish courts as a principle of law as well as policy.[9] The "release" of children in long-term care for adoption is a rare event[10] (see below on recent changes to the Constitution in respect to children in care for longer than three years, irrespective of the parents' marital status). This family-centric policy places a positive onus on the Child and Family Agency to continuously consider the option of re-unification. From a child's point of view, however, this may inhibit permanence planning and lead to "drift" for some children in care.

CHALLENGES, REFORMS, AND BLIND SPOTS

The ongoing significant use of voluntary care nationally raises questions vis-à-vis the extent to which parents' rights are safeguarded, and may suggest concerns regarding the transparency and accountability of this system. Although all professionals accept that independent legal advice is absolutely essential for parents who are defending applications for child protection orders before the courts, there is no requirement of such advice being provided before parents consent to a voluntary care placement. No safeguards are in place to ensure that parents know what they are consenting to or that they are not pressured into consenting. This potentially raises concerns regarding the procedural rights of parents, as protected by the Irish Constitution and the ECHR. We are not suggesting impropriety in the usage by the Child and Family Agency of this section of the Act; however, it is an area of practice and legislation that requires further research and critical examination.

The establishment of the Child and Family Agency is a key systemic reform that should lead to significant positive changes in child protection in Ireland. In addition to this, it is proposed to establish a specialist family court system. Although the precise shape of this proposed reform is unclear at present, we have argued elsewhere that the weight of opinion and available evidence clearly demonstrates the need for child care proceedings to be dealt with by specialist judges in dedicated facilities (O'Mahony et al. 2016b). A number of steps have been taken to improve the transparency of child care proceedings, including the establishment of the Child Care Law Reporting Project, which since 2013 has conducted research into child care proceedings using a case observation methodology backed up by the use of quantitative data. Case histories were published online, and a series of reports were published based on these histories and statistics with a view to identifying trends and problems and making recommendations (Child Care Law Reporting Project 2013-2015; Coulter 2013, 2014; Coulter et al. 2015). Finally, legislation was passed to allow representatives of the media to attend family law proceedings in certain circumstances.[11] In the immediate aftermath of this change coming into effect in January 2014, newspapers regularly published reports on child care cases; this early enthusiasm has somewhat diminished, but reports continue to appear most weeks in the *Irish Times*. Over time, it is to be hoped that the Child Care Law Reporting Project, research studies, media access, and the publication of a greater number of judgments in child care cases on the Courts service website (see Courts Service 2008–2015) will result in greater transparency in child care proceedings in Ireland, but these reforms will have a limited impact until a critical mass of information becomes available.

The highest-profile legal reform was the approval by the Irish electorate in November 2012 of the insertion of a new provision on children's rights—Article 42A—into the Irish Constitution. The main impact this will have on child protection proceedings will be to make it mandatory that the views of any child who is capable of forming them shall be ascertained and given due weight according to the age and maturity of the child. This will be a positive move away from the current position whereby it is discretionary for the court to ascertain the views of the child. The precise mechanism through which this will occur is not specified, and the Special Rapporteur on Child Protection has recommended that a variety of mechanisms should be provided for, including the appointment of a guardian ad litem and the meeting of the child by the judge in chambers (Shannon 2013). The other significant reform included in the amendment is to allow for the children of married parents (see note 11 below) to be placed for adoption with the consent of the parents (previously impossible due to the description of the rights of the marital family as "inalienable"), and to make it easier for such children to be placed for adoption without the consent of their parents. The previous regime under the Adoption Acts 1988 and 2010 made this virtually impossible, with the effect that many children remained in the twilight zone of long-term foster care up to their eighteenth birthday. It is proposed that the amendment will allow for an adoption placement after a period of thirty-six months of parental abandonment, where the best interests of the child so require and the child has been in the care of the potential adoptive parents for at least eighteen months. Finally, the amendment makes a broad guarantee that the State will protect and vindicate the rights of the child, and slightly rephrases the provision authorizing State intervention in the family to protect children. It is unclear at present, however, whether these amendments will have any real effect on law and practice.

Inconsistency continues to be a problem in the child care proceedings system (see Coulter 2014; Coulter et al. 2015; O'Mahony et al. 2016a,b). In granting a care order, the District Court confers the Child and Family Agency (acting on behalf of the State) with the powers of the parent to make decisions regarding the type of care, travel, education, medical treatment, and the issuing of passports for the child. Even when a judge is satisfied that the grounds for a care order are met, he/she may not grant the order for the length of time requested by the Child and

Family Agency. Accounts from social workers and solicitors around the country indicate that judicial practices vary considerably in respect to both the readiness of judges to grant orders and the length of time for which orders are granted. In addition, there appears to be reluctance among some judges to grant care orders in respect to children until their eighteenth birthday. Some judges, of their own volition, have taken on a role of reviewing care orders in order to receive updates from the Child and Family Agency on the child's progress and care plan, and to review whether a child can return home. These reviews are in addition to the statutory child care reviews examining children's care plans undertaken internally by the Child and Family Agency with family, professionals, and carers. There is no basis in the Child Care Acts for judge-led reviews of care orders; while the Act delegates to the Minister the power to make regulations governing reviews (s.42), the relevant regulations (Statutory Instruments 259 and 260 of 1995) currently provide only for internal reviews by the Child and Family Agency and make no reference to court-led reviews. Our research indicates that where judges impose such reviews, they do so via a condition being attached to the care order that the court at a set point in the future reviews the order, which is not expressly provided for in the Act. Such reviews are taking up an increasing amount of social workers' and courts' workloads and time; however, these independent reviews bolster accountability and can contribute to safeguarding the rights of parents and children. Social workers in our qualitative study reported that these extra court reviews impacted time-wise on their availability to work with children and families in the community, but at the same time, most professionals expressed positive feelings about the effect of these reviews on individual cases.

Finally, two high-profile cases have raised questions regarding the use of s.12 by An Garda Síochána in cases involving children from the Roma community. The subsequent inquiry by the Ombudsman for Children (2014) into the removal of these children from their families using s.12 was critical of Garda practice. It highlighted the inappropriate use of the families' ethnicity in decision-making leading to the removals. The Ombudsman and the Special Rapporteur on Child Protection (Shannon 2014) have both recommended the development and publication of guidelines regarding how An Garda Síochána exercise their powers under s.12. Furthermore, whether s.12 is used in a manner unintended by the Act due to the unavailability of a national out-of-hours social work service is unclear. Overall, this area requires greater transparency and further research.

CONCLUSION

This chapter explored child care proceedings legislation and practice in Ireland and charted the emerging shift in culture toward transparency, specialization, and the recognition of children's rights. At the same time, the system is endeavoring to preserve the traditional emphasis on protecting the rights of parents and the family unit and the privacy of the individuals involved. All of this is occurring in a context where increasing demands are being placed on the system from all angles—most obviously through the number of children and families who are coming into contact with it, but also through the need to respond to legislative and structural reforms and various critical reports—in a harsh economic climate where resources are in short supply.

From a legal and policy perspective, the Irish child protection system is broadly moving in the right direction, although room for improvement still remains. The Minister for Children and Youth Affairs (Reilly 2015) has initiated a review of the Child Care Act 1991 that will being in 2016 with a view to modernizing the Act; it is hoped this will address some of the issues raised in this chapter. This review of the Act follows recommendations made by the Special Rapporteur concerning the modernization of the law relating to child protection removals and related child protection matters (Shannon, 2014). A detailed study of practices and trends in the area of voluntary care is overdue, and the manner in which the system responds to emergency situations (including both the s.12 procedure and the establishment of an out-of-hours social work service) needs to be addressed in a coherent manner. If, however, the constitutional amendment on children's rights is fully implemented, genuinely specialist family courts are established as promised, and media access, research studies, published judgments and the Child Care Law Reporting Project contribute to a more transparent and consistent system, very significant progress could be made in a relatively short period of time. But none of this will prove to be effective unless the necessary resources are provided to deliver on the potential of these reform measures. In particular, a specialist family court system must be more than an organizational arrangement with a building of its own. Facilities must be purpose-designed and staff (including judges and lawyers) must be provided with specialist training in dealing with children at risk. Potentially, things could be far better in 2026 than they were in 2016; only time will tell by how much.

ACKNOWLEDGMENTS

The authors would like to acknowledge the support and participation of staff in the Child and Family Agency, Courts Service, Legal Aid Boards, and Barnardos, as well as of a number of individual solicitors and barristers. We also would like to thank Donna O'Leary, Alastair Christie, and the Child and Family Agency for providing us with access to unpublished statistical data. The authors also would like to acknowledge the financial support received from the College of Arts, Celtic Studies and Social Science, the Head of Law Strategic Fund, and the Strategic Research Fund at University College Cork for their research on District Court child care proceedings in Ireland. For more details see:

http://www.ucc.ie/en/appsoc/resconf/res/childcareproceedingsinthedistrict-court/.

LEGISLATION. STATUTORY INSTRUMENTS AND CASE LAW

Adoption Acts 1998, 2010.

Child Care (Amendment Act) 2013.
Child Care (Amendment Act) 2011.
Child Care (Amendment Act) 2007.
Children Act 2001.
Child Care Act 1991.
Children First Act 2015.
S. I. No. 259/1995—Child Care (Placement of Children in Residential Care) Regulations, 1995.
S. I. No. 260/1995—Child Care (Placement of Children in Foster Care) Regulations, 1995.
Southern Health Board v. CH [1996] 1 IR 21

NOTES

1   Ireland refers to the twenty-six counties of the Republic of Ireland; the legal and child protection systems in Northern Ireland (which is part of the United Kingdom) are not addressed.
2   See Thirty-First Amendment to the Constitution (Children) Act 2015.
3   See, for example, *Re JH (an infant)* [1985] IR 375; *North Western Health Board v. HW* [2001] 3 IR 622; and *N v. Health Services Executive* [2006] 4 IR 374, as discussed in U. Kilkelly and C. O'Mahony, "The Proposed Children's Rights Amendment: Running to Stand Still?" (2007) 10(2) *Irish Journal of Family Law* 19.
4   In *North Western Health Board v. HW* [2001] 3 IR 622, the majority judges all referred to circumstances approximating an immediate threat to the child's life; an immediate threat of serious injury; or an immediate threat to the child's capacity to function as a human person. The thresholds set in sections 13, 17, 18, and 19 of the Child Care Act 1991 for the granting of the various child protection orders are phrased somewhat differently, referring to children being assaulted, ill-treated, neglected, or sexually abused, and children whose health, development, or welfare has been, is being, or is likely to be avoidably impaired or neglected.

5 In *State (DC) v. Midland Health Board* (High Court, unreported, July 31, 1986), Keane J. held that a statutory provision that allowed for the removal of a child from the custody of his parents for longer than was necessary to carry out an assessment of his welfare would constitute a breach of his parents' constitutional rights.

6 See, for example, *Keating v. Crowley* [2003] 1 ILRM 88, where a provision allowing for an interim barring order to be granted ex parte without any time limit on its effect was declared unconstitutional as a disproportionate interference with the principle of *audi alterem partem*. The Court specifically referred to the eight-day time limit in provisions of the Child Care Act 1991 dealing with emergency and interim care orders as a model of how ex parte applications can adequately balance constitutional rights.

7 All of the *Growing up in Ireland: National Longitudinal Study of Children* reports are available on this website: http://www.growingup.ie

8 *Southern Health Board v. CH* [1996] 1 IR 219, at 237 (emphasis in original). The Court justified this position on the grounds that the child's welfare is the first and paramount consideration for the court, and takes priority over any right that the parents wish to assert through the adversarial process. This approach manifests itself in a variety of ways, including, for example, relaxed rules of evidence that allow for the admission of hearsay evidence at the discretion of the court (ibid at 239). See also *Health Services Executive v. OA* [2013] IEHC 172 at [63] to [64], where the High Court echoed this aspiration, but added the caveat that although the notion that there are no winners and losers is appropriate for professional participants, it "asks a degree of detachment that is very unlikely to be shared by a parent. The procedure is, as a matter of fact, adversarial."

9 *Health Service Executive (Southern Area) v. SS (a minor)* [2007] IEHC 189 at [94] to [95].

10 Irish law, until the implementation of the constitutional amendment on children in 2015, treated children of married and unmarried parents differently in various ways. One such difference is that children of married parents cannot be voluntarily placed for adoption, and the threshold for placing them for adoption without the parents' consent in cases of abandonment is extraordinarily high (see Adoption Act 1988). In practice, however, few Irish children in care have been placed for adoption irrespective of parental marital status. The constitutional amendment on children will introduce reforms on these issues, permitting voluntary placement for adoption of all children and reducing the threshold for involuntary adoption.

11 Courts and Civil Law (Miscellaneous Provisions) Act 2013, section 8. This provision gives the Court the discretion to decide whether to exclude the media from a particular case having regard to a range of competing considerations, including the desirability of promoting public confidence in the administration of justice, the best interests of a child who is the subject of

proceedings, the views of such a child or of any party to the proceedings (including witnesses), and the likely impact on the child or on parties to the proceedings of the presence of the media at the proceedings.

REFERENCES

Buckley, H. and Burns, K. (2015). "Child Welfare and Protection in Ireland: Déjà Vu All Over Again." In Christie, A., Featherstone, B., Quin, S., and Walsh, T. (Eds.), *Social Work in Ireland: Continuities and Changes*. Basingstoke: Palgrave Macmillan.

Burns, K., O'Mahony, C., Shore, C., and Parkes, A. (2013). "Fit for Purpose? Professional Perspectives on District Court Child Care Proceedings." *13th ISPCAN European Regional Conference on Child Abuse and Neglect*, Dublin, Ireland, September 15–18, 2013.

Burns, K. and Lynch, D. (2012). "Politics, Democracy and Protecting Children." In Lynch, D. and Burns, K. *Children's Rights and Child Protection: Critical Times, Critical Issues in Ireland*. Manchester: Manchester University Press.

Central Statistics Office. (2012). *This is Ireland. Highlights from Census 2011, Part 1*. Dublin: Stationery Office.

Child Care Law Reporting Project. (2014). *Courts Service Child Care Statistics*. Retrieved March 25, 2014 from http://www.childlawproject.ie/statistics/.

Child Care Law Reporting Project. (2013–2015.) *Case Histories Archive 2013–2015*. Retrieved April 20, 2016 from http://www.childlawproject.ie/archive/.

Considine, M. and Dukelow, F. (2013). "Ireland's Economic Crises in Recent Historical Perspective: From Resilience to Retrenchment in the Irish Welfare State?" In Jónsson, G. and Stefánsson, K. (Eds.), *Retrenchment or Renewal? Welfare States in Times of Economic Crisis*. Helsinki: Norwel Studies in Historical Welfare State Research 6.

Coulter, C., Colfer, L., Healy, K., and MacMahon, M. (2015). *Final Report. Child Care Law Reporting Project*. Retrieved November 30, 2015 from http://www. childlawproject.ie/interim-reports/.

Coulter, C. (2014). *Second Interim Report. Child Care Law Reporting Project*. Retrieved November 30, 2014 from http://www.childlawproject. ie/ interim-reports/

Coulter, C. (2013). *First Interim Report. Child Care Law Reporting Project*. Retrieved March 25, 2014 from http://www.childlawproject.ie/interim-reports/.

Courts Service. (2008–2015). *All Judgements by Court (District Court)*. Retrieved April 20, 2016 from http://www.courts.ie/Judgments.nsf/FrmJu dgmentsByCourtAll?OpenForm&Start=1&Count=35&Expand=5&Seq=1.

Courts Service. (2007–2014). *Courts Service Annual Reports 2008, 2009, 2010, 2011, 2012 and 2013*. Retrieved March 25, 2014 from http://www.courts.ie/ courts.ie/library3.nsf/pagecurrent/5D12A39F06827AD080256DA60033FE8 7?opendocument&l=en.

Daly, A. (2010). "Limited Guidance. The Provision of Guardian ad Litem Services in Ireland." *Irish Journal of Family Law.* 13(1): 8–11.

Department of Children and Youth Affairs. (2014). *Better Outcomes, Brighter Future: The National Policy Framework for Children and Young People, 2014–2020.* Dublin: Government Publications.

Department of Children and Youth Affairs. (2013). *State of the Nation's Children.* Dublin: Government Publications.

Department of Children and Youth Affairs. (2011). *Children First: National Guidance for the Protection and Welfare of Children.* Dublin: Stationery Office.

Garrett, P. M. (2013). "Beyond the Community of Persons to be Accorded 'Respect'? Messages from the Past for Social Work in the Republic of Ireland." In Carey, M. and Green, L. (Eds.), *Practical Social Work Ethics: Complex Dilemmas within Applied Social Care.* Farnham: Ashgate.

Gilbert, N., Parton, N., and Skivenes, M. (Eds.) (2011). *Child Protection Systems: International Trends and Orientations.* New York: Oxford University Press.

Health Service Executive. (2013). *Review of Adequacy for HSE Children and Family Services 2011.* Retrieved April 29, 2014 from http://www.tusla.ie/publications/review-of-adequacy-reports.

Health Service Executive. (2009a). *HSE Child Welfare and Protection Social Work Departments Business Processes. Report of the NCCIS Business Process Standardisation Project October 2009.* Dublin: Health Service Executive.

Health Service Executive. (2009b). *Review of Adequacy of Services for Children and Families 2008.* Retrieved April 29, 2014 from http://www.tusla.ie/publications/review-of-adequacy-reports.

Kelly, F. (2013). "Social workers to get training to act instead of solicitors." *The Irish Times,* December 28. Retrieved May 18, 2014 from: http://www.irishtimes.com/news/politics/social-workers-get-training-to-act-instead-of-solicitors-1.1638799.

Kilkelly, U. (2008). *Children's Rights in Ireland: Law, Practice and Policy.* Sussex: Tottel Publishing.

Nestor, J. (2007). *An Introduction to Irish Family Law* (3rd ed.). Dublin: Gill and MacMillan.

O'Brien, V. and Ahonen, H. (2015). *Pathways and Outcomes: A Study of 335 Referrals to the Family Welfare Conference (FWC) Service in Dublin 2011–2013.* Dublin: Tusla, Child and Family Agency.

O'Leary, D. and Christie, A. (2014). "Pathways In Care: Knowledge Production through Dialogue with Social Workers." *4th European Conference for Social Work Research,* Free University of Bozen-Bolzano, Italy, April 2014.

Ombudsman for Children. (2014). *Emily Logan Submits Special Inquiry Report to Justice Minister.* Retrieved May 29, 2014 from: http://specialinquiry.ie/news-item-one/and http://www.oco.ie/2014/04/emily-logan-submits-special-inquiry-report-to-justice-minister/.

Ombudsman for Children. (2012). *Ombudsman for Children Annual Report 2011*. Dublin: Ombudsman for Children's Office.

O'Mahony, C., Burns, K., Parkes, A., and Shore, C. (2016a). "Representation and Participation in Child Care Proceedings: What about the Voice of the Parents?" *Journal of Social Welfare and Family Law*, Vol. 2 (in press).

O'Mahony, C., Burns, K., Parkes, A., and Shore, C. (2016b). "Child Care Proceedings in Non-Specialist Courts: The Experience in Ireland." *International Journal of Law Policy and The Family*, Vol. 2: 1–27, doi: 10.1093/lawfam/ebw001.

Parkes, A., Shore, C., O'Mahony, C., and Burns, K. (2015). "The Right of the Child to Be Heard? Professional Experiences of Child Care Proceedings in the Irish District Court." *Child and Family Law Quarterly*, 27 (4): 423–444.

Reilly, J. (2015). "Official Opening." International Conference: Child Protection and the Law, Law Society of Ireland, Blackhall Place, Dublin, April 13.

Ryan, S. (2009). *Commission to Inquire into Child Abuse Report* (Volumes I–V). Dublin: Stationery Office.

Shannon, G. (2014). *Seventh Report of the Special Rapporteur on Child Protection. A Report Submitted to the Oireachtas.* Dublin: Department of Children and Youth Affairs.

Shannon, G. (2013). *Sixth Report of the Special Rapporteur on Child Protection. A Report Submitted to the Oireachtas.* Dublin: Department of Children and Youth Affairs.

Shannon, G. (2011). *Child Care Law*. Dublin: Thomson Reuters.

Skehill, C. (2004). *History of the Present of Child Protection and Welfare Social Work in Ireland*. New York: Edwin Mellen Press.

Tusla, Child and Family Agency. (2015a). *Quarterly Management Data Activity Report—Quarter 1 2015*. Retrieved December 29, 2015 from http://www.tusla.ie/data-figures.

Tusla, Child and Family Agency. (2015b). *Review of Adequacy in Respect of Child Care and Family Support Services Provided by the Health Service Executive 2013*. Dublin: Tusla, Child and Family Agency.

Tusla, Child and Family Agency. (2015c). *Monthly National Performance Activity—September 2015*. Retrieved January 2, 2016 from http://www.tusla.ie/data-figures.

Tusla, Child and Family Agency. (2014a). *Monthly National Performance Activity—January 2014*. Retrieved April 29, 2014 from http://www.tusla.ie/data-figures.

Tusla, Child and Family Agency. (2014b). *Review of Adequacy for HSE Children and Family Services 2012*. Dublin: Tusla, Child and Family Agency.

Tusla, Child and Family Agency. (2014c). *Monthly National Performance Activity—December 2014*. Retrieved May 2, 2015 from http://www.tusla.ie/data-figures.

Tusla, Child and Family Agency. (2014d). *Report on the Number of Interventions Notified under Section 12 of the Child Care Act 1991 for the Years 2012 and 2013* (unpublished report). Dublin: Tusla, Child and Family Agency.

Tusla, Child and Family Agency. (2013a). *Suite of Policy and Guidance Documents for the Child and Family Agency.* Retrieved May 1, 2014 from: http://www. childandfamilyresearch.ie/publications/policy-practice.

Tusla, Child and Family Agency. (2013b). *Guidance for the Implementation of an Area Based Approach to Prevention, Partnership and Family Support.* Dublin: Tusla, Child and Family Agency.

UNICEF. (2010). *Innocenti Report Card 9: The Children Left Behind.* Retrieved September 1, 2014 from: http://www.unicef-irc.org/files/documents/d-3796-The-Children-Left-Behind-.pdf.

UNICEF. (2013). *Innocenti Report Card 11: Child Well-Being in Rich Countries— A Comparative Review,* Retrieved September 1, 2014 from: http://www. unicef.org.uk/Images/Campaigns/FINAL_RC11-ENG-LORES-fnl2.pdf.

UNICEF. (2014). *Innocenti Report Card 12: Children of the Recession: The Impact of the Economic Crisis on Child Well-Being in Rich Countries.* Retrieved November 4, 2014 from: http://www.unicef-irc.org/publications/series/16

UNICEF. (2016). *Innocenti Report Card 13: Fairness for Children: A League Table of Inequality in Child Well-Being in Rich Countries.* Retrieved April 20, 2016 from: https://www.unicef-irc.org/publications/pdf/RC13_eng.pdf

8

STATE INTERVENTION IN FAMILY LIFE IN ENGLAND

SAFEGUARDING CHILDREN THROUGH CARE PROCEEDINGS AND ADOPTION

Karen Broadhurst

INTRODUCTION

The law sanctions compulsory state intervention in family life in England in situations where a child is deemed to be suffering or likely to suffer "significant harm." In addition, harm must be attributable to serious failings in parental care or to the fact that the child is beyond parental control. Children can be removed on a short-term or permanent basis from their birth parents and placed in kinship or foster care, or with adopters. Although many children enter care on a voluntary basis, the majority of children who remain in public care on a long-term basis will be subject to care orders. A care order places the child under the care of the local authority, and in the majority of cases, the child will be removed from parents' care. The past two decades have witnessed increased policy emphasis on adoption as the preferred permanency option for young children, and the court can approve a plan for adoption with or *without* parental consent (Allen 2007). Although few would question that the child's welfare must be the court's paramount consideration when faced with a case of proven child maltreatment or neglect, compulsory intervention in family life continues to be a fiercely contested matter, evidenced by multiple high-profile reviews and amendments to existing legislation and policy (Munro 2011, 2012).

The child protection legislative and policy landscape is shaped by a *battle of ideas*—ideas that are theoretical, moral, and political. At the heart of this battle is the intractable problem of ensuring respect for private and family life, but at the same time, safeguarding children from harm. Although the Children Act 1989 has been deemed compatible with the European Convention on Human Rights (ECHR) given the emphasis within the Act on supporting the upbringing of children by their families of origin, parental rights can be infringed where there are child safeguarding concerns. English child protection policy places front and center the child's needs for permanence, defined as a right to lifelong secure relationships of care. Critics have argued, however, that support for permanency *at home* has received far less attention (Hunt and Waterhouse 2012). Child welfare systems can be categorized into two types: child-protection systems and family-service systems (Gilbert et al. 2011). The English system has been described as having a child-protection orientation, characterized by a relatively high threshold for intervention and the mitigation of serious risks to children's health and safety (Parton and Berridge 2011). Although in-home services are vital to prevention, family support is delivered largely on a short-term basis with an expectation that parents will become independent of services. England's particular incarnation of neoliberalism has resulted in increasing emphasis on private self-reliance and reluctant public support for those in need (Broadhurst et al. 2009; White et al. 2014). Social divisions are arguably further entrenched in the context of austerity, because public sector cuts hit the poorest in society the hardest (Institute for Fiscal Studies [IFS] 2013). For all the emphasis on early intervention or early help, local authority social workers increasingly complain that their work is focused on child safety rather than child welfare (Association of Director's of Children's Services [ADCS] 2014). Recent years have seen an unprecedented rise in care proceedings, commonly attributed to the impact of the tragic death of baby Peter (Hall and Guy 2009; Macleod et al. 2010), but which also coincide with harsher living conditions that undermine parenting capacity (Utting 2007).

This chapter will provide an overview of the policy and legislative framework concerning the reception of children in England into public care and adoption. The chapter will cover compulsory intervention, whether planned or taken on an emergency basis, as well as the voluntary accommodation of children. The opening sections will provide the reader with relevant background context, describing England's population profile, as well as children-in-care statistics. The Children Act 1989 will be introduced, which remains the single primary Act of parliament most referenced in child-care decisions. The chapter also will consider in some detail how decisions within care and adoption proceedings are made, to include the threshold for formal legal intervention and the child's right to separate representation. Discussion also will turn to enduring concerns about delay in social work and judicial decision-making and recent efforts to radically reform the English Family Court. That children wait "in limbo" while the court directs further evidence of parenting capacity has been a matter of considerable concern for the English Family Justice system (Ministry of Justice, the Department of Education and the Welsh Government 2011). Now, with the passage of the Children and Families Act 2014, courts are required to resolve care proceedings within twenty-six weeks so that swifter decisions can be made about long-term out-of-home care or adoption. Frontline workers within the family justice system face radical system redesign, in the context of a continued high volume of care applications coupled with an increasingly complex population demographic. Thus, critics have argued that this is a time of considerable mismatch between demand and resourcing, with the roadmap for public services continuing to be uncertain.

ENGLAND: POPULATION PROFILE AND CHARACTERISTICS

According to the mid-year estimates produced by the Office of National Statistics, population count at June 30, 2013 indicated that the population of the United Kingdom surpassed the 64 million mark, standing at 64,105,700, with by far the largest percentage of residents (84 percent) living in England (ONS 2014). Growing more rapidly than any other European nation state, England has experienced a spike in population expansion since 2001, to a figure of 53,865,800 residents, attributed in part to net inward migration and rising birth rate. Not only are large urban conurbations of England now densely populated, they are also complex in respect to cultural makeup and the geography of family ties and obligations. An increasing number of children who come to the attention of children's services and the courts are members of transnational family networks and are caught between the contradictory legislative frameworks of immigration and child protection.

Census population counts are collected in age bands, and for the 2011 census, there were 3,914,000 children aged zero to four years, 3,517,000 aged five to nine years, 3,670,000 aged ten to fourteen years, and 3,997,000 aged fifteen to nineteen years living in England. This equates to over 12 million children and young people, or just under one-quarter of the population (Office for National Statistics 2011). The age structure of the English population is gradually becoming older, because people are living significantly longer. A clear challenge for governments is to meet the care demands of old age, while ensuring sufficient resources are allocated to the protection of children. Dementia alone costs England an estimated 19 billion annually, compared with 2.5 billion for children in public care (Children in Care England Statistics 2014).

Despite retaining an A-listed economy, England's place among the richest countries on the globe masks high levels of social polarization. Concerns about concentrations of child poverty are once again to the fore, given the impact of the global economic downturn. Responding to the introduction of austerity measures in the United Kingdom in 2011, the IFS

predicted that relative child poverty rates would soar above 3 million children by 2016, rising to at least 25 percent of all children (IFS 2011, 2013).
The most recent analysis based on national data ("Households Below Average
Incomes" [HBAI]) certainly does confirm a picture of worsening inequality, comparable to that seen in the late 1990s, under the previous right-wing
Thatcher government, with more children predicted to live in relative poverty by 2020 (IFS 2013). Relative child poverty is most acutely evidenced in
the major urban conurbations—parts of London, Manchester, Nottingham,
and Birmingham. In this context, it is not surprising that the Association of
Directors of Children's Services (ADCS 2014) has reported rising referrals
concerning both children in need and those at risk of significant harm, with
little indication that this increase is slowing.

CHILDREN IN CARE IN ENGLAND

Children in care are described as "looked after" by the state, whether they
enter care on a voluntary or compulsory basis. According to government statistics for the year ending March 31, 2013, some 68,110 children were looked
after by the State, which equates to a rate of six children, per every thousand (DfE 2013). This figure constitutes an increase of 2 percent on the previous year, but an increase of *12 percent* when compared with the year ending
March 31, 2009 (see Table 8.1 for trends since 2009). The rate for the year
ending March 31, 2009 was 5.4 per 1,000 children. The number of looked-after
children (LAC) in England has increased consistently since 2009 and has now
reached an all-time high. Not only is England witnessing an increase in the

Table 8.1. Children in Care in England (fiscal years ending 2009–2013)

Year Ending	Total Number of Looked-After Children in Given Year (per 1,000 children)	Foster Placements (including family and friends care) (per 1,000 children)	Placed for Adoption (per 1,000 children)	Placement with Parents (per 1,000 children)	Secure Units Children's Homes and Hostels (per 1,000 children)
2013	68,110 (5.6)	50,900 (4.2)	3,350 (0.28)	3,260 (0.27)	6,000 (0.49)
2012	67,080 (5.6)	50,060 (4.1)	2,880 (0.24)	3,590 (0.3)	5,970 (0.49)
2011	65,500 (5.5)	48,150 (4.0)	2,710 (0.21)	3,990 (0.33)	6,010 (0.50)
2010	64,450 (5.5)	46,880 (3.9)	2,520 (0.21)	4,210 (0.35)	6,220 (0.52)
2009	60,900 (5.1)	43,900 (3.7)	2,690 (0.23)	4,170 (0.35)	6,110 (0.51)

NB: In any given year, a small percentage of children are reported "missing" to the police or are in other
community settings including mother and baby units and young offender institutions and residential
schools, the detail of which is beyond the scope of this chapter. Fuller details of these statistics can be
found at Children in Care in England: Statistics, House of Commons Library (Last update, August 13, 2014).

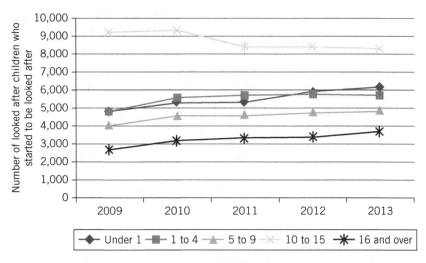

Figure 8.1. Age of children on starting to be looked after, years 2009 to 2013.

number of children in care, but, equally, the age profile of children entering care is changing. National statistics concerning the age distribution of children entering care reveal this changing picture (DfE 2013). For the year ending March 31, 2013, some 6,150 children younger than one year old started to be looked after, which as Figure 8.1 illustrates, is the age group demonstrating the largest increase in number, although still a minority of all looked-after children (6 percent). Whereas, in contrast, the trend for children aged ten to fifteen years (although this category remains the largest annual intake) is of a reducing number of care entrants. There are far fewer young people aged sixteen years and older in care, although again statistics indicate something of an increase. For the year ending March 31, 2013, overall, some 28,830 children (2.4 children per 1,000 children) started being looked after in England.

Although the majority of the looked-after population are White (78 percent at year ending March 31, 2013), there is a history of over- and under-representation of minority ethnic children who are looked after. Black and mixed ethnicity children begin to be looked after at higher rates than their presence in the population, while Asian children start to be looked after at lower rates (Owen and Statham 2009; Selwyn et al. 2010).

There are a variety of routes into public care and adoption, as will be described in detail in this chapter. In short, however, the majority of children (62 percent) are looked after because of child abuse or neglect, and the majority of these children will be subjects of formal court orders (care orders). Figure 8.2 illustrates the variety of reasons why children become looked after:

By far the majority of the LAC population are looked after by foster carers (50,900 [4.19 per 1,000 children] as of March 31, 2013), with the number increasing from 72 percent in 2009 to 75 percent in 2013. This percentage indicates that foster

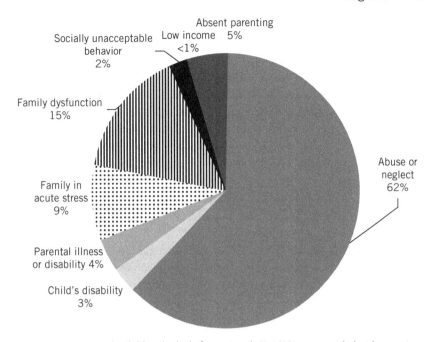

Figure 8.2. Reasons why children looked after at March 31, 2013 were provided with a service.

care remains the mainstay of substitute family care in England (Care Inquiry 2013). It is important, however, to recognize the role that family and friends play in the provision of foster care. Of the total population of 50,900 children in foster care, 7,240 children (0.60 per 1,000 children) were placed with approved foster carers who were family members or friends. Children also can be placed *at home* on care orders with parents. The most common reason for a child returning home on a care order is that the court deems parents to be sufficiently improved in their ability to care for the child, and that he/she is returned home during care proceedings or at the final hearing. This small subgroup comprised 3,260 children (0.27 children per 1,000 children) (approximately 5 percent of 68,110) as of March 31, 2013. Pending an adoption order, children in care, but residing with their adoptive parents, remain classified as looked-after children. Some 3,350 children (0.28 per 1,000 children) were "placed for adoption" pending an adoption order during the year ending March 31, 2013. This latter group of children will be subject to care and placement orders.

The DfE uses the category "secure units, children's homes and hostels" to classify the remainder of children (DfE 2013, p. 4). This group of children and young people constitute 9 percent of the total care population in the year ending March 31, 2013. This equates to a figure of 6,000 (0.49 per 1,000 children) children, which is a slight reduction in number (2 percent) since 2009.

Due to changes in the law on account of the Legal Aid, Sentencing and Punishment of Offenders Act in December 2012, children and young people who have committed criminal offenses and are on remand or committed for trial, are now classed as looked-after children. This population also contributes to the total count of children now in State care, although numbers are very small (310 children [0.03 per 1,000 children], year ending March 2013). Table 8.1 summarizes the placement type for children classified as "looked after."

For children in care (both kinship and nonkinship placements), placement stability is a key measure of performance for local authorities, because instability is linked to adverse outcomes. Numerous central government initiatives aimed at increasing the stability of out-of-home care have had some positive results (Rushton 2007). The picture reported by the DfE for the year ending 2013 was of relative stability for 66 percent of children looked after who had only one placement during the year. However, 34 percent in total recorded some instability: 23 percent of children experienced two placements and 11 percent appear to have a less stable pattern with three or more placements. Children in residential children's homes are of particular national concern and tend to have the most problematic placement histories (Berridge et al. 2012). Recently described as "out of sight and out of mind" by the *All-Party Parliamentary Group Inquiry into Children Missing from Care* (All Parliamentary Group [APPG] for Runaway and Missing Children and Adults and the APPG for Looked After Children and Care Leavers 2012), children in this sector who are often placed at a significant distance from their family networks in out-of-area placements are at heightened risk of sexual exploitation, gang-related activity, and going missing.

Cost information is available for the fiscal year 2013/2014, with a reported £2.5 billion spent on looked-after children services in England. Of that total, £1.4 billion (55 percent) was spent on foster care and 0.9 billion (36 percent) on children's homes. The costs of state care for children has increased year on year, with each child estimating to cost the State £36,534 for fiscal year 2013/2014.

ENTERING PUBLIC CARE: VOLUNTARY AND COMPULSORY ADMISSION AND EMERGENCY ACTION

Despite multiple amendments, the Children Act 1989, which came into effect in October 1991, remains the single primary Act of parliament most referenced in respect to decisions concerning children (Doughty 2010). The Act is broad ranging and covers both private and public law proceedings. In addition, the Act enables the local authority to "accommodate" children on a voluntary basis, but also to remove children on a compulsory basis through court order. In respect to compulsory intervention in family life, statutory duties and powers enshrined in the Act are designed to ensure that all decisions concerning children's futures are timely and proportionate and clearly determine who holds parental responsibility for children. In respect to *all* court decisions concerning children, the court (irrespective of court level) must ensure that the child's welfare is the paramount consideration. Although the court realizes that any delay in determining questions about a child's future may prejudice the child's welfare, it must also be satisfied that the making of an order is better than no order at all. The latter "no order principle" indicates the English Family Court's commitment to Article 8 of the European Convention on Human Rights (1950), which requires "respect for private and family life." The Children Act 1989 has been subject to a number of important amendments in relation to court decisions, which will be detailed later.

As stated above, the majority of children residing on a long-term basis in State care will be subject to care orders. In the year ending March 31, 2013, some 40,180 children (3.3 per 1,000 children) were in care on care orders (interim and full order), of a total of 68,110 (5.6 per 1,000 children) children looked after. This constitutes an increase when compared with 2009, where 36,250 children (3.0 per 1,000 children) were subject to care orders. Care orders only can be made where it is clear that the threshold for compulsory state intervention is met. The threshold for compulsory intervention is laid out in s.31 of the Children Act 1989, which governs both care and supervision orders:

> s.31 A court may only make a care order or supervision order if it is satisfied—
>
> (a) that the child concerned is suffering, or is likely to suffer, significant harm; and
> (b) that the harm, or likelihood of harm, is attributable to—
>   (i) the care given to the child, or likely to be given to him if the order were not made, not being what it would be reasonable to expect a parent to give to him; or
>   (ii) the child's being beyond parental control.

It is noteworthy that the same threshold applies for care and supervision orders, despite the fact that the making of a supervision order does not result in the removal of a child from his/her family of origin. When a local authority applies for a care order, the court will, in most cases, make an *interim* care order (ICO), pending the outcome of further assessment of parents. ICOs are made under s.38 of the Children Act 1989 and since the passage of the Children and Families Act 2014 (which brought forth important amendments to the Children Act 1989) the requirement that an ICO be renewed on a monthly basis is removed. Instead, the judge can issue an ICO for a period that he/she considers appropriate, as long as it does not exceed the new twenty-six weeks rule for the final resolution of care proceedings. A full care order is made under s.31 of the Act where the court deems that the child's long-term care needs require the protection of the state; a full care order lasts until the child is eighteen years of age. Under both interim and full care orders, the local authority acquires parental responsibility (PR) for the child, although it must work in partnership with parents, who *retain* PR.

A large number of children enter care on a *voluntary* basis under s.20 of the Children Act 1989. For the year ending March 31, 2013, some 28,830 children (2.4 per 1,000 children) started to be looked after, and of those, 16,980 (1.4 per 1,000 children) or 59 percent were on a voluntary basis. This is a far larger percentage than those children who *start* to be looked after on a care order (6,980 [0.57 per 1,000 children] or 24 percent). However, more of this cohort of children will *return home*, than children subject to care orders. In addition, many children may start their care journey on a voluntary basis, but the local authority then swiftly brings care proceedings (Masson et al. 2008). Thus children *in care* subject to voluntary agreements constituted only 27 percent of all children in care at year ending March 31, 2013. There has been a slight reduction in the number of children in care subject to voluntary agreement, from 19,260 children (1.6 per 1,000 children) in 2009, to 18,190 children (1.5 per 1,000 children) in 2013. In respect to voluntary care, the statute refers to the provision of "accommodation," although all children in care are deemed "looked after" irrespective of their legal status:

> s.20 Every local authority shall provide accommodation for any child in need within their area who appears to them to require accommodation as a result of:
> a) there being no person who has responsibility for him;
> b) his being lost or having been abandoned;
> c) the person who has been caring for him being prevented (whether or not permanently, and for whatever reason) from providing him with suitable accommodation or care.

Where a child is in voluntary accommodation, the local authority does *not* acquire parental responsibility for the child—hence, this is a far less intrusive measure than an application for a care order. A person holding PR can terminate an arrangement for accommodation at any time and without notice (Children Act 1989 s.28(8)). However, the provision of accommodation through voluntary agreement must be based on a written agreement with parents, which will likely specify actions that the local authority will take should termination of accommodation suggest that the child will be at risk of significant harm. An agreement to voluntary accommodation can be made with the young person himself/herself in cases where the child is older than sixteen years of age and the parent is objecting to this provision. Accommodation can consist of a single or multiple episodes of varying length; all children are deemed looked after whenever they are in the care of the State for more than twenty-four hours (Children Act 1989 s.22(2)). Although s.20 voluntary accommodation is seen as in keeping with the spirit of the "no order" principle within the Children Act 1989, reservations have been raised in cases where it appears the local authority is using s.20 coercively while an application for a care order is being put together. The issue at stake is that parents are not guaranteed any legal representation in cases where a child enters care on a "voluntary" basis; whereas in the court arena, parents must be afforded this protection. There is particular controversy about the use of s.20 to remove a newborn infant from a mother's care. It is not uncommon for the local authority to remove infants on this basis, given that care proceedings cannot be brought prior to a child's birth. In this context, however, s.20 accommodation can be used as a staging post en route to compulsory action (Luckock and Broadhurst, 2013). A number of high profile appeals court cases have raised significant disquiet about action that aims to secure a mother's agreement to the "voluntary" removal of her infant, within hours of actual delivery (Freel 2010). Can informed consent truly be given in these circumstances?

Children also can be removed from their parents on an emergency basis through the use of police protection powers (s.46 Children Act 1989) or through an Emergency Protection Order (EPO) granted by the court (s.44 of the Children Act 1989). Emergency action only sanctions short-term removal of a child. An EPO lasts for eight days (the local authority can apply for a limited extension but this is rarely done) whereas a child can be taken into police protection for only seventy-two hours. An application for an EPO is made by the local authority and must be sanctioned by the court, whereas this is not necessary in the case of police protection. Where a child is removed on an EPO, although this is for a limited period, the local authority must consider the child's contact with birth families and other relevant persons. The issue that has raised some controversy is that with leave (permission) of the court, the local authority can make an EPO application without first notifying parents or other persons holding parental responsibility. This has been considered to be a potential breach of parents' rights to a "fair trial" under Article 6 of the Human Rights Act 1998, but the court must balance the child's immediate need for protection with any consideration of parents' rights. Independent legal representation for the child is a key consideration regarding any EPO application, which affords an important safeguard in these circumstances. In order to secure the longer-term care of a child in out-of-home care who has been removed on an emergency basis, the local authority must apply for a care order.

CARE PROCEEDINGS: THE COURT PROCESS, SIGNIFICANT HARM, AND TIMING

The court process
The local authority applies to the court for a care order when there is concern that a child is suffering significant harm or that harm is likely without compulsory intervention. Prior to making an application, in many cases a formal

pre-proceedings process will have determined that all options other than care proceedings have been tried and have failed (cf. Broadhurst and Holt 2010 or Masson et al. 2013 for a fuller discussion). During the formal pre-proceedings process, parents will have received a letter spelling out the agency's concerns (Letter Before Proceedings) and will have had the opportunity to respond to concerns over a number of weeks or months subsequent to a formal pre-proceedings meeting. At this juncture, parents are entitled to independent legal advice. Thus, save for cases of emergency action, escalation to care proceedings following a period of pre-proceedings assessment/intervention should be of no surprise to parties in situations where positive change is not achieved.

Until very recently, all care proceedings cases started in a lower court, termed a Magistrates or Family Proceedings Court, but moved to a County or Higher court when case complexity or appeal warranted this. This three-tier court system is now replaced (from April 2014) with the single Family Court. Lay justices (magistrates) as well as judges will continue to oversee cases and make decisions, but cases will be allocated at the outset to the appropriate level of judge. Previously, delay occurred when cases transferred between tiers of the court system. A children's Guardian (specialist social worker) is appointed from the outside to ensure that the child's welfare is central to care proceedings (s.41 CA 1989) and this practice will continue in the new single Family Court.

When care proceedings are issued, the local authority brings the case and parents are the "respondents"—parents are entitled to independent legal representation throughout. The role of the court is to determine whether the threshold is met for compulsory intervention, to consider the local authority's interim and final plan for children, as well as whether that plan is in the best interests of the child. The court also will direct further assessments of parents, where additional evidence will help the court make a decision about the child's future. The care proceedings process must now be completed within twenty-six weeks, ideally comprising not more than four court hearings (DfE, 2014). In the majority of cases, a single judge will preside over cases at each sitting, unless cases are appealed and hearings take place in the High Court or Appeal Court.

Significant harm (the threshold test)

Compulsory intervention to remove a child from his or her birth parents requires that the local authority prove to the court that the child is suffering or likely to suffer significant harm. Introduced as a central concept within the Children Act 1989, this broad definition was welcomed with the implementation of the Act in 1991 (Harwin and Madge 2010). Significant harm is defined under s.31(9) of the Children Act 1989 and refers to "ill-treatment or the 'impairment of health and development.' Development is further defined as 'physical, intellectual, emotional, social or behavioural development,' health is further defined as 'physical or mental,' and ill-treatment refers to sexual abuse and forms of ill-treatment which are not physical." A key amendment to the definition of significant harm was brought forth with the Adoption and Children Act 2002, to include harm that results from seeing or hearing the ill-treatment or abuse of another in the household. This latter amendment resulted from a growing recognition of the emotional toll of domestic violence on children and impetus within the law to hold parents to account for this form of harm.

In practice, however, we are dealing not with definition but with *interpretation,* and therein lies the problem. Particular difficulties arise for both local authorities and the courts when required to consider *likely* rather than actual harm. Whereas a serious injury has a clear material reality upon which to make a case of significant harm, future developmental impairment arising from parental neglect, for example, is far harder to both measure and evidence. This difficulty explains why social workers (as an enduring trend) often appear to wait for a serious incident or event before applying to the court for care orders (Brandon et al. 2008). It is also important to grasp an "escalating threshold" in respect to how the court thinks about significant harm. Depending on the finality of the legal order in question, different evidence requirements apply. For example, the evidence requirements for interim removal will be quite different from the court's requirements at a final order hearing (for further discussion, see Prest and Wildblood 2005).

Timing

As stated, the courts are now under an obligation to start and conclude cases of care proceedings within twenty-six weeks (Children and Families Act 2014), save for the most exceptional circumstances. However, the history of care proceedings within the family court is of expensive and lengthy care proceedings (Booth 1996; Doughty 2014). The final report of the Family Justice Review (Ministry of Justice, the Department of Education and the Welsh Government 2011, para. 2.10, p. 42) reported a national average of fifty-six weeks (HMCTS FamilyMan data, January to June, 2011) for the resolution of care and supervision proceedings. Difficulties in establishing the threshold for permanent removal of children from birth parents, but also the disquiet about "draconian" intervention in family life, have resulted in protracted and expensive court proceedings. As Pearce et al. (2011) outlined, the court's preference (in recent history) has been for a consensual approach to settlement of final plans for children. Thus, the court has conceded to further, and in some cases, duplicate assessments of parents, in order to ensure a felt sense of fairness for adult parties in particular. Of course, the consequences of a settlement culture are that children have been left to drift in interim placements. Evidence in support of the changes now ushered in with the Children and Families Act 2014, which requires cases to be dealt with far more swiftly (twenty-six weeks) is that children have been left in limbo for far too long, which has served to reduce their chances of forming successful attachments in a permanent placement. Conclusions drawn from the Department for Education's *Safeguarding Research Initiative* (Ward et al. 2012), which documented significant weaknesses in local authority care planning, suggested that social workers were overly optimistic in respect to parents' capacity for change, thereby leaving children in situations of harm for too long. The problem is that longitudinal follow-up studies are scant, and many of those that are published are based on rather small, unrepresentative samples, which limits the value of follow-up work.

However, the question that lies at the heart of debate about the *timing* of child removal, is whether developmental harm resulting from neglectful parenting is *reversible* (Rutter and O'Conner 2004; Sroufe et al. 2010). This question is not new, but remains unresolved (Broadhurst and Mason, 2014). Recent policy documents indicate that neuroscientific explanations are gaining traction in policy circles. We are witnessing further emphasis on early infant development (zero to three years), based on a premise that early brain architecture is deterministic in respect to subsequent life chances (Brown and Ward 2013). Debates continue to rage, however, as to the extent to which typical childhood neglect does lead to the patterns of brain and neural impairment found in children reared in conditions of severe institutional neglect upon which such premises are based (Belsky and de Haan 2010; Wastell and White 2012). A recent comprehensive review of the empirical literature reported several limitations with studies that specifically link *child maltreatment* and brain development, suggesting that basing policy on current neuroscientific evidence is premature (McCrory et al. 2012).

EXIT ROUTES FROM PUBLIC CARE: KINSHIP CARE

For all children subject to care proceedings, the court will consider the possibility of reuniting parent and child. If reunification is not possible, however, the court will look to a placement within the extended family as the next best option. Kinship care provides a vital resource in terms of providing long-term substitute family care in England. Typically, family members or friends carers have applied for either a residence order (RO) under the Children Act 1989, or a special guardianship order (SGO) under the Adoption and Children Act 2002. With the passage of the Children and Families Act 2014, previous private law provisions under s.8 of the Children Act 1989 (notably residence and contact orders) are replaced by new statutes introduced with the Child Arrangements Programme (CAP 2014; Ministry of Justice 2014). The Child Arrangements Programme (CAP) is a further attempt to encourage families to settle safe and child-focused arrangements for children, without recourse to a court order; a "settlement" culture applies to both parents/families in dispute but also in respect to safeguarding concerns. It is recognized that negotiated agreements between adults generally enhance long-term cooperation and are better for children. Where there are safeguarding concerns, however, and an order is necessary, the court can make a child arrangements order (Children Act 1989, s.8(1) as revised by the Children and Families Act, 2014, s.12). A child arrangements order will prescribe "with whom a child is to live, spend time or otherwise have contact." Critics have suggested that the change from provisions previously provided under s.8 of the Children Act 1989 may be purely semantic—but only time will tell.

Special Guardianship was introduced with the Adoption and Children Act 2002, although not formally implemented until 2005. Research indicated that there was a significant group, comprising mainly older children, who did not wish to make the absolute legal break with their birth family that is associated with adoption, but who would benefit from a legal status that would offer a more lasting sense of permanence. Special Guardianship was seen to provide a greater level of legal security than long-term fostering (DfE 2005). Where a special guardianship order (SGO) is made, the special guardian gains parental responsibility for the child until he/she reaches the age of eighteen years. In the case of either a child arrangement order or an SGO, where a child was previously in the care of the state, they are no longer the responsibility of the local authority. The advantage of these extended family arrangements is that they are seen to provide greater continuity for children, often resulting in less disruption to schooling and peer networks and affording contact with birth parents. There is long-standing concern, however, that kin networks are not properly supported by local authorities and are treated as a "second class" service when compared with foster care (Hunt and Waterhouse 2012). This is concerning, because the evidence remains strong that kinship placements can deliver more positive outcomes for children, than non-kin placements (Winokur et al. 2014). Where the local authority feels that there are residual concerns about a family or friends placement, a Supervision Order can be made, in tandem with the private law order (Children Act 1989).

The Children Act 1989 is now in its twenty-third year since implementation, but the law has changed little in respect to the *positive duty* to promote contact between a looked-after child and those closely connected with the child—birth parents and family and friends networks. S.34 of the Children Act 1989 lays out the statute relating to this duty based on the notion of "reasonable" contact. Successive case law precedents have given further weight to the general principle that during the early weeks of a child's entry to care, reasonable contact ought to mean *frequent contact*, with a view to reunification of parent and child. In this context, kinship care also is favored because it is seen to offer the best chance of maintaining family ties.

EXIT FROM PUBLIC CARE: ADOPTION

Recent years have seen cross-party political support for adoption as the preferred permanency option for infants and young children who cannot be cared for by their birth parents or within extended family networks. Since the launch of the former Blair Government's review of adoption (Performance and Innovation Unit 2000), there has been sustained policy interest in speeding up the adoption process and increasing the number of infants and children adopted from public care. Successive governments have set targets for local authorities to incentivize adoption, with the Blair government initially proposing that 40 percent of all children in care should be placed for adoption. The current Coalition Government has again sought to stimulate this permanency option, in light of falling numbers of children placed for adoption. A significant overhaul of legislation and statutory guidance has taken place. The single over-riding goal made explicit in the recent Adoption Action Plan (DfE 2012), is that infants and children should be placed as soon as possible with a permanent family. Indeed, foster carers who also are approved as potential adopters should be considered for all infants and young children entering care, under the government's controversial "foster to adopt" scheme. This is a further attempt to avoid what is seen as long-term drift in public care (see "Placement of looked after children with prospective adopters," Children and Families Act 2014, s.2).

Statutory duties and powers in respect of adoption are set out in the Adoption and Children Act 2002. Controversial at the time of its inception, was the proposed threshold for the making of a "placement order"—that is, an order made prior to the placement of a child for adoption, which serves to dispense with parental consent to adoption (where parents do not offer this freely). The threshold for making a placement order is that:

(a) The case must satisfy the conditions for the making of a care order (s.31(2) of the CA 1989) and
(b) The welfare of the child requires that parental consent is dispensed with (ACA 2002 Act, s.52(1)(b)).

Parents can contest a placement order, and the majority of cases of adoption can be described as nonconsensual. For the year ending 2013, only 330 cases record "placed for adoption with consent" out of 3,350 children (0.28 per 1,000 children) subject to a plan for adoption. Parents who do not actively contest may formally disagree with a plan for adoption in their final evidence—but the precise number of parents who opt for this position at the final hearing is not known (Luckock and Broadhurst 2012).

The Act also has been controversial because once a placement order is made, parents have no subsequent automatic right to contest an adoption order— rather, they must apply for leave of the court to oppose an application made by adopters. Birth parents are only granted leave if they can evidence change of circumstances (s.47(7) Adoption and Children Act 2002). There has been little systematic research analysis of how many birth parents seek leave to contest at this later stage—although some evidence that even when parents do show change in circumstances, this will most likely be deemed too late if children are settled with adopters (Luckock and Broadhurst 2012). Although children subject to placement orders are the smallest population (9,240 year ending March 31, 2013), there is a marked upward trend in the use of these orders. Between 2009 and 2013, was a *95 percent increase* in the number of children subject to placement orders, which is most likely accounted for by the further endorsement and incentivization of adoption by the current Coalition Government (DfE 2013).

Final legal status is profoundly consequential because of the impact on parental rights and contact. If a child is adopted, birth parents have their rights removed, permanently. When an adoption order is made, the court must sanction the local authority's plan for contact and, in the case of infants and very young children, the court will frequently agree to indirect (letter box) contact only. Although there is clear evidence that the general stability of a positive adoptive placement can lead to marked improvement for children who have experienced developmental harm (Rushton 2007), nonconsensual adoption brings issues of proportionality and fairness into sharp focus because birth parents typically will lose direct contact with their children. The Supreme Court recently has reiterated that nonconsensual adoption must always be a last resort, only sanctioned when all other placement options have been explored and the child's welfare demands this option (Re B-S (Children) [2013] EWCA Civ 1146). New findings from Neil et al. (2014) have raised further questions about established practice, because longitudinal research has shown that direct contact can benefit all parties in cases of adoption.

The largely nonconsensual adoption process in England and Wales has much in common with policy in the United States, but stands in strong contrast to that in many European countries. "Forced adoption" is not an option in Finland or Germany and rarely used in Sweden. That young children appear at an increasing risk of being removed from their birth parents is of national concern, particularly in cases where vulnerable birth mothers lose *successive* infants to public care and adoption. Recent research has found that in 42 percent of these cases infants became subject to proceedings at or very close to birth, which raises the question of what chance this population of mothers (and fathers) have of being reunified with their infants. In only a very small percentage of cases were supervision orders made (9 percent), suggesting that in the vast majority of cases infants found permanency in out-of-home care (Broadhurst et al. 2014).

SEPARATE REPRESENTATION OF CHILDREN

Separate representation for children is an important cornerstone of public law proceedings in England (s.41, Children Act 1989). In 1984, the role of the Guardian ad litem in care proceedings was created. The stimulus for this landmark development was the death of Maria Colwell—a child returned to the care of her mother but subsequently killed by her mother's partner. Following a Public Inquiry (DHSS, 1974), formal legislative change served to augment children's rights within public law proceedings. Every child subject to care proceedings now has full party status and is entitled to separate representation. In 1991, England agreed to be bound by the United Nations Convention on the Rights of the Child (UNCRC), giving further emphasis to the voice of the child within family proceedings. In 2001, a new centrally managed Children's Guardian service was created named the Child and Family Court Advisory and Support Service (Cafcass). Despite a somewhat checkered history and suffering acute shortage in funding in the context of rising care demand, the "in tandem"[1] model of support for children delivered by Cafcass aims to ensure that the child's welfare is the court's paramount consideration. Independent representation for children remains a vital safeguard within the English family court, ensuring the child's best interests remain central to proceedings.

THE FAMILY COURT IN ENGLAND: NEW DIRECTIONS AND ALTERNATIVE MODELS

Given England's commitment, within law and policy, to placing the child at the center of legislation, the passage of recent legislation (Children and Families Act 2014) that has led to the setting up of a dedicated single Family Court appears long overdue. The fact that cases concerning children are now much more likely to be overseen by the same judge is undoubtedly a very welcome development and will ensure more effective adjudication. In many respects, however, new legislation shores up, rather than radically reimagines child welfare and family justice. It is yet to be seen whether systemic change will prevail, but arguably for parents and children, the tradition of the court in respect to the complexity of legal language and rules will continue to alienate. Hunt's (2010) recent and comprehensive review of the literature concerning parental perspectives on family justice documents this alienation in detail.

A promising new direction has emerged, however, in the form of the Family Drug and Alcohol Court or FDAC. This alternative court model is based on a problem-solving approach to care proceedings—the input of lawyers is radically reduced in favor of close and regular engagement of the judge with families working alongside an interdisciplinary, independent treatment team. Detailed evidence from a five-year evaluation reveals that the families graduating from FDAC are more likely to be reunified with their children and have a far more positive experience of the court process (Harwin et al. 2013; 2014). Of particular importance is the fact that the President of the Family Division (England's leading judge, L. J. Munby) very recently expressed his wish for FDACs to be set up in all forty-four Designated Family Judge areas in England. This was swiftly followed by major central government funding, which has seen the launch of the Family Drug and Alcohol Court Development National Unit. Embedding FDACs nationally will introduce a radically different approach to family justice in cases where care proceedings are brought. The FDAC court has the authority to make the same decisions as those made in ordinary courts, but the emphasis is on the court's rehabilitative potential, which is where practice departs from routine proceedings. In addition, the FDAC court will recommend that proceedings extend beyond twenty-six weeks, where parents clearly show potential for change. Closer, more effective engagement of parents enables the FDAC court to have a realistic sense of parents' capacity for change and the likelihood of child reunification. Parental substance misuse is the leading cause of child abuse and neglect in the United Kingdom, but parents can clearly benefit from evidence-based treatments, which FDAC currently delivers.

CONCLUSION

Constant reform is a consistent feature of the English child protection system. The Children Act 1989, which came into effect in October 1991, has survived successive reforms but there are few sections of the Act's 108 original sections that have not been subject to amendment (Doughty 2010). Endless reform of primary and secondary legislation creates a hugely challenging environment for practitioners who are quickly called to account where a child falls through the net of protective services. Austerity has undoubtedly magnified the challenges of child protection work, such that problems of staff retention are again to the fore (ADCS 2014). For all the aspirations toward an evidence-based system of family justice, a dearth of robust longitudinal studies or even the administrative structures to enable analysts to link essential datasets across government departments means that political/ideological ideas can often hold sway in the absence of good science (McGhee et al. 2013). England is still searching for the answers to long-standing debates about the reversibility of early adversity, the factors that lead to positive turning points for high-risk parents (Broadhurst and Mason 2014), and the reasons why public care is unable to deliver better outcomes for a larger percentage of children. Where the volume of applications for care proceedings remains high, however, resources inevitably are devoted to compulsory intervention, at the expense of prevention. Long-term support for children on the "edge of care" has become politically unpalatable in England, yet evidence from tried and tested preventative interventions (Grant et al. 2014) suggests that sustained support for parents over a period of three years is required to effect lasting change. As I write, England has embarked on an ambitious program of transforming children's services; it will be interesting to see whether promising new directions can be fostered and sustained through this innovative program.

NOTE

1

REFERENCES

Allen, G. (2007). *Making Sense of the New Adoption Law: A Guide for Social and Welfare Services.* Dorset: Russell House Publishing.

All Parliamentary Group (APPG) for Runaway and Missing Children and Adults and the APPG for Looked After Children and Care Leavers. (2012). *Report from the Joint Inquiry into Children Missing from Care.* Retrieved September 1, 2014 from http://www.childrenssociety.org.uk/sites/default/files/tcs/u32/joint_appg_inquiry_-_report...pdf

Association of Directors of Children's Services (ADCS). (2014). *Safeguarding Pressures, Phase 4.* Retrieved September 9, 2014 from http://www.adcs.org.uk/download/news/adcs-sg-pressures-p4-report-final.pdf

Belsky, J. and de Haan, M. (2010)."Annual Research Review: Parenting and Children's Brain Development: The End of the Beginning." *The Journal of Child Psychology and Psychiatry* 53(4): 409–428.

Berridge, D., Biehal, N., and Henry, L. W. (2012). *Living in Residential Care.* London: Department for Education.

Booth, D. M. (1996). *Avoiding Delay in Children Act Cases,* London: Lord Chancellor's Department.

Brandon, M., Belderson, P., Warren, C., Howe, D., Gardner, R., Dodsworth, J., and Black, J. (2008). *Analysing Child Deaths and Serious Injury through Abuse and Neglect: What Can We Learn? A Biennial Analysis of Serious Case Reviews 2003–2005.* London: Department for Children Schools and Families. Retrieved September 5, 2014 from http://dera.ioe.ac.uk/7190/1/dcsf-rr023.pdf

Broadhurst, K., Grover, C., and Jamieson, J. (2009). *Critical Perspectives on Safeguarding Children.* Oxford: Wiley-Blackwell.

Broadhurst, K. and Holt, K. E. (2010). "Partnership and the Limitations of Procedure: Prospects for Parents and Professionals under the New Public Law Outline." *Child and Family Social Work,* 15(1): 97–106.

Broadhurst, K. and Mason, C. (2014). "11 Birth Mothers against the Odds: Turning Points for Women Who Have Lost Children to Public Care." *Family Law,* November: 1572–1576.

Broadhurst, K., Harwin, J., Alrouh, B., and Shaw, M. (2014). "Capturing the Scale and Pattern of Recurrent Care Proceedings: Initial Observations from a Feasibility Study." *Family Law,* June. Retrieved September 10, 2013 from: http://www.familylaw.co.uk/news_and_comment/capturing-the-scale-and-pattern-of-recurrent-care-proceedings-initial-observations-from-a-feasibility-study#.

Brown, R. and Ward, H. (2013). *Decision-making Within a Child's Timeframe: An Overview of Current Research Evidence for Family Justice Professionals Concerning Child Development and the Impact of Maltreatment*. Working Paper 16. Childhood Wellbeing Research Centre. Retrieved September 10, 2013 from http://www.cwrc.ac.uk/resources/773.html

The Care Inquiry. (2013). *Making Not Breaking: Building Relationships for Our Most Vulnerable Children*. London: The Nuffield Foundation. Retrieved August 28, 2014 from http://www.frg.org.uk/images/Policy_Papers/care-inquiry-full-report-april-2013.pdf

Department for Education. (2012). *An Action Plan for Adoption: Tackling Delay*. London: Department for Education. Retrieved September 30, 2014 from http://media.education.gov.uk/assets/files/pdf/a/an%20action%20plan%20for%20adoption.pdf

Department for Education. (2013). *Children Looked After in England, Including Adoption*. London: Department for Education. Retrieved September 1, 2014 from https://www.gov.uk/government/statistics/children-looked-after-in-england-including-adoption

Department for Education. (2014). *Court Orders and Pre-Proceedings for Local Authorities*. Retrieved November 17, 2014 from https://www.gov.uk/government/uploads/system/uploads/attachment_data/file/306282/Statutory_guidance_on_court_orders_and_pre-proceedings.pdf

Department of Health and Social Security (DHSS). (1974). *Report of the Committee of Inquiry into the Care and Supervision Provided in Relation to Maria Colwell*. London: Department of Health and Social Security.

Doughty, J. (2010). "Amendments to the Legislation 1989–2009." *Journal of Children's Services*, 5(2): 7–16.

Doughty, J. (2014). "Care Proceedings: Is There a Better Way?" *Child and Family Law Quarterly*, 26(2): 113–131.

Freel, M. (201) "Baby K's Unlawful Removal: Practice Issues in the Emergency Protection of Children." *Child Abuse Review*, 19: 158–168.

McGhee, J., Mitchell, F., Daniel, B., and Taylor, J. (2013). "Taking a Long View in Child Welfare: How Can we Evaluate Intervention and Child Wellbeing over Time?" *Child Abuse Review*, 24(2): 95–106.

Gilbert, N., Parton, N., and Skivenes, M. (2011). *Child Protection Systems: International Trends and Emerging Orientations*. New York: Oxford University Press.

Grant, T. M., Graham, J. C., Ernst, C. C., Peavy, K. M., and Brown, N. N. (2014). Improving Pregnancy Outcomes Among High-Risk Mothers Who Abuse Alcohol and Drugs: Factors Associated with Subsequent Exposed Births. *Children and Youth Services Review*, 46: 11–18.

Hall, E. and Guy, J. (2009). *The Baby Peter Effect and the Increase in S.31 Care Order Applications*. London: Cafcass.

Harwin, J., Alrouh, B., Ryan, M., and Tunnard, J. (2014). *Changing Lifestyles, Keeping Children Safe: An Evaluation of the First Family Drug and Alcohol Court (FDAC) in Care Proceedings.* London: Brunel University. Retrieved September 10, 2014 from www.nuffieldfoundation.org/evaluation-pilot-family-drug-and-alcohol-court).

Harwin, J., Alrouh, B., Ryan, M., and Tunnard, J. (2013). "Strengthening Prospects for Safe and Lasting Family Reunification: Can a Family Drug and Alcohol Court Make a Contribution?" *Journal of Social Welfare and Family Law,* 35(4): 459–474.

Harwin, J. and Madge, N. (2010). "The Concept of Significant Harm in Law and Practice." *Journal of Children's Services,* 5(2): 73–83.

House of Commons Home Affairs Committee. (2013). *Child Sexual Exploitation and the Response to Localized Grooming, Second Report of Session 2013–2014.* Retrieved 1. 0. 2014 from http://www.publications.parliament.uk/pa/cm201314/cmselect/cmhaff/68/68i.pdf

Hunt, J. (2010). "Parental Perspectives on the Family Justice System in England and Wales: A Review of Research." Retrieved September 10, 2014 from http://www.judiciary.gov.uk/wp-content/uploads/JCO/Documents/FJC/Publications/Parental_Perspectives_final.pdf

Hunt, J. and Waterhouse, S. (2012). "Understanding Family and Friends Care: The Relationship between Need Support and Legal Status—Carer's Experiences." (FRG/Oxford Centre for Family Law and Policy) http://www.frg.org.uk/images/e-publications/ffc-report-1.pdf

Institute for Fiscal Studies. (2011). "Child and Working-age Poverty from 2010–2020." Retrieved September 10, 2014 from http://www.ifs.org.uk/comms/comm121.pdf

Institute for Fiscal Studies. (2013). "Living Standards, Poverty and Inequality in the UK." Retrieved September 11, 2014 from http://www.ifs.org.uk/comms/r81.pdf

Lord Chancellor's Department. (2012). *Scoping Study on Delay in Children Act Cases: Findings and Actions Taken.* London: Lord Chancellor's Department. 2002; Ofsted, *Right on Time: Exploring Delays in adoption, Ofsted, 2012*: www.ofsted.gov.uk

Luckock, B. and Broadhurst, K. (2013). *Adoption Cases Reviewed: An Indicative Study of Process and Practice.* Project Report. London: Department of Education. Retrieved September 6, 2014 from https://www.gov.uk/government/uploads/system/uploads/attachment_data/file/191002/DfE-RR270.pdf

Macleod, S., Hart, R., Jeffes, J., and Wilkin, A. (2010). *Local Government Education and Children's Services Research Programme: The Impact of the Baby Peter Case on Applications for Care Orders.* London: Local Government Association.

Masson, J., Pearce, J., Bader, K., Joyner, O., Marsden, J., and Westlake, D. (2008). Care Profiling Study. Ministry of Justice. Retrieved November 11, 2014 from http://www.bristol.ac.uk/media-library/sites/law/migrated/documents/care-profiling-study-report.pdf

Masson, J. and Dickens, J. (with K. Bader and J. Young). (2013). *Partnership by Law? The Pre-Proceedings Process for Families on the Edge of Care Proceedings* (Report of ESRC RES-062-2226). Bristol: School of Law, University of Bristol and Centre for Research on Children and Families, University of East Anglia.

McCrory, S. De Brito, and Viding, E. (2012). "The Link between Child Abuse and Psychopathology: A Review of Neurobiological and Genetic Research." *Journal of the Royal Society of Medicine,* 105: 151–156.

Ministry of Justice, the Department of Education, and the Welsh Government. (2011). *Family Justice Review.* Final Report. Retrieved September 9, 2014 from https://www.gov.uk/government/uploads/system/uploads/attachment_data/file/217343/family-justice-review-final-report.pdf

Ministry of Justice, Practice Direction 12B, Child Arrangements Programme. http://www.justice.gov.uk/courts/procedure-rules/family/practice_directions/pd_part_12b

Munro, E. (2011). *The Munro Review of Child Protection: Final Report.* London: Department for Education.

Munro, E. (2012). *Progress Report: Moving Towards a Child-Centred System.* London: Department for Education.

National Scientific Council on the Developing Child. (2004). *Children's Emotional Development is Built into the Architecture of the Brain*: Working Paper No. 2. Retrieved August 1, 2014 from http://www.developingchild.net.

Neil, B., Beek, M., and Ward, E. (2014). *Contact after Adoption: A Longitudinal Study of Adopted Young People and Their Adoptive Parents and Birth Relatives.* London: BAAF.

Office of National Statistics. (2014). Annual Mid-year Population Estimates 2013. Statistical Bulletin. Retrieved July 9, 2014 from http://www.ons.gov.uk/ons/dcp171778_367167.pdf

Owen, C. and Statham, J. (2009). *Disproportionality in Child Welfare: The Prevalence of Black and Minority Ethnic Children within the "Looked After" and "Children in Need" Populations and on Child Protection Registers in England.* Research Report DCSF-RR124. Retrieved September 9, 2014 from http://dera.ioe.ac.uk/11152/1/DCSF-RR124.pdf

Parton, N. and Berridge, D. (2011). "Child Protection in England." In Gilbert, N., Parton, N., and Skivenes, M. (Eds.), *Child Protection Systems: International Trends and Emerging Orientations*), pp. 60–85. New York: Oxford University Press.

Pearce, J., Masson, J., and Bader, K. (2011). "Just Following Instructions? The Representation of Parents in Care Proceedings." Retrieved September 9, 2014 from http://www.bristol.ac.uk/law/people/judith-m-masson/pub/2860102

Performance and Innovation Unit. (2000). *Prime Minister's Review of Adoption: Report from the Performance Unit.* London: HMSO.

Prest, C. and Wildblood, S. (2005). *Children Law: An Interdisciplinary Handbook*. London: Jordan Publishing.

Re, B-S (Children) [2013] EWCA Civ 1146). Retrieved September 19, 2014 from http://www.bailii.org/ew/cases/EWCA/Civ/2013/1146.html

Rushton, A. (2007). "Outcomes of Adoption from Public Care: Research and Practice Issues." *Advances in Psychiatric Treatment*, 13: 305–311.

Rutter, M. and O'Connor, T. G. (2004). "Are There Biological Programming Effects for Psychological Development? Findings from a Study of Romanian Adoptees." *Developmental Psychology* 40: 81–94.

Selwyn, J., Quinton, D., Harris, P., Wijedesa, D., Nawaz, S., and Wood, M. (2010). *Pathways to Permanence for Black, Asian and Mixed Ethnicity Children*. London: British Association of Adoption and Fostering

Sroufe, L. A., Coffino, B., and Carlson, E. A. (2010). "Conceptualising the Role of Early Experience: Lessons from the Minnesota Longitudinal Study." *Developmental Review* 30: 36–51.

Utting, D. 2007. *Parenting and the Different Ways It Can Affect Children's Lives: Research Evidence*. Joseph Rowntree Foundation.

Wade, I., Sinclair, J., Dixon, A., and Richards, A. (2009). *Characteristics, Outcomes and Meanings of Three Types of Permanent Placements: Adoption by Strangers, Adoption by Carers and Long-Term Foster Care*. Research Brief DCSF-RBX-09-11. Retrieved July 1, 2014 from www.adoptionresearchinitiative.org.uk/study1.html.

Ward, H., Brown, R., and Westlake, D. (2012). *Safeguarding Babies and Very Young Children from Abuse and Neglect*. London: Jessica Kingsley Publishers.

Wastell, D. and White, S. (2012). "Blinded by Neuroscience: Social Policy, the Family and the Infant Brain." *Families, Relationships and Societies*, 18: 397–414.

White, S., Morris, K., Featherstone, B., Brandon, M., and Thoburn, J. (2014). "Re-imagining Early Help: Looking Forward, Looking Back." In Blyth, M. (Ed.), *Moving on from Munro: Improving Children's Services*. Bristol: Policy Press.

Winokur, M., Holtan, A., and Batchelder, K. (2014). *Kinship Care for the Safety, Permanence and Well-Being of Children Removed from the Home for Maltreatment: A Systematic Review*. The Campbell Library. Retrieved September 9, 2014 from http://www.campbellcollaboration.org/lib/project/51/

9

HOW CHILDREN ARE REMOVED FROM HOME IN THE UNITED STATES

Katrin Križ, Janese Free, and Grant Kuehl

INTRODUCTION

It is certainly no exaggeration to state that the United States fares poorly in terms of children's well-being compared with other countries in the developed world: The 2013 UNICEF *Innocenti Report Card*, which measures child well-being along five dimensions, including material well-being, ranks the United States as number 26 out of 29 Organization for Economic Co-operation and Development (OECD) countries overall—followed only by Lithuania, Latvia, and Romania. The most recent *Report Card* (2014), which examines the impact of the economic recession on children in the developed world, showed that child poverty rose in thirty-four U.S. states between 2006 and 2011. These statistics are concerning because it is well-documented that poverty is associated with child maltreatment (Drake and Rank 2009; Duva and Metzger 2010; Fluke et al. 2011; Pelton 1978; Shook 1999); and that child abuse and neglect may entail long-term negative consequences for children and society overall (Goldman et al. 2003; Pecora et al. 2013). In the United States, 16.1 million children (or 21.9 percent of all children under the age of eighteen years) live in poverty (DeNavas-Walt et al. 2012). Given the high number of children in poverty, it is salient to analyze the processes by which the state, through public child protection agencies and the courts, makes decisions affecting the lives of children who have been neglected and abused—especially when removing children from their caregivers to protect them from abuse and neglect.

This chapter examines how these decisions are made in the context of the United States. It does so in the following way: First, we will provide some background information about the policy framework and legal platform that undergird the child protection system in the United States before mapping out the key agents, institutional processes, and main steps involved in the process of removing children from home. We will use the Commonwealth of Massachusetts, the state the authors live in, as the case to illustrate the institutions and processes involved in decisions about removing children. We will analyze the challenges and blind spots of the system and provide statistics related to child removals.

POLICY FRAMEWORK AND LEGISLATION

Child protection policy

The United States is considered a liberal or residual welfare regime—a social policy regime type that targets public services primarily at the most disadvantaged with the help of means-testing. This targeted public funding is at a level that is less generous than in the Scandinavian countries, where public services tend to be generous and universal (i.e., not means-tested) (Aspalter 2011; Esping-Anderson 1990). Given that the U.S. child protection system is embedded within a liberal welfare regime, it is not surprising that it is primarily focused on intervening to protect children—targeting those who are most at risk, with comparatively high thresholds for intervention—and then providing services toward family reunification, instead of offering generous universal services that aim at preventing child abuse and neglect in the first place, as family service-oriented countries do (Gilbert et al. 2011).

The principles guiding child protection services in the United States, as defined by federal law, are children's safety, permanency, and well-being with the goal of meeting the "best interests of the child" (Berrick 2011). The safety principle underscores that children must be protected from abuse and neglect and cared for safely in their homes whenever possible. Children are supposed to live in a stable living environment that maintains family connections and continuity in relationships with a caregiver—this is what the law views as "permanency" (Berrick 2011). In cases where a child needs to be removed from home because of safety concerns, the law underscores that the primary permanency goal is to reunify the child with a birth parent or other extended family members (Berrick 2011). The principle "child and family well-being" means that children should receive services that meet their educational, physical, and mental health needs; and that their families should have access to services that ensure that they are able to take care of their children (Berrick 2011; Reed and Karpilow 2009).

In the U.S. context, however, it is also important to mention the large variation in the implementation of federal child protection policy in public child protection agencies across the country—there is no centralized or national child protection system. There are federally mandated regulations and minimum standards to address child abuse, services, out-of-home placements, and adoption; however, each state interprets and implements the legislation differently (Berrick 2011). It is, therefore, not surprising that states and counties show different trends regarding the number of children in out-of-home care; for instance, in terms of outcomes at the county level, only ten counties (out of 3,000 counties and county equivalents) accounted for one-half of the decline in foster care rates between 2002 and 2012. In terms of state variation, three states (California, New York, and Florida) were responsible for over 50 percent of the decline in the number of children in foster care in the country during the same time period (U.S. Department of Health and Human Services 2013a). Similarly, there was wide variation in the use of congregate care (i.e., group home or institution) across U.S. states between 2004 and 2013: Five states increased congregate care use, twenty-two states decreased it by 7 percent to 36 percent, and twenty-four states decreased it by more than 37 percent (U.S. Department of Health and Human Services 2015).

Federal legislation

Several important laws outline how children ought to be protected in the United States by defining the minimum threshold for abuse and neglect and establishing timelines for the review of the case process: the Child Abuse Prevention and Treatment Act of 1974 (PL 93-247) (CAPTA), the Adoption Assistance and Child Welfare Act of 1980 (PL-96-272), and the Adoptions and Safe Families Act (ASFA) of 1997 (PL-105-89). We will discuss these laws below.

CAPTA

CAPTA (1974), as amended by the 2010 CAPTA Reauthorization Act, is salient in the context of child removal because it defines the minimum thresholds for child abuse and neglect under federal law. States that accept CAPTA funding develop their own definitions of abuse and neglect within their civil and criminal statutes (Child Welfare Information Gateway [CWIG] 2011a). Under CAPTA (1974) (42 U.S.C.A. § 5106g), child abuse and neglect are defined as "any recent act or failure to act on the part of a parent or caretaker, which results in death, serious physical or emotional harm, sexual abuse, or exploitation, or an act or failure to act which presents an imminent risk of serious harm" (CWIG 2011a, pp. 1–2). The Commonwealth of Massachusetts defines child abuse and neglect in regulation, while all other states provide civil definitions in statute (CWIG 2011a).

CAPTA ensures that court proceedings and agency records remain confidential; it also guarantees that a child who has been maltreated and whose case is heard in court is entitled to a Guardian ad Litem (GAL), an attorney, or a Court-Appointed Special Advocate (CASA) (CWIG 2012; Jones 2006). CASAs are often professionals with a background in education, nursing, or psychology (Child Welfare Information Gateway 2014; Jones 2006).[1] In lieu of a GAL or a CASA, children also may be represented by a lawyer in court, depending on State law or local practice (Jones 2006). In Massachusetts, a lawyer is automatically appointed to children and parents in care and protection proceedings (Parents Helping Parents 2010); if parents are unable to afford a lawyer—these parents are defined as "indigent" in regulations, procedures, and the academic literature—they have a right to a court-appointed lawyer. Poor and low-income parents, however, do not have the right to a free court-appointed attorney in all States (CWIG n.d. *The Court System and Child Abuse and Neglect*).

The 1980 Adoption Assistance and Child Welfare Act

This piece of legislation is particularly pertinent to the topic of child removal because it nationalized many rules pertaining to foster care and sought "to prevent the unnecessary placement of children in foster care; reunify families whenever possible; and reduce the time that children spend in foster care by encouraging adoption when reunification was not possible" (Freundlich 1999, p. 97). The Act reduced timelines in the permanency planning process by making States' receipt of federal foster care matching funds conditional on the fact that "States make 'reasonable efforts' to prevent removal of the child from home and return those who have been removed as soon as possible" (CWIG n.d. *Adoption Assistance and Child Welfare Act of 1980 P.L. 96-272*). Importantly, the law outlined review timelines for children in care: the status of every child who had been placed in a setting that was not permanent required a court or agency review (also called administrative review) every six months. The review was to be conducted with the best interests of the child in mind, and with a focus on returning the child home as soon as possible. In addition, the court was required to determine the future status of the child (return home, continued foster care, or adoption) within eighteen months after the child was first placed into foster care (CWIG n.d. *Adoption Assistance and Child Welfare Act of 1980 P.L. 96-272*).

The 1997 Adoptions and Safe Families Act (ASFA)

ASFA was the legislative result of a shift in child welfare policy in the 1990s that favored the use of termination of parental rights more frequently and more quickly (Freundlich 1999). The law, which sought to encourage the adoption of children in foster care through incentive funds and a requirement for States to make reasonable efforts toward the permanent placement of children in foster care, tightened timelines to accelerate permanency placements: If a child is in foster care for at least fifteen of the most recent twenty-two months (except in cases where the child is cared for by a relative or it is not in the best interest of the child), States are required to commence Termination of Parental Rights (TPR) court proceedings so a child can move toward adoption (CWIG n.d. *Adoption and Safe Families Act of 1997*). Freundlich (1999) describes a possible unintended consequence of the TPR process as outlined in the law:

"The adversarial process through which a birth parent is stripped of all rights to her child necessarily carries with it financial and psychological burdens including the court, attorney, expert witness, and other costs associated with litigation. In some cases, there are, as well, appeals and heavy emotional toll on birth parents, children, and agency staff exacted by a process designed to prove the parent a failure." (p. 104)

This quote suggests that the adversarial nature of the process may have hidden emotional and financial costs to children, parents, and society overall.

DECISION-MAKING AGENTS

Child protection agencies

In the following, we will discuss how child protection agencies and the courts are involved in making decisions about removing children from their homes on a temporary and permanent basis. We will use examples from the Department of Children and Families (DCF), the public agency charged with child protection in the Commonwealth of Massachusetts, and from the Massachusetts juvenile courts to describe the role of these institutions in the decision-making processes involved in removing children from home. Child protection agencies and courts must take numerous steps when removing a child from home for safety concerns. These are summarized in the following quote from an online training manual for child protection caseworkers by *Child and Family Services Reviews Information Portal (2007)*:

"Cases begin with a petition, or **initial pleading**, before a court. Following that, there is an **initial hearing**, which is where the court determines whether the child should be placed into foster care or remain in the home. If the child is to be placed in foster care or receive additional services from the agency, then an **adjudication hearing** will be scheduled to hear evidence supporting the petition. At the **disposition hearing**, which may occur simultaneously with the adjudication hearing or shortly afterward, the court determines which specific services the child and family should receive. **Review hearings,** to review progress in the case, take place, at a minimum, every six months. **Permanency hearings** must begin within twelve months of adjudication, and after that are held every twelve months to determine progress toward achieving permanency for the child and family." (no page number)

The intake and investigation processes follow this trajectory: Child protection agencies respond to an allegation of child maltreatment with an investigation that gathers evidence about cases of child maltreatment; assesses children's safety and future risk of harm; and decides on the level of services and/or intervention (Berrick 2011). The social worker and/or law enforcement officer can remove a child from home (Pence and Wilson 1992; U.S. Department of Justice 2001). In most states, Child Protective Services (CPS) workers and police officers work together formally or informally during an investigation. Two states, Arkansas and Florida (in several counties), established special offices in police departments (Arkansas) and sheriff's offices (Florida) in the late 1990s to deal with child protection investigations (Cross, Finkelhor, and Ormrod 2005). In the course of an investigation into the reported maltreatment, it is typically a public child protection agency, in consultation with the agency attorney or an intake officer (a court employee), that makes the decision to remove a child from home if the child's safety is at risk; the agency then files a petition with the court to take custody of the child if it considers it necessary to protect the child from significant harm (CWIG n.d. *The Court System and Child Abuse and Neglect*). Children can be removed without advance notice to parents through so-called "emergency custody orders" (CWIG n.d. *The Court System and Child Abuse and Neglect*). According to Jones (2006), "most removals are authorized by *ex parte* orders and the first hearing is conducted after the removal has occurred" (p. 25).

In Massachusetts, the most frequent process through which a child can be removed from home is through court custody pursuant a care and protection petition in juvenile court. (This process is referred to as "protective care.") Children also first come into the care of DCF as a result of a Voluntary Placement Agreement (VPA); as a result of parents signing an adoption surrender; and as a result of a third party seeking custody of the child (Commonwealth of Massachusetts DCF 2013). VPAs are used in cases that do not involve protective concerns or questions about parental competency; they revolve primarily around the child's developmental or behavioral disability and when the parent requests the placement or agrees to it (Commonwealth of Massachusetts DCF 2013; Children First Advocacy 2011). Child in Need of Services (CHINS) cases (termed "Child Requiring Assistance" [CRA] cases after a change in law in 2012) are cases in which parents or a school seek services. CRA cases involve children between six and eighteen years of age who repeatedly fail to follow reasonable home rules or repeatedly run away from home; repeatedly fail to follow school rules or fail to attend school for more than eight days in a school quarter; and children who have been subjected to sexual exploitation (Children's Law Center of Massachusetts 2013).

Most care and protection cases begin as a result of DCF receiving a report of child abuse and neglect, called a "51A report." DCF will either "screen in" or "screen out" the report. DCF will screen out a report if the reported actions are not considered child abuse or neglect as stipulated by law (Children's Law Center of Massachusetts 2014). If a report is screened in, it either can be screened

in for initial assessment (following the "alternative response" route), or for investigation. If a case is screened in for initial assessment, DCF begins a "family
assessment" and will offer services to the family (Massachusetts Law Reform
Institute 2005). Alternative response is a CPS practice that allows for multiple
methods of initial response to reports of child abuse and neglect. It is also referred to as "differential response" or "dual track." This approach recognizes
the variation in severity of reports and allows for different responses to different
types of cases (CWIG 2008). If, on the other hand, the report is screened in for
investigation, DCF conducts an investigation and decides whether or not the
child is currently unsafe and an emergency response is required to protect the
child from immediate risk of harm. If this is the case and DCF seeks to obtain
temporary custody of the child, the social worker prepares a written statement (an affidavit), which is reviewed and revised by the Department Attorney
before it is filed with the court (Children's Law Center of Massachusetts 2014;
Commonwealth of Massachusetts, Department of Children and Families 2013).
Emergency custody hearings should be held within seventy-two hours after the
child has been removed (Massachusetts Trial Court Law Libraries 2007).

The courts
The roles and functions of courts
Juvenile courts make decisions about whether children have been maltreated
and whether children should be (temporarily or permanently) removed from
home. Courts also intervene in family life in cases involving a child's labor,
school attendance, or other situations that affect the well-being of a child. They
monitor cases by reviewing the progress of the family and assessing the performance of the child protection services agency involved in a case. Most juvenile courts also hear Termination of Parental Rights (TPR) cases and deal
with adoptions. Cases of child abuse and neglect also may be heard in so-called
Family Courts and Juvenile and Family Drug Courts, depending on the county
and State in which families live (Jones 2006).

In their monitoring and oversight role, courts can hold in contempt child
protection workers who, for instance, refuse to arrange for a particular evaluation; courts also have the power to determine whether the child protection
agency has made "reasonable efforts" to avoid child removal, reunite a child
with his or her family, and secure a permanent placement or adoption—with
potentially negative effects for CPS, especially if the court reaches a negative
reasonable efforts finding. As a result, action could be taken against CPS, such
as a report to the State and Federal oversight agencies (Jones 2006). According
to Guggenheim (2007), "many judges joust with child welfare agencies and
surely regard themselves as overseeing and critically engaging agency practice"
(p. 507). In their supportive role (to child protection agencies), courts can order
witnesses to testify based on their power to subpoena, and they can obtain

formal documents and other information that child protection agencies may need for their investigations. In some states, courts have the statutory power to order parents to participate in certain services that may be a condition for a child not to be removed or to be returned to their parent(s) or other caregiver(s) (Jones 2006).

There is great variety across the United States in terms of the power and discretion held by courts and judges. According to Jones (2006), "some courts exercise the authority to dictate to CPS where children should be placed, sometimes including specific foster homes. Other States are more prescriptive in their statutory laws about placement options for children in State custody and give less discretion and authority to the courts" (p. 10).

Decision-making processes

Courts make important decisions during all stages of a child protection case. In the investigation stage, they may issue a court order sought by agency investigators if investigators need, for example, to interview a child or search a home. In some States, children are removed from their families with the help of a court order if investigators determine that children will not be safe if they stay at home; in some States, child protection agencies can remove children without a court order (CWIG 2011b). In the "initial hearing," which occurs shortly after the child protection agency's petition with the court to remove the child from home or the child's removal, a judge or a judicial hearing officer hears evidence from the child protection agency that determines the child's harm or risk of harm (Berrick 2011; CWIG 2011b).[2] The judge or hearing officer decides whether the child should be removed from home, and if so, where the child will be placed until the trial (Berrick 2011; CWIG 2011b; Jones 2006). If the child is removed from home, parents, or foster parents, the child and DCF sign a "service plan" that details what family members and DCF must do so the child can be returned home. The service plan may require parents, for example, to take parenting or anger management classes, go to counseling, or find suitable housing (Children's Law Center of Massachusetts 2014).

In Massachusetts, once a child has entered (or re-entered) DCF care, DCF organizes a so-called six-week placement review with parents and DCF staff to review records, reports, and assessments and determine the likelihood and timeframe in which the child may return home (Commonwealth of Massachusetts, DCF 2013). The meeting reviews and revises the service plan together with the family and determines whether it is appropriate to commence expedited TPR or concurrent permanency planning (Commonwealth of Massachusetts, DCF 2013). Within four to six months, and ten to twelve months after a child enters placement, DCF holds a foster care review, in which a panel reviews the service plan and status of the family (Commonwealth of Massachusetts, DCF 2013).

At the trial or adjudicatory hearing, also referred to as "jurisdictional" or "fact-finding hearing," which in Massachusetts takes place twelve to fifteen months after filing (Massachusetts Trial Court Law Libraries 2007), the judge decides, based on the facts s/he heard, whether child abuse, neglect, or abandonment occurred (CWIG 2011b) and gives the parents the opportunity to oppose the removal (CWIG n.d. *The Court System and Abuse and Neglect*). The child's removal either can continue, or the court can dismiss the application and the child can be returned home (Children's Law Center of Massachusetts 2014; Jones 2006). Some courts use pretrial settlement conferences that may avoid the contested and adversarial process of adjudicatory hearings (Jones 2006). If the case is not dismissed, then the judge decides in a "dispositional hearing" what will need to happen in order to remove the conditions that led to the petition in the first place, and whether to return the child home or to remove the child (even temporarily) (Jones 2006). The adjudicatory and dispositional hearings may occur simultaneously or separately. According to CWIG (2011b):

> "At the dispositional hearing, the judge may allow the children to return home under agency supervision, or the children may be placed in the custody of the State or county child welfare agency (legal custody) and then placed with kin in kinship foster care or in other foster care. The judge will also determine what services the children and parents should receive and will likely review the children's case plan in which the agency has indicated what requirements the parents need to meet in order to have the children returned to their home." (no page number)

Judges or an administrative review panel are supposed to review the progress of the case (toward permanency for the child) every six months in "review hearings," in which they consider how the child is doing in placement, how parents are progressing (in terms of participating in services), and whether a revision of the case plan is necessary (CWIG 2011b). As a result, children may be returned home or remain in placement (Jones 2006). Colorado is one of the states in which review hearings are carried out by an administrative review panel, namely, Colorado's Administrative Review Division (ARD). Review members are staff employed by the Colorado Department of Human Services who "maintain notable academic and professional credentials" (Colorado Department of Human Services 2015, n.p.).

In a "permanency hearing," which should occur every twelve to fourteen months after the child has been removed and every twelve months thereafter, a judge determines the permanent placement of the child. The goals of the permanency hearing could be to (1) reunify the child with her parents; (2) terminate parental rights and move to adoption; (3) find a permanent placement other than adoption (Jones 2006). In Massachusetts, a pretrial conference called a "permanency planning conference" takes place within the first nine months after placement. There, DCF, children, parents, and their attorneys prepare for and select a date for the "permanency hearing," which takes place within twelve months after the initial placement. When a child has been in placement for fifteen of the previous twenty-two months, TPR initiation is required unless an exception applies and has been approved (Commonwealth of Massachusetts, DCF 2013).

STATISTICS

Overall Trends

Children represent almost a quarter of the U.S. population: There were about 74 million children (under age 18 years) in 2012 (Federal Interagency Forum on Child and Family Statistics 2013). Statistics about children in foster care in the United States show several noteworthy characteristics and trends. First, there were 397,122 children in foster care on September 30, 2012, as table 9.1. shows (U.S. Department of Health and Human Services 2013a); this number equals a rate of 5.4 out of 1,000 children younger than 18 years (Child Trends Database 2014). Second, children of color are over-represented among children in foster care (U.S. Department of Health and Human Services 2013a).[3] Although the number of African American children in foster care has decreased from 37 percent in 2002 to 26 percent in 2012 (whereas the number of Hispanic children in foster care has increased during that time period from 17 percent to 21 percent), the proportion of African American children is still almost twice the average of all children in care. The rates of American Indian/Alaska Native children in foster care only dropped slightly—from

Table 9.1. Number of Children in Foster Care in the United States (2008–2013)

Year	Number of children	Number of children in foster care on Sept. 30[3]	Per 1,000 children
2008	74,104,602[1]	463,792	6.2
2009	74,134,167[1]	420,415	5.6
2010	74,119,556[2]	405,330	5.5
2011	73,902,222[2]	397,885	5.4
2012	73,708,179[2]	397,122	5.4
2013	73,610,207[4]	402,378[5]	5.5

Sources:

[1] U.S. Census Bureau (2012).

[2] U.S. Census Bureau (2014a).

[3] U.S. Department of Health and Human Services (2013b).

[4] U.S. Census Bureau (2016b).

[5] U.S. Department of Health and Human Services (2014).

14.1 percent to 13.0 percent—between 2002 and 2012 (U.S. Department of Health and Human Services 2013a).

Third, the United States saw an increase in the number of children in foster care during the 1990s, but this number has continuously declined since 1999: The rate of children in foster care increased from 6.2 per 1,000 in 1990 to 7.9 per 1,000 in 1999 (Child Trends Databank 2014). Between 2008 and 2012, the number of children in foster care declined from a rate of 6.3/1,000 to 5.4/1,000 (Child Trends Databank 2014). Fourth, between 2002 and 2012, the number of children entering foster care declined, and, fifth, children's average length of stay in foster care declined from 31.3 months in 2002 to 22.4 months in 2012 (U.S. Department of Health and Human Services 2013a). Sixth, in the past decade, the number of children in congregate care decreased at an even faster rate than the decrease in foster care (U.S. Department of Health and Human Services 2015). The decline of children in foster and congregate care between 2002 and 2012 may be a result of the changing legal landscape, which focused on children's permanency through family preservation and timelier permanency planning, the monitoring of child welfare systems through the Child and Family Services Review process, and the increased flexibility that states have had to pursue family preservation and timelier permanency through Title IV-E waiver demonstration projects (U.S. Department of Health and Human Services 2013a).

Types of placements

Because federal-level statistics about voluntary and involuntary care placements are, to our knowledge, not available, we used data from Massachusetts. We have not located statistics about the number of removal cases presented to courts in the entire United States per year, or about how many removal cases per year are appealed in the United States or Massachusetts. Table 9.2 presents data on the number of children in placement in Massachusetts overall, as well as the number of children in voluntary and protective care in Massachusetts from 2008 to 2012. Table 9.2 shows that the number of children in care decreased between 2008 and 2012, mirroring national trends. Table 9.3 shows that most of the children who had been taken into DCF care come into care following a Care and Protection order by the court. The table also illustrates that this trend generally has remained the same between 2008 and 2012.

Costs

Although the costs related to court proceedings in dependency cases are not readily available, we do know that under the Title IV-E of the Social Security Act, annual state and federal expenditures in the United States for foster care total more than $9 billion or €7 billion (Zill 2011).[4] The federal foster care program also provides a portion of the funding for States' costs for children who are removed from welfare-eligible homes due to maltreatment.

Table 9.2. Children (0–18 years of age) in Care in Massachusetts, 4th Quarter of Financial Fiscal Years 2008–2013

Years	Number of Children	Children on Caseload in 4th Quarter	Children in Placement	Children in Placement by 1,000 Children	Foster Care (n)	Foster Care by 1,000 Children	Congregate Care (n)	Congregate Care by 1,000 Children	Median Age of Children in Placement
2008[1]	1,500,064	45,730	9,281	6.1	6,864	4.8	1,908	1.3	12.1
2009[2]	1,500,064	46,288	8,694	5.8	6,606	4.4	1,673	1.1	11.6
2010[3]	1,500,064	39,479	8,097	5.4	6,213	4.1	1,514	1	11.5
2011[4]	1,407,240[5]	37,162	7,841	5.6	6,084	4.3	1,769	1.2	11.2
2012[6]	1,399,417[5]	35,046	7,467	5.2	5,803	4.1	1,369	1	11.0
2013[7]	1,392,955[8]	35,707	7,368	5.3	6,983	5	1,683	1	10.4

Sources:

[1] Massachusetts Department of Children and Families (2008a)

[2] Massachusetts Department of Children and Families (2009a)

[3] Massachusetts Department of Children and Families (2010a)

[4] Massachusetts Department of Children and Families (2011a)

[5] U.S. Children's Bureau (2013)

[6] Massachusetts Department of Children and Families (2013a)

[7] Massachusetts Department of Children and Families (2014)

[8] U.S. Census Bureau (2016a)

Table 9.3. Types of Intake of Children in Placement on December 31 of Calendar Year

Year	Total Children in Placement	Protective (Care and Protection Proceeding)	Court Referral[1] and Other/Unspecified	CHINS Referrals	Voluntary Request	Alternative Response
2008	8,729/100%	7,163/82%	Other/Unspecified: 295/3%	538/6%	733/8%	N.d
2009[2]	8,024/100%	6,638/83%	Other/Unspecified: 279/3%	456/6%	651/8%	N.d.
2010[4]	7,845/100%	6,869/88%	Court Referral: 159/2% Other/Unspecified: 79/1%	374/5%	364/5%	N.d.
2011[5]	7,355/100%	6,430/87%	Court Referral: 188/3% Other/Unspecified: 77/1%	368/5%	292/4%	N.d.
2012[6]	7,302/100%	6,036/83%	Court Referral: 201/3% Other/Unspecified: 43/1%	370/5%	272/4%	380/5%
2013[7]	7,677/100%	6,424/84%	Court Referral: 201/3% Other/Unspecified: 27/ less than 1% after rounding off	299/4%	254/3%	472/6%

Sources:

[1] A probation officer of a court in which a CHINS petition has been filed refers a child or her or his family to DCF for services (Children First Advocacy 2011).

[2] Massachusetts Department of Children and Families (2008b)

[2] Massachusetts Department of Children and Families (2009b)

[3] Massachusetts Department of Children and Families (2010b)

[4] Massachusetts Department of Children and Families (2011b)

[5] Massachusetts Department of Children and Families (2012)

[7] Massachusetts Department of Children and Families (2013b)

This funding, equal to approximately $5 billion or €4 billion per year, is an uncapped entitlement: qualified State expenditures are partially reimbursed (U.S. Department of Health and Human Services 2005, p. 1). These costs result in a national average maintenance cost per child per year of $19,107 or €15,133 (under Title IV-E) and a national average administrative cost per child per year of $6,675 or €5,290. Therefore, the total of maintenance costs and administrative costs per child per year in the United States is $25,782 or €20,420 (Rosman et al. 2011).[5]

CHALLENGES AND BLIND SPOTS

In the removal process, children and parents are entitled to certain rights, including the right to family integrity; to notice of the proceedings; to a hearing and to counsel. However, as we will show below, there are systematic barriers to children and parents exercising their rights, especially delays and backlogs in the court system. Challenges also include ensuring that children's voices are included and represented in the court process; that the voices of parents who cannot afford legal representation are heard in court; and that the courts do not discriminate against children, youth, and families of color, thus potentially building a "foster care to prison pipeline" for children of color.

Disempowerment of children

One of the many challenges of the court system in the United States is its ambivalent record in terms of involving children in the decisions that affect their lives. Empirical research has shown that a large proportion of children who have gone through the courts for care and protection proceedings report feeling unheard. Block et al. (2010) researched children's knowledge and attitudes, in a juvenile dependency court in a large urban area in a western state, through interviews with seven-to-ten-year-old children right after they emerged from such proceedings. The researchers found that children lacked an understanding of the court process and expressed negative attitudes toward the court. (Younger children had less court-related knowledge than older children.) The more knowledge children had about the court, the more positive attitudes they expressed; and the more anxious children felt, the more negative their attitudes. Over half of the children (54 percent) did not know whether they would return home or remain in foster care; over one-third of them (37 percent) did not feel that they were believed or listened to in the courtroom. This study suggests that children want to be empowered and listened to. The authors also concluded that "maltreated children might profit from greater understanding of dependency court" (Block et al. 2010, p. 668), for instance through brief preparation programs. In addition, those children who lack knowledge about the court system and hold negative attitudes may need counseling or other interventions, or they might otherwise be negatively affected as they adjust to foster care and interact with courts in the future (Block et al. 2010).

This finding parallels the research findings by Weisz et al. (2011), who compared the reactions of children in foster care who attended dispositional review hearings in the dependency court system in a Midwestern State with children who did not attend. This study showed that the children in foster care who attended the hearings felt more positively about the court process in terms of their comfort level with their GALs and caseworkers, their perception that the judge's decision was fair, and their trust in the judge. Interestingly (but not surprisingly), "children who attended their hearings had a better self-perceived understanding of the details of their case [. . .] and reported higher perceptions of knowing what their family's case plan was" (Weisz et al. 2011, p. 270). The study did not find evidence of children being highly distressed immediately before or after their hearings; and found that children (in both groups) responded more positively to the process when judges were more actively engaged through questions or interactions. The researchers concluded that "judges can make the court experience less stressful and more comfortable for children by adopting brief and encouraging direct interactions with the children in the courtroom" (p. 271).

With regard to children's representatives in court, research findings about the role of GALs in representing children's views are ambivalent. Karatekin et al.'s (2014) study of court records of cases referred to juvenile court in Minnesota demonstrated that almost all children had a GAL, and that judges followed the recommendations of GALs in their orders in a large majority of the cases analyzed. Litzelfelner's (2000) study of CASAs in Kansas showed that although permanency outcomes did not differ depending on whether a child had a CASA, children with CASAs received more services. Other studies have shown that the views of GALs rarely differed from those of county attorneys; that they rarely expressed their views in court (Anderson et al. 2010); that volunteer GALs are more likely than private attorneys acting as GALs to attend family support team meetings; and that cases involving private attorney-GALS were more likely to be dismissed earlier and re-reported for maltreatment (Loman and Siegel 2003).

The disempowerment of children in the courts is also reflected in the fact that many children do not have a say in whether adoption is their permanency goal, nor do many have a say in who will adopt them. A study that analyzed the views of twenty judges representing eighteen different U.S. States found that 75 percent of judges do not require a child to consent to the goal of adoption; however, 60 percent required or desired the child's consent to an adoption by a particular family before they made their decision (Ellis et al. 2009).

Delays, backlogs, and decision-making bias
Delays in court proceedings resulting in families not being referred to the services they needed, as well as customer dissatisfaction and parental disengagement as a result of lawyers' lack of engagement with parents between court

appearances (Guggenheim 2007), were reported as features of the New York Family Courts in the late 1990s and early 2000s (Guggenheim and Gottlieb 2005; Guggenheim 2007; Vittulo-Martin 1999). Parties reported enduring long waits before spending a few minutes in the courtroom (Vittulo-Martin 1999). Some parties also reported that they experienced delays and obstacles related to caseworkers. Some caseworkers were found to arrive at court late and unprepared to testify or did not appear at all (Guggenheim and Gottlieb 2005); caseworkers themselves found that structural obstacles, such as high caseloads, competing goals, and time pressures due to child welfare policy changes that mandate reduced time frames for CPS cases hindered their ability to perform their duties and adhere to guidelines presented during their training (Smith and Donovan 2003, p. 549). Additionally, due to intense time constraints, some caseworkers felt the need to deprioritize aspects of their jobs (e.g., working collaboratively with parents to assess needs, arranging services for parents and children, and providing support to help parents improve their parenting) for the sake of the "core job requirements" (Smith and Donovan 2003, p. 549).

The New York Family Court has, along with the Center for Court Innovation, created a "Blueprint for Change" that acknowledged the courts' challenges and laid out a strategic plan for improvement. These improvements included the need to strengthen administrative and judicial leadership with the necessary tools and skills to spearhead reform; provide more staff and resources to match the current needs of the clients and the system; clarify the roles of all parties involved in the family court process; develop an internal capacity for multidisciplinary training; and enhance collaboration among key players, the community, and the families the court serves (State of New York Unified Court System 2010).

Due to resource gaps and full dockets, judicial officers often make decisions in protective hearings for many cases at a very quick pace, which introduces bias in the decision-making process (Payne 2006). Russell and Summers (2013) reported that according to the Washington Administrative Offices of the Courts (2010), "in King County, Washington, [. . .] 2.3 full-time equivalent judicial officers hear more than a thousand preliminary protective hearings in juvenile dependency cases each year" (p. 3). Russell and Summers (2013) evaluated the impact of two court interventions—a training program for judicial decision-makers on implicit and institutional bias with a focus on reflective decision-making; and a judicial "bench card" that judges used during preliminary protective court hearings to guide their practice during the hearing. "Bench cards provide ready reference to relevant laws and accepted practices to ensure that the judge is conducting a thorough hearing, providing effective due process, providing opportunities for engagement of parties in the hearing, and issuing and enforcing appropriate and comprehensive court orders" (Russell and Summers 2013, p. 4). The researchers' evaluation found that, over time, the use of both interventions together resulted in increases in parent placements and decreases in foster care placements (Russell and Summers 2013). Relatedly, Outley's (2006) work showed that fewer than half of the judges working in dependency courts in the United States had any child protection related training. This is significant in the light of Beal et al.'s (2014) study, which found that judges do make a difference in terms of the length of time children spend in foster care: "it is likely that when judges are more active in controlling case progression, resolution of cases occurs more speedily" (p. 11).

In summary, there is evidence of the disempowerment of children; evidence also exists of negative time-related dynamics in judges' decision-making processes related to the removal of children, including delays and backlogs in the system that may lead to parental disengagement, high caseloads resulting in a decision-making pace that may lead to decision-making bias, and lack of child protection-related training, which may affect how judges make decisions.

Disempowerment of parents in poverty

According to CWIG (n.d. *The Court System and Child Abuse and Neglect*), "while most States give indigent parents a right to free court-appointed counsel in abuse or neglect cases, not all States do. The Supreme Court held in the *Lassiter* case [*Lassiter vs. Department of Social Services*, 452 U.S. 18 (1981)] that parents have a constitutional right to a lawyer in at least some termination of parental rights cases, depending on the circumstances of the particular case" (no page number). However, according to the Lassiter ruling, there is no federal constitutional right to counsel for indigent parents (Jones, 2006). Vasser (2007) argues that, even though juvenile courts prefer all parties to be represented by counsel and states are moving in the direction of providing full rights for indigent parents, *Lassiter* should be overturned because the rights of indigent parents in TPR proceedings will not be secure until *Lassiter* is overruled: "until indigent parents are given the right to litigate their cases with the same access to the courts as affluent parents, the often-prohibitive expense of civil litigation will continue to close the door of the courts to the poor" (Vasser 2007, p. 331). But securing the representation of indigent parents is possible: Courtney and Hook (2012), who studied the pilot Parent Representation Program in Washington State, which supported indigent parents, found that the program resulted in an increase in the rate of family reunification and a near doubling of the speed to adoption and legal guardianship (Courtney and Hook 2012).

Over-representation of children of color in care

As already mentioned, the disproportionality of children of color in foster care is a noteworthy fact in the U.S. context: children of color are more likely to be caught in limbo in the child protection system, less likely to be reunited with their families, less likely to be adopted, and more likely to experience negative life outcomes such as poverty, joblessness, and involvement in the criminal justice system (Roberts 2002). A recent study of a Midwest sample of young adults who aged out of the foster care system found that 81 percent of the young men in long-term foster care had been arrested (compared with 17 percent of all young men in the United States overall), and 59 percent had been convicted on a minimum of one crime (compared with 10 percent in the United States overall) (Zill 2011). Although there is scholarly agreement on racial disparity and disproportionality in the foster care system, scholars do not agree on the *causes*; this has led to a heated debate spanning decades (Fluke et al. 2011). On the one hand, proponents of the "disproportionate and disparate need" view argue that children and families of color have a disproportionately greater need for child protective services than white children and families because they are likely to be affected more by structural problems such as poverty, homelessness, unemployment, a lack of education, and incarceration than whites (Bartholet 2009; Fluke et al. 2011). The underlying major factor cited in this argument is the role that poverty plays in the lives of people of color, who are over-represented among the poor (Macartney et al. 2013). This overrepresentation could (among other significant reasons related to structural racial discrimination) be interpreted as the result of a welfare state that does not provide universal services to all, which relates back to our discussion on the U.S. policy background. Scholars on the other side of the argument embrace a "racial bias and discrimination" perspective. This position holds that there are disproportionately more children of color in the child protection system because the child protection system is racially biased and discriminates toward families and children of color (Roberts 2002).

CONCLUDING REMARKS

To conclude, this chapter discussed how child removals in the United States occur in a structural context in which child protection agencies work alongside courts to protect children from child abuse and neglect in a country that targets public services only to the most disadvantaged, at a level that is far less generous than in other developed countries (Aspalter 2011; Esping-Anderson 1999), and through a child protection system whose thresholds for removing children from home are comparatively high (Gilbert et al. 2011). UNICEF data confirm that children's well-being in the United States is lower than in many other OECD countries (UNICEF 2013). This chapter evidenced several significant blind spots in the system, including racial and class-based bias and discrimination, and delays in decision-making. Thus, it showed the need for further research on how these blind spots impact children and their families, and on the impact of programs that aim at improving it. Further, this chapter also underscored the need for systemic change to ensure that bias can be eliminated and all disadvantaged children and parents, especially those with the least amount of resources, can also be engaged and empowered users of the system.

ACKNOWLEDGMENTS

We would like to thank Aastha Mahajan, Alyssa Sands, and Brittany Bye for their invaluable assistance in finding and annotating sources for this chapter. We also would like to thank Dr. Elspeth Slayter for her thoughtful comments on the first draft of this chapter. We are grateful for the Emmanuel College Faculty Development funds that fund students' research assistantships for projects like these.

NOTES

1 Until the 1970s, it was quite common that children did not participate in the court process, and that none of the parties involved, including CPS, worked with a legal representative. The only people present in the court were the caseworker, the judge, and sometimes the child's parent(s). Now, State law outlines who represents a child in a child maltreatment case—it could be a lawyer, a GAL, or a CASA (Jones 2006).

2 If a child is seriously harmed, the person who abused the child may be arrested and prosecuted in criminal court (Berrick 2011).

3 Although we know that 8.6 percent of children who came to the attention of the child protection system in the United States between 1999 and 2000 were children of immigrants (Dettlaff and Earner 2012; Lincroft and Dettlaff 2010), there are no statistics about how many children of immigrants and immigrant foreign-born children are in foster care in the United States; these research gaps about the representation of these children in the child welfare system in general have been documented (Earner and Križ 2015). To the authors' knowledge, there are also no national data on the precise number of lesbian, gay, bisexual, transgender, and questioning (LGBTQ) youth in the foster care system. The National Resource Center for Youth Development estimates that they comprise at least 5 percent to 10 percent of the total foster care population (The National Resource Center for Youth Development 2014).

4 This figure does not include the monies spent on publicly funded medical care for foster children, food stamps, and payment to the families who care for foster children. Also not included in that figure are other long-term costs paid by society due to developmental risks associated with foster care, family disruption, and family abuse and neglect (Zill 2011).

5 For a full explanation of the savings that would result from an increase in foster care adoptions, see Rosman et al. (2011).

REFERENCES

Anderson, M., Coulter, S., and McNamara, D. (2010). *Reasonable Efforts or Unreasonable Expectations. A Look at Hennepin County Child Protection Cases.* Retrieved on June 16, 2014 at http://www.ncdsv.org/images/WATCH_ ReasonableEffortsOrUnrealisticExpectations_2010.pdf.

Aspalter, C. (2011). "The Development of Ideal-Typical Welfare Regime Theory." *International Social Work,* 54(6): 735–750.

Bartholet, E. (2009). "The Racial Disproportionality Movement in Child Welfare: False Facts and Dangerous Directions." *Arizona Law Review,* 51: 871–932.

Berrick, J. D. (2011). "Trends and Issues in the U.S. Child Welfare System." In Gilbert, N., Parton, N., and Skivenes, M. (Eds.), *Child Protection Systems: International Trends and Orientations,* pp. 17–35. Oxford: Oxford University Press.

Block, S. D., Oran, H., Oran, D., Baumrind, N., and Goodman, G. (2010). "Abused and Neglected Children in Court." *Child Abuse & Neglect,* 34: 659–670.

Child and Family Services Review Information Portal. (2007). *Court Petition.* Retrieved on November 6, 2014 at https://training.cfsrportal.org/section-2-understanding-child-welfare-system/3019.

Children's Bureau. (2013). *Child Welfare Reports Outcome Data— Demographics: Child Welfare Summary Massachusetts: 2009–2012.* Washington DC: U.S. Department of Health and Human Services, Administration for Children and Families. Retrieved on June 12, 2014 at http://cwoutcomes.acf. hhs.gov/data/tables/demo_stats?states%5B%5D=22&state=&region=.

Children First Advocacy. (2011). *CHINS: Child in Need of Service.* Retrieved on May 28, 2015 at http://www.childrenfirstadvocacy.com/care-protection/ child-in-need-of-service/.

Children's Law Center of Massachusetts. (2014). *Care and Protection Cases.* Retrieved September 20, 2014 at http://www.clcm.org/2014/C-P_2014.pdf.

Children's Law Center of Massachusetts. (2013). *Quick Reference on CRA (Child Requiring Assistance): Guide for Child Advocates in Massachusetts.* Retrieved September 14, 2014 at http://www.clcm.org/CRA_guide_5-30-12.pdf.

Child Trends Databank. (2014). *Foster Care.* Retrieved on October 5, 2014 at http://www.childtrends.org/?indicators=foster-care#sthash.kFvhiHWz.dpuf

Child Welfare Information Gateway (CWIG). (2014). *Representation of Children in Child Abuse and Neglect Proceedings.* Washington, DC: U.S. Department of Health and Human Services, Children's Bureau. Retrieved on May 28, 2015 at https://www.childwelfare.gov/pubPDFs/represent.pdf.

CWIG. (2012). *Major Federal Legislation Concerned With Child Protection, Child Welfare and Adoption.* Retrieved on March 31, 2013 at https://www. childwelfare.gov/pubs/otherpubs/majorfedlegis.cfm.

CWIG. (2011a). *Definitions of Child Abuse and Neglect.* Retrieved on June 14, 2014 at https://www.childwelfare.gov/systemwide/laws_policies/statutes/ define.cfm.

CWIG. (2011b.) *Understanding Child Welfare and the Courts*. Retrieved on June 12, 2014 at https://www.childwelfare.gov/pubs/factsheets/cwandcourts.cfm.

CWIG. (2008). Differential Response to Reports of Child Abuse and Neglect. Retrieved on January 12, 2016 at https://www.childwelfare.gov/pubs/issue-briefs/differential-response/.

CWIG. (n.d.). *Adoption Assistance and Child Welfare Act of 1980*. Retrieved on June 13, 2014 at https://www.childwelfare.gov/systemwide/laws_policies/federal/index.cfm?event=federalLegislation.viewLegis&id=22.

CWIG. (n.d). *Adoption and Safe Families Act of 1997*. Retrieved on June 13, 2014 at https://www.childwelfare.gov/systemwide/laws_policies/federal/index.cfm?event=federalLegislation.viewLegis&id=4.

CWIG. (n.d.). *Court Process Flowchart: Working With the Courts in Child Protection*. Retrieved September 21, 2014 at https://www.childwelfare.gov/pubs/usermanuals/courts_92/figure1.cfm.

CWIG. (n.d.). *The Court System and Child Abuse and Neglect*. Retrieved on June 13, 2014 at https://www.childwelfare.gov/pubs/usermanuals/courts_92/courtsc.cfm.

Colorado Department of Human Services. (2015). *Vision and Mission*. Retrieved May 29, 2015 at http://www.colorado.gov/cs/Satellite/CDHS-Emp/CBON/1251579376536.

Commonwealth of Massachusetts, Department of Children and Families. (2013). Permanency Planning Policy. Retrieved June 16, 2014 at http://www.mass.gov/eohhs/docs/dcf/policies/permanency-planning-policy.pdf.

Courtney, M. E. and Hook, J. L. (2012). "Evaluation of the Impact of Enhanced Parental Legal Representation on the Timing of Permanency Outcomes for Children in Foster Care." *Children and Youth Services Review*, 34: 1337–1343.

Cross, T.P., Finkelhor, D., and Ormrod, R. (2005). "Police Involvement in Child Protective Services Investigations: Literature Review and Secondary Data Analysis." *Child Maltreatment*, 10(3): 1–21.

DeNavas-Walt, C., Proctor, B., and Smith, J. (2012). *Income, Poverty and Health Insurance Coverage in the United States: 2011*. Washington, DC: US Census Bureau. Retrieved on January 3, 2013 at http://www.census.gov/prod/2012pubs/p60-243.pdf.

Dettlaff, A. J. and Earner, I. (2012). *Children of Immigrants in the Child Welfare System: Findings from the National Survey of Child and Adolescent Well-being. Migration and Child Welfare National Network Research Brief.* Retrieved on January 3, 2013 at http://www.americanhumane.org/assets/pdfs/children/pc-childofimmigrantpdf.pdf.

Drake, B. and Rank, M. R. (2009). "The Racial Divide among American Children in Poverty: Reassessing the Importance of Neighborhood." *Children and Youth Services Review*, 31(12): 1264–1271.

Duva, J., and Metzger, S. (2010). "Addressing Poverty as a Major Risk Factor in Child Neglect: Promising Policy and Practice." *Protecting Children*, 25(1): 63–74.

Earner, I. and Križ, K. (2015). "The United States: Child Protection in the Context of Competing Policy Mandates." In Skivenes, M., Barn, R., Križ, K., and Pösö, T. (Eds.), *Child Welfare Systems and Migrant Children*, pp. 157–178. Oxford: Oxford University Press.

Ellis, R., Malm, K., and Bishop, E. (2009). "The Timing of Termination of Parental Rights: A Balancing Act for Children's Best Interests." *Child Trends Research Brief*. Retrieved on June 7, 2014 at http://childtrends.org/wp-content/uploads/2009/09/Child_Trends-2009_09_09_RB_LegalOrphans.pdf.

Esping-Anderson, G. (1990). *The Three Worlds of Welfare Capitalism*. Princeton, NJ: Princeton University Press.

Federal Interagency Forum on Child and Family Statistics. (2013). "Table Pop1–Child Population." In *America's Children: Key National Indicators of Well-Being*. Washington, DC: U.S. Government Printing Office. Retrieved June 11, 2014 at http://www.childstats.gov/americaschildren/tables/pop1.asp.

Fluke, J., Harden, B. J., Jenkins, M., and Ruehrdanz, A. (2011). "Research Synthesis on Child Welfare: Disproportionality and Disparities." In *Disparities and Disproportionality in Child Welfare: Analysis of the Research*, pp. 1–93. Research Symposium: Alliance for Racial Equity in Child Welfare.

Freundlich, M. (1999). "Expediting Termination of Parental Rights: Solving a Problem or Sowing the Seeds of a New Predicament?" *Capital University Law Review*, 28: 97–110.

Gilbert, N., Parton, N., and Skivenes, M. (2011). "Changing Patterns of Response and Emerging Orientations." In Gilbert, N., Parton, N., and Skivenes, M. (Eds.), *Child Protection Systems: International Trends and Orientations*, pp. 243–257. Oxford: Oxford University Press.

Goldman, J., Salus, M. K., Wolcott, D., and Kennedy, K. Y. (2003). "What Are the Consequences of Child Abuse and Neglect?" In *A Coordinated Response to Child Abuse and Neglect: The Foundation for Practice*. Washington, DC: U. S. Department of Health and Human Services.

Guggenheim, M. (2007). "Parental Rights in Child Welfare Cases in New York City Family Courts." *Columbia Journal of Law and Social Problems*, 40: 507–525.

Guggenheim, M. and Gottlieb, C. (2005). "Justice Denied: Delays in Child Protection Cases in New York." *The Virginia Journal of Social Policy and the Law*, 12(3): 546–576.

Jones, W. (2006). *Working with the Courts in Child Protection*. U.S. Department of Health and Human Services. Retrieved February 11, 2014 at https://www.childwelfare.gov/pubs/usermanuals/courts/courts.pdf.

Karatekin, C., Gehrman, R., and Lawler, J. (2014). "A Study of Maltreated Children and their Families in Juvenile Court: I. Court Performance Measures." *Children and Youth Services Review*, 41: 62–74.

Lincroft, Y. and Dettlaff, A. J. (2010). "Children of Immigrants in the U.S. Child Welfare System." Retrieved on January 3, 2012 at http://www.firstfocus.net/library/fact-sheets/children-of-immigrants-in-the-us-child-welfare-system.

Litzelfelner, P. (2000). "The Effectiveness of CASAs in Achieving Positive Outcomes for Children." *Child Welfare*, 79(2): 179–193.

Loman, L. A. and Siegel, G. L. (2003). *Evaluation of the Missouri Juvenile Court Improvement Project, City of St. Louis, June 2003*. Institute of Applied Research. Retrieved June 12, 2014 at http://www.iarstl.org/papers.htm.

Macartney, S., Bishaw, A., and Fontenot, K. (2013). *Poverty Rates for Selected Detailed Race and Hispanic Groups by State and Place: 2007–2011*. Washington, DC: U.S. Census Bureau. Retrieved June 12, 2014 at http://www.census.gov/prod/2013pubs/acsbr11-17.pdf.

Massachusetts Law Reform Institute. (2005). *Abuse and Neglect: Your Rights and DCF*. Retrieved on September 14, 2014 at http://www.masslegalhelp.org/children-and-families/abuse-neglect-claims-your-rights-and-dss.

Massachusetts Department of Children and Families. (2013b). *Annual Profile*. Retrieved on January 12, 2016 at http://www.mass.gov/eohhs/docs/dcf/reports/annual/annual-data-profile-cy2013.pdf

Massachusetts Department of Children and Families. (2012). *Annual Profile*. Retrieved on June 12, 2014 at http://www.mass.gov/eohhs/researcher/family-services/dcf/annual-data-profiles.html.

Massachusetts Department of Children and Families. (2011b). *Annual Profile*. Retrieved on June 12, 2014 at http://www.mass.gov/eohhs/researcher/family-services/dcf/annual-data-profiles.html.

Massachusetts Department of Children and Families. (2010b). *Annual Profile*. Retrieved on June 12, 2014 at http://www.mass.gov/eohhs/researcher/family-services/dcf/annual-data-profiles.html.

Massachusetts Department of Children and Families. (2009b). *Annual Profile*. Retrieved on June 12, 2014 at http://www.mass.gov/eohhs/researcher/family-services/dcf/annual-data-profiles.html.

Massachusetts Department of Children and Families. (2008b). *Annual Profile*. Retrieved on June 12, 2014 at http://www.mass.gov/eohhs/researcher/family-services/dcf/annual-data-profiles.html.

Massachusetts Department of Children and Families. (2014). *Quarterly Report Fiscal Year 2013 4th Quarter. 4/1/2013 – 6/30/2013*. Retrieved on January 12, 2016 at http://archives.lib.state.ma.us/handle/2452/238435

Massachusetts Department of Children and Families. (2013a). *Quarterly Report Fiscal Year 2012 4th Quarter. 4/1/2012 – 6/30/2012*. Retrieved on May 28, 2015 at http://www.mass.gov/eohhs/researcher/family-services/dcf/dcf-quarterly-reports.html.

Massachusetts Department of Children and Families. (2011a). *Quarterly Report Fiscal Year 2011 4th Quarter. 4/1/2011 – 6/30/2011*. Retrieved on May 28, 2015 at http://www.mass.gov/eohhs/researcher/family-services/dcf/dcf-quarterly-reports.html.

Massachusetts Department of Children and Families. (2010a). *Quarterly Report Fiscal Year 2010 4th Quarter. 4/1/2010 – 6/30/2010.* Retrieved on May 28, 2015 at http://www.mass.gov/eohhs/researcher/family-services/dcf/dcf-quarterly-reports.html.

Massachusetts Department of Children and Families. (2009a). *Quarterly Report Fiscal Year 2008 4th Quarter. 4/1/2009 – 6/30/2009.* Retrieved on May 28, 2015 at http://www.mass.gov/eohhs/researcher/family-services/dcf/dcf-quarterly-reports.html.

Massachusetts Department of Children and Families. (2008a). *Quarterly Report Fiscal Year 2008 4th Quarter. 4/1/2008 – 6/30/2008.* Retrieved on May 28, 2015 at http://www.mass.gov/eohhs/researcher/family-services/dcf/dcf-quarterly-reports.html.

Massachusetts Department of Children and Families. (n.d.). *A Family's Guide to Protective Services for Children.* Retrieved on September 10, 2014 at http://www.mass.gov/eohhs/docs/dcf/can-family-guide.pdf.

Massachusetts Executive Office of Health and Human Services. (2014). *Definitions of Child Abuse and Neglect.* Retrieved on September 10, 2014 at http://www.mass.gov/eohhs/gov/departments/dcf/child-abuse-neglect/definitions.html.

Massachusetts Trial Court Law Libraries. (2007). *Massachusetts Juvenile Court Standing Order 2-07: Time Standards.* Retrieved on September 15, 2014 at http://www.lawlib.state.ma.us/source/mass/rules/juvenile/standingorders/2-07.html.

Outley, A. (2006). "Overcoming Barriers to Permanency: Recommendations for Juvenile and Dependency Courts." *Family Court Review,* 44: 244–257.

Parents Helping Parents. (2010). *You Are Not Alone: An Empowering Guide for Parents Whose Children Are in DCF Foster Care.* Retrieved on September 15, 2014 at http://media.wix.com/ugd/ff0e80_69c1da9f939ed9b8c66d8d-98bad8c0f8.pdf.

Payne, B. K. (2006). "Weapon-bias: Split-second Decisions and Unintended Stereotyping." *Current Directions in Psychological Science,* 15: 287–291.

Pecora, P. J., Williams, J., Kessler, R. C., Downs, A. C., O'Brien, K., Hiripi, E., and and Morello, S. 2013. "Assessing the Effects of Foster Care: Early Results from the Casey National Alumni Study." Retrieved on June 11, 2014 at http://www.casey.org/Resources/Publications/pdf/CaseyNationalAlumniStudy_FullReport.pdf.

Pelton, L. (1978). "Child Abuse and Neglect: The Myth of Classlessness." *American Journal of Orthopsychiatry,* 48(4): 608–617.

Roberts, D. (2002). *Shattered Bonds: The Color of Child Welfare.* New York: Basic Civitas Books.

Reed, D. F. and Karpilow, K. (2009). *Understanding the Child Welfare System in California*. Retrieved on January 3, 2013 at http://ccrwf.org/wp-content/uploads/2009/03/final_web_pdf.

Rosman, E., Callahan, N., and Johnson, C. (2011). *Adoption Advocate No. 35: Better Prospects, Lower Cost: The Case for Increasing Foster Care Adoption*. Retrieved on June 14, 2014 at https://www.adoptioncouncil.org/publications/adoption-advocate-no-35.html.

Russell, J. and Summers, A. (2013). *Reflective Decision-making and Foster Care Placements*. Reno, NV: National Council of Juvenile and Family Court Judges. Retrieved June 10, 2014 at http://www.nccdglobal.org/sites/default/files/publication_pdf/russell_summers_article.pdf.

Shook, K. (1999). "Does the Loss of Welfare Income Increase the Risk of Involvement with the Child Welfare Service System?" *Children and Youth Services Review*, 21:781–814.

Smith, B. and Donovan, S. (2003). "Child Welfare Practice in Organizational and Institutional Context." *Social Service Review*, 77(4): 541–563.

State of New York Unified Court System and Center for Court Innovation. (2010). *New York City Family Court Blueprint for Change*. New York: State of New York Unified Court System.

The National Resource Center for Youth Development. (2014). *LGBTQ Youth in Care: Information & Resources*. Tulsa, OK: The National Resource Center for Youth Development. Retrieved on June 11, 2014 at http://www.nrcyd.ou.edu/lgbtq-youth.

UNICEF Office of Research. (2014). *Children of the Recession. The Impact of the Economic Crisis on Child Well-being in Rich Countries. Innocenti Report Card 12*. Florence: UNICEF Office of Research.

UNICEF Office of Research. (2013). *Child Well-Being in Rich Countries: An Overview. Innocenti Report Card 11*. Florence: UNICEF Office of Research.

U.S. Census Bureau. (2016b). *Annual Estimates of the Resident Population for Selected Age Groups by Sex for the United States, States, Counties, and Puerto Rico Commonwealth and Municipios: April 1, 2010 to July 1, 2014*.

U.S. Census Bureau. (2016a). *ACS Demographic and Housing Estimates. 2013 American Community Survey 1–3 Year Estimates*. Retrieved January 12, 2016 at http://factfinder.census.gov/faces/tableservices/jsf/pages/productview.xhtml?src=bkmk

U.S. Census Bureau, Population Division. (2014a). 2013 Postcensal Population Estimates. Retrieved May 29, 2015 at http://www.census.gov/popest/data/national/asrh/2013/index.html.

U.S. Census Bureau, Population Division. National Intercensal Estimates (2000–2010). (2012). Retrieved May 29, 2015 at http://www.census.gov/popest/data/intercensal/national/nat2010.html.

U.S. Department of Health and Human Services. (2015). "A National Look at the Use of Congregate Care in Child Welfare." Retrieved on May 28, 2015 at http://www.acf.hhs.gov/sites/default/files/cb/cbcongregatecare_brief.pdf.

U.S. Department of Health and Human Services. (2014). *The AFCARS Report*. Retrieved January 12, 2016 at https://www.acf.hhs.gov/sites/default/files/cb/afcarsreport21.pdf

U.S. Department of Health and Human Services. (2013a). *ACYF Office of Data, Analysis, Research, and Evaluation Data Brief 2013-1*. Retrieved September 20, 2014 at http://www.acf.hhs.gov/sites/default/files/cb/data_brief_foster_care_trends1.pdf.

U.S. Department of Health and Human Services. (2013b). *The AFCARS Report*. Retrieved June 10, 2014 at http://www.acf.hhs.gov/sites/default/files/cb/afcarsreport20.pdf.

U.S. Department of Health and Human Services. (2005). *ASPE Issue Brief: How and Why the Current Funding Structure Fails to Meet the Needs of the Child Welfare Field*. Retrieved on June 14, 2014 at http://aspe.hhs.gov/hsp/05/fc-financing-ib/ib.pdf

U.S. Department of Justice. (2001). *Law Enforcement Response to Child Abuse*. Retrieved on September 26, 2014 at https://www.ncjrs.gov/pdffiles/162425.pdf.

Vasser, N. (2007). "Termination of Parental Right: The Indigent Parent's Right to Counsel in Termination of Parental Rights Proceedings." *The Journal of Contemporary Legal Issues*, 16: 329–332.

Vitullo-Martin, J. (1999). *New York Family Court: Court User Perspectives*. Retrieved on September 20, 2014 at http://www.vera.org/pubs/new-york-family-court-court-user-perspectives

Washington Administrative Offices of the Courts. (2010). *Caseloads of the Courts of Washington: Juvenile Dependency Proceedings by Type of Proceeding—2010 Annual Report*. Retrieved on October 12, 2014 at http://www.courts.wa.gov/caseload/?fa=.caseload.showReport&level=s&freq=a&^tab=juvDep&fileID=jdpproyr.

Weisz, V., Wingrove, T., Beal, S., and Faith-Slaker, A. (2011). "Children's Participation in Foster Care Hearings." *Child Abuse & Neglect*, 35: 267–272.

Zill, N. (2011). *Adoption from Foster Care: Aiding Children While Saving Public Money*. Brookings—Center on Children and Families. Retrieved on June 13, 2014 at http://www.brookings.edu/~/media/research/files/reports/2011/5/adoption%20foster%20care%20zill/05_adoption_foster_care_zill.pdf.

10

REMOVALS OF CHILDREN BY THE CHILD WELFARE SYSTEM—VARIATIONS AND DIFFERENCES ACROSS COUNTRIES

Kenneth Burns, Tarja Pösö, and Marit Skivenes

INTRODUCTION

The comprehensive examination of sociolegal decision-making processes in child welfare removals in the eight nation states examined in this book has demonstrated how policies, law, and professional practices vary considerably among these high-income countries. The analysis highlights that decisions to remove children are a mix of sociolegal reasoning. There is no dominant model of child removal decision-making: Although there are some shared features among countries, each country seems to have its unique approach on decision-making bodies, processes, decision-makers, and knowledge bases. In this final chapter, we examine the differences and similarities among these systems and countries; we highlight surprises and contradictions, blind spots, and critical features of countries' systems; and we conclude the chapter with a research agenda and a series of reflective questions for those considering reforming systems in their country.

A VARIETY OF REMOVALS OF CHILDREN OUT OF THEIR HOMES

There were three types of child welfare removals examined in this book, as displayed in Figure 10.1, including: (1) emergency removals, (2) voluntary

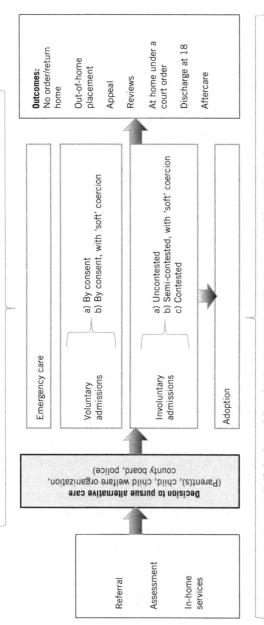

A mix of police, administrative, court or court-*like* decision-making bodies

Referral

Assessment

In-home services

Decision to pursue alternative care
(Parent(s), child, child welfare organization, county board, police)

Emergency care

Voluntary admissions
a) By consent
b) By consent, with 'soft' coercion

Involuntary admissions
a) Uncontested
b) Semi-contested, with 'soft' coercion
c) Contested

Adoption

Outcomes:
No order/return home

Out-of-home placement

Appeal

Reviews

At home under a court order

Discharge at 18

Aftercare

Mediating factors influencing the culture and practices of removal decision-making bodies:

Child welfare orientation, best interests of the child, welfare state model, poverty and deprivation, values, children's rights, parents' rights, protected status of the 'family', threshold for entry into care, no order principle, social policy, legal and constitutional systems, adversarial/inquiry/inquisitorial approach, transparency, UNCRC, ECtHR, theory and research

Figure 10.1. Types of child removal decision-making systems and outcomes.

admissions (of varying degrees of "voluntariness"), and (3) involuntary removals, involving police, administrative, court, and court-*like* decision-making bodies, with a range of possible outcomes indicated. In terms of the outcome of these decisions, children are in "care," "alternative care," "looked after," "out-of-home care," or "adopted" as a result of the removal decisions.

Emergency removals are instigated by the police or social workers to remove a child to a place of safety outside his/her home for a short-term or medium-term period of time. The aim is to provide immediate security for the child, and quite often an emergency removal is the route to a care order. Although there is scarce information regarding the process, anecdotal evidence indicates that emergency removals function as hard evidence in borderline cases where the child welfare agency has been unsure whether to send a care order application.

The aim of a voluntary admission of children is to support the family over a short period of time; for example, to create space for parents to address their health problems. These removals may, however, include some elements of "soft" coercion, given that the refusal of a supportive, voluntary admission may be interpreted as a parent's lack of commitment to change. The offer of voluntary care may be accompanied by a contingency plan for the removal of a child involuntarily should the voluntary admission option be rejected, because the child staying with a parent(s) at that time may not be safe. To what extent—ostensibly, in the best interests of children—some parents are "softly" coerced into consenting to a "voluntary" admission is unclear due to a lack of empirical research on these voluntary processes. Countries profiled in this book also indicate, however, that parents often initiate voluntary admissions themselves and voluntary systems clearly have a valid place. Voluntary processes are less adversarial, there is greater potential for partnership, potentially fewer people are involved, and voluntary systems can support and reduce stress on parents at a difficult period in their lives. For children, a voluntary placement may offer much needed respite from the troubles in their family and everyday environment, as well as an opportunity to find new sources of support. The problem is that we do not know much about how these types of voluntary placements are experienced by children and families. For example, we do not know whether the parents feel forced to place the children, and whether the children are insecure about the placement and the length of time it will last. We also know very little about the placements themselves; for example, whether children and parents are sufficiently informed about what is going on and about their rights or whether voluntary placements are substitutes for placements that should have been decided by the courts.

Regarding involuntary removals, we argue that it is necessary to differentiate among decisions that are uncontested, semicontested, and contested (see Figure 10.1). Involuntary removals that are semicontested with "soft" coercion do not officially exist; but there is some indication that parents are engaged with as part of the decision-making process to see beyond conflict with the child welfare agency, and their own circumstances and difficulties, to reach a decision to relinquish care in the best interests of their child at that specific point in time.

Child removals can mean different things: In some countries, care is more likely to lead to a permanent separation (e.g., England and the United States), whereas in other countries, family reunification remains an active policy and practice imperative even with a care order in place. Permanent separation through adoption is used most actively in England and the United States, and is a rarely used or nonexistent option in other countries. Norway is increasingly arguing, however, that adoptions should be used more often, and Ireland will soon have legal mechanisms in place to allow for the adoption of children in long-term care.

The boundary between private and public responsibility for children is drawn differently within the various systems. As we can see in Figure 10.1, mediating factors such as system features, parents' rights, children's rights, and what is meant by the best interests of the child, are significant in setting the overall *context* for these child-removal decision-making systems. It is noteworthy that the key principles covering child removals are labeled quite similarly across the countries studied in this book. They can, however, mean different things in different sociohistorical contexts, and the adoption of children in care provides an illustrative example of such differences. Dependent on context, one can interpret the legal and policy initiatives to facilitate children in long-term care to be placed for adoption in a number of ways: allowing children in care to be placed for adoption is a child-centric development that will promote permanency and one that gives paramount consideration to the child's best interest; it is a shift away from family-centric policies toward a practice that is "punitive" toward parents; it is a pragmatic decision that recognizes that some children will never be able to return home to their parents; it is a research-based decision; it is a mechanism to reduce the overall number of children in state care, and/or a neoliberal-inspired economic policy for states to save money in their child welfare budgets by transferring some of the responsibility for children in long-term care from the state back to the community.

DIFFERENCES IN VOLUNTARY AND INVOLUNTARY REMOVAL RATES AMONG COUNTRIES

A striking finding in this book is the unexpectedly large proportion of children who come into care through voluntary processes. Table 10.1 collates the numbers of child removals in involuntary and voluntary care from earlier chapters. The numbers of children in voluntary care includes all forms of removal that are based on consent. Because the countries differ in how they record removals and present their statistical data, the categories might not be fully comparable

Table 10.1. Numbers of children (0–17 years of age) in care at year end by country

Country	Year	Children placed out-of-home and per 1,000 children	Number of children per 1,000 children and the proportion of children in involuntary care of all children in care (%)	Number of children per 1,000 children and the proportion of children in voluntary care of all children in care (%)
Switzerland[i]	2012	793 (10.4)	2.5 (39%)	3.8 (61%)
Norway	2013	11,405 (10.1)	7.2 (71%)[ii]	2.9 (29%)
Finland	2012	10,365 (9.6)	1.8 (19%)	7.8 (81%)[iii]
Germany	2012	118,530 (9)	1 (10%)	8 (90%)
Sweden	2012	15,646 (8.2)	2.36 (26%)	6.65 (74%)
England	2013 (March)	68,110 (6)	4.25 (71%)	1.75 (29%)
Ireland	2012	6,332 (5.5)	3.2 (58%)	2.3 (42%)
Massachusetts (United States)	2012 (2013)	7,302 (5.2) (398,482 [5.4])	4.3 (83%) (–)	0.9 (17%) (–)

(–) = Data not available

[i] Cantons Basel-Landschaft & Basel-Stadt only, and entries per year for involuntary and voluntary placements.

[ii] Involuntary removals consists of all the care orders that are made by the county board, and per definition they are categorized as involuntary even in cases when they *de facto* are voluntary.

[iii] The Finnish number includes both voluntary care orders and removals as part of in-home services. In both types the child enters the care based on consent. The voluntary removal by a care order, however, may not be terminated by the parents' or child's decision only.

and the numbers in this table should be compared with caution. They do, however, present some interesting tendencies within and among countries:

If we look at the removal decisions per 1,000 children, we see that the removal numbers for the Nordic countries, Germany, and Switzerland, are much higher than for England, Ireland, or the United States. As we already know, the threshold for interventions or services from child welfare systems varies a great deal among countries and this reflects the different system orientations (see Gilbert 1997; Gilbert et al. 2011). The Nordic countries have a sliding transition from universal welfare services to services that are provided by the child welfare system (Pösö et al. 2014), and Germany is not very different. However, the picture changes to a risk-orientation with a higher threshold and a different motivation for intervention in Switzerland, Ireland, England, and the United States. The first contact point between the service user and the child welfare system, therefore, usually has different aims. A puzzle that has been pointed out by Gilbert et al. (2011) and Pösö et al. (2014), among others, is the relatively high numbers of out-of-home placements in service-oriented child welfare systems. This is interesting because these systems have a strong emphasis on preventing harm, providing service, and making sure removals are not necessary. Contrary to expectations, however, this preventive approach and service delivery has not led to fewer removals. We believe several explanations are possible: for example, the living standards for children in Nordic countries are high and perhaps, therefore, the threshold for interventions and acceptance of particular living conditions and parenting approaches toward children are relatively lower than other countries. The degree of child-centrism in a country also may be of importance, and both Norway and Finland have been categorized as child-centric in their child welfare system orientation.

Decisions about removals of children are perceived differently in the eight countries, as is reflected in the numbers of voluntary versus involuntary removals in Table 10.1. Some countries use removals as a form of service provision as is evident in, for example, Finland and Germany. Further, Finland, Germany, Cantons of Basel-Landschaft & Basel-Stadt (Switzerland), and Sweden had significantly more children in voluntary than involuntary care at year end, whereas in other countries more children were in involuntary care at year end as a result of a contested removal decision. Readers should be careful, however, not to generalize from year-end data. For example, in Ireland only four in ten children were in voluntary care at year end, yet six in ten children come into care during the year through voluntary care. The Irish authors also argued that we should be trying to capture data on differences between voluntary and involuntary care between *first* and subsequent admissions to care for a child to facilitate even finer levels of analysis among countries on the use of voluntary versus involuntary (coercive) care. They also highlighted differences among regions within Ireland on the use of voluntary versus involuntary care, and similarly, most chapter authors have generally highlighted internal differences in child removal practices among regions. The limited datasets provided by social services and court records regarding child removals within countries, differences in record keeping practices, and fundamental differences in the nature of removal systems among countries, has meant that one of the aims of this book, which was to provide a comprehensive analysis of statistical data on child removals, was not fully realized.

The similarities and dissimilarities among countries' child removal systems, who makes removal decisions, how and where these decisions are made, whether parents, children, and young people participate, and whether these removal decisions can be appealed, are examined in the next section.

SOCIOLEGAL VARIETIES OF CHILD REMOVAL DECISION-MAKING

Another surprising finding of this book is that there is a wider diversity of decision-making systems and decision-making bodies to remove children from their family homes than we expected. A key message of this book is that court-based care orders make up only one part of all the removals and may even be one of the smallest parts of many countries' child removal systems. In the countries we have studied, in general, the decision-making practice regarding child removals is a mixture of social-work-led decisions at the local level (social welfare agencies or similar child welfare agencies) and legal decisions (courts or court-*like* agencies) on the regional/national level. The matrices presented below summarize the key features of voluntary removals decision-making bodies (Table 10.2) and involuntary removal decision-making bodies (Table 10.3).

As we can see from Table 10.2 and Table 10.3, the authority to undertake or facilitate removals of children—with or without parental and/or a child's consent—differs among countries and forms of removal. Parents, children, social workers, and other family and community members can initiate voluntary removals. These removal decisions are consented to by a parent or parents, and/or by children in some countries, and are made in conjunction with social workers in most countries. The parents, and/or children, can cancel the removal at any time. Many countries have, however, specified practices for the child welfare agencies to continue with the removal if the concerns about the child's situation persist; these may involve an application by the state welfare agency/youth office to a court or court-like body. The Finnish "voluntary care order" complicates the picture of voluntary care even further: In the Finnish child welfare system, a child may enter care based on consent, but the decision to terminate care is made by social workers. This means that what begins as voluntary care becomes involuntary as soon as care has started.

Involuntary removals

In case of involuntary removals, juridical agencies—general courts or specialized courts—are involved in the decision-making. In Switzerland the decision-making body is the Child and Adult Protection Authorities (CAPA), which differs fundamentally from all the other countries included in this book as it emphasizes the expertise of child welfare professionals and does not necessarily include any members with legal education. The composition of decision-makers in courts in other countries is not uniform—legally trained judges or/and other lay and professional members—and thus the spectrum of knowledge bases in courts, and other (final) decision-making bodies, is varied. The courts employ juridical knowledge, child welfare knowledge, and the knowledge of "every citizen" (lay members, lay judges). This is to say that on a continuum, these

Table 10.2. Matrix of key features of voluntary decision-making bodies

Country	Agency type	Type of body	Who can initiate a voluntary care process?	Decision-maker(s)	Appeal body	Primary legislation
Norway	Child Welfare Agency	Child Welfare Organization	Parent(s), Child Welfare Organization,	Parent(s), social worker; all children should be heard, but a child 15 years or older must consent to care	Parent(s) can cancel anytime. Child Welfare Agency can bring care order application to County Social Welfare Board if concerns persist	Child Welfare Act 1992
Sweden	Social Welfare Board (SWB)	Administrative body	Parent(s), Child 15 years or older, Social Service (social worker)	Laypersons, political appointees (5–8)	County Administrative Court	Social Services Act 2001 (SoL)
Switzerland	Social Service/Child Welfare Agency/Youth Office/Children and Family Counselling Agencies/School Authorities/Social Authorities (varies by Canton)	Social Service/Child Welfare Organization/School Authorities/Social Authorities (varies by Canton)	Parent(s), Social Service/Child Welfare Agency/Head of School;	Parent(s), social worker, representatives of school authorities, laypersons (in cases where responsibility is with social authorities)	Parent(s) can cancel anytime. CAPA can intervene if such an action might pose a serious risk to the development of the child. Social Service/Child Welfare Agency/Youth Office/Children and Family Counselling Agencies School Authority, etc., can refer the case to Child and Adult Protection Authority if concerns persist	Swiss Civil Code; Cantonal legislation (degree of differentiation varies; legislation is often limited to matters of financial responsibility)
Finland	Social Welfare Agency	Child Welfare Organization	Parent(s), Child 12 years or older, Social Welfare Agency	Social workers, parent(s), all children should be heard, but a child 12 years or older must consent to care	Regional administrative court deals with the appeals. If the removal is a part of in-home services, parents and/or child 12 years or older can cancel anytime. If the removal is a voluntary care order, the decision to terminate the removal is made by social workers.	Child Welfare Act 2007

Ireland	Child and Family Agency (CFA)	Child Welfare Organization	Parent(s), Child and Family Agency	Parent(s), social worker	Parent(s) can cancel anytime. CFA can bring care order application to District Court if concerns persist	Child Care Act 1991 (as amended)
England	Local Authority	Child Welfare Organization	Parent(s), Local Authority, child 16+ where parent does not consent	Parent(s), social worker, child 16 years or older where parent does not consent	Parent(s) can cancel anytime. Local authority can bring care order application to Family Court if concerns persist	Children Act 1989
Germany	Youth Office	Child Welfare Organization	Parent(s), Youth Office	Parent(s), social worker, children should be consulted	Parent(s) can cancel anytime. Local authority can bring care order application to Family Court if concerns persist	German Child and Youth Welfare Code (SGB VIII)
United States (Massachusetts)	A parent, legal guardian, custodian, school, or police officer may file an application with the Juvenile Court (Child Requiring Assistance cases) A parent or the child protection agency; a parent and by a court, if the child is of Indian/Native American origin. (VPA)	Juvenile Court (Child Requiring Assistance cases) Child protection agency (VPA)	Parent(s) or a person who represents the school district can file an application (Child Requiring Assistance cases) Parent or child protection agency (VPA)	A Juvenile Court judge (Child Requiring Assistance cases) A parent, young adult in the care or custody of the child protection agency, or child protection agency, or family and child protection agency (VPA)	A child, parent, legal guardian, or custodian may appeal to the Massachusetts Appeals Court (Child Requiring Assistance cases). A parent, young adult, or the child protection agency can revoke the VPA at any time. (VPA)	*Federal laws:* Indian Child Welfare Act of 1978; Adoption Assistance and Child Welfare Act of 1980 (PL-96-272); Keeping Children and Families Safe Act of 2003 (P.L. 108-36) *Massachusetts:* 2013 Massachusetts General Law, part I, Title XVII, Chapter 119; 110 Code of Massachusetts Regulations: Department of Children and Families (2015)

Table 10.3. Matrix of key features of involuntary [compulsory] decision-making bodies

Country	Decision-making body	Type of body	Applicant	Decision-maker(s) and number of persons	Appeal body	Primary Legislation
Norway	County Social Welfare Board	Specialist Court-"like" Body	Child Welfare Agency	Judge (chair), expert, and lay-person (3)	District Court	Child Welfare Act 1992
Sweden	County Administrative Court	Court	Social Welfare Board (SWB)	Judge and three lay persons (4)	Regional Administrative Court	Care of Young Persons Act, LVU 1990
Switzerland	Child and Adult Protection Authorities (CAPA)	Six Cantons set up their CAPA as a Specialist Court; 20 Cantons set up their CAPA as an Administrative Body	Anyone can report a child in danger or at risk to a CAPA; legislation defines no organization with special application rights; a reporting person or referring organization has no rights against the CAPA; the CAPA acts *ex officio*	Professionals from law, social work, psychology, pedagogy (3); 13 of 26 Cantons require chair to be a jurist	Cantonal Court/ Cantonal Administrative Court or other (Varies according to Cantonal legislation)	Swiss Civil Code & Each Canton has its own legislation
Finland	Regional Administrative Court	Non-Specialist Administrative Court	Child Welfare Agency	Two judges and one expert member (3)	Supreme Administrative Court	Child Welfare Act 2007
Ireland	District Court	Non-Specialist District Court (One Specialist Court in the Dublin Metropolitan District)	Child and Family Agency	Single Judge (1)	Circuit Court	Child Care Act 1991 (as amended)

	Court	Specialist Court	Local Authority	Composition	Appeal Court	Legislation
England	Family Court	Specialist Court	Local Authority	Single Lay Justice (Magistrates) or Judge (1)	Appeal Court	Children Act 1989
Germany	Family Courts	Specialist Family Law District Court	Anyone can report to court. Most reports by youth office. Court acts *ex officio*	Single Judge (1)	Appellate Court or Federal Court of Justice	German Civil Code (BGB)
United States (Massachusetts)	Juvenile Court (can also be heard in Family Courts and Juvenile and Family Drug Courts)	Specialist Court	Department of Children and Families (DCF)	Singe Judge (1) Singe Judge (1) or Judicial Hearing Officer (1) for initial hearing	Intermediate appellate courts or State Supreme Court (depending on State)	Adoption Assistance and Child Welfare Act of 1980 Adoption and Safe Families Act of 1997 Indian Child Welfare Act 1978 Child Abuse Prevention and Treatment Act of 1974 (PL 93-247)

bodies may employ *mainly* legal knowledge (e.g., England, Ireland, the United States) to *mainly,* or only, child-welfare knowledge (Switzerland). In between, the knowledge base also can mix legal, child welfare, and/or lay knowledge, as is done in Norway, Finland, and Sweden—all countries with an emphasis on family services in child welfare. These countries are at the "social" end of the sociolegal spectrum along which the "social" element plays an important and integral part in care order decision-making. This finding suggests that in the family-service systems, removal decisions, when made by the court, are seen to require a wider knowledge base than the decisions in more child protection focused systems in which the knowledge base is primarily juridical.[1] However, both the German family-service system and the risk oriented Swiss system differ from this rationale.

At the "legal" end of the sociolegal spectrum, employing only legally trained members in the court, we have countries such as England, Ireland, Germany, and the United States, which have a clear emphasis on court-led decision-making for removals, with a strong emphasis on the juridical nature of the decisions. This picture becomes, however, more complicated if we look at *all* forms of child removals, as the apparent extensive use of voluntary removals are more social-work-led decisions, but not exclusively so as in the case of Germany.

In all countries, court decisions are preceded by applications from the child welfare agency. The "legal" decision-making bodies are thus dependent on social welfare agencies' inputs, knowledge, and proposals. The interaction between the courts and the social welfare agencies differs among the countries. In Finland and Norway, the court makes decisions based on the applications and does not interact with the social welfare agency otherwise. In Germany, the court is involved in the cases by actively reviewing the process of the cases and guiding the work in the social welfare agency. In England, Ireland, and the United States the courts make several (interim) decisions during the decision-making process and thereby regularly review the development of the removal cases. In Germany and Ireland, court reviews can continue after the care order is granted, but in Ireland this practice is not explicitly provided for in law and is not a consistent practice across all District Courts. In Sweden, the social welfare board interacts between the social welfare agencies and the courts, deciding whether to take the proposals by the social welfare agencies to court, and making decisions on voluntary removals. The role of the Swedish social welfare boards, which consist of politically appointed members, is distinctive among the countries studied in this book.

Child participation and child-centeredness

The removal of children by a state from their family is about promoting the rights, safety, and welfare of children; and in the center of all such decisions is a child or young person. Some countries decision-making systems set specific age criteria for children's participation in decision-making, so that a child of twelve (Finland), fifteen (Norway, Sweden), or sixteen (England) years of age can be a full party to the decision-making process and express his/her view on the voluntary/involuntary nature of a decision. Because children's participation is more involved than just contributing to a decision, a key finding of this book is that there seem to be considerable differences— and a distinct lack of knowledge—regarding the quality and frequency of how children and young people's direct participation (e.g., decision-making meetings about voluntary removals, attendance at court, or meeting a judge in chambers) and indirect participation (e.g., letter to a judge, legal representation, guardian *ad litem,* or voice of the child in a social work report) are facilitated (see UNCRC report number 12 [2009] for a comprehensive outline of the meaning of CRC Article 12). Although a country such as Germany is instituting progressive child-centered reforms in care order cases, none of the other countries profiled in this book could be held up as exemplars in facilitating children's participation, whereby chapter authors highlighted issues with: practice methods, facilities, the adversarial nature of some court systems, overly adult-centric processes, the imposition of age limits for participation, and a lack of training for professionals. Furthermore, considerable empirical research is required in all countries to provide a more accurate picture of children and young people's participation, and the child-centeredness of these processes. Equally important would be an exploration of the quality and extent to which children and young people are involved in voluntary removal decisions.

Appeals, legitimacy, and the European Court of Human Rights

Various practices guarantee and monitor the legitimacy of court decisions: child welfare removal decisions made by the various country courts can be appealed to higher courts, with certain restrictions. In earlier chapters and as outlined in Table 10.3, all countries have clear pathways for parents, and children in some countries, to appeal decisions to higher courts. As displayed in Table 10.2, parents—and in some countries, children—retain the right to cancel voluntary care. Although the state agency can proceed to another decision-making body or court should voluntary care be cancelled while a child welfare concern still exists. In voluntary systems, it is less clear where or to whom parents and children appeal if they are unhappy with the voluntary care process.

In European countries, in very few cases, a child welfare case also eventually may involve an application to the European Court of Human Rights in Strasbourg. From the perspective of the sociolegal orientation that is a central feature of the child welfare removal decision, it is interesting to note that the ECtHR is a strictly legal institution. Renowned jurists from European countries serve as judges, and usually attorneys general from the countries in question represent the state that is accused of human rights violations. Thus, the review of human rights violations and the child's best interests are evaluated according to the legal and juridical knowledge base within a strictly legal system. Although only 4 percent of the applications to the ECtHR are accepted, there were just less than 17,000 court rulings between 1959 and 2013 (ECtHR 2014). Just over 1,000 of these were cases concerning violations of Article 8, "Respect for private and family life," the article that is most likely to be violated in child welfare, removing children, or terminating parental rights and responsibilities. In the seven European countries examined in this book, there are 150 cases of violations of Article 8 recorded between 1959 and 2013 (Ireland 5, Norway 6, Sweden 9, Germany 20, Switzerland 21, Finland 23 and Great Britain 66), but only a relatively small number of these cases were cases relating exclusively to child removals by the state. The subscription to a higher court is an important issue because it raises questions concerning a nation-state's autonomy and people's democratic sovereignty, which are balanced against human rights and the legal sovereignty both within the nation-state and also between the nation-state and the supranational body. The potential tensions between politics and law that are currently occurring in Europe concerning the child's best interests and child welfare systems, are important to explore further.

BLIND SPOTS AND CRITICAL FEATURES OF THE SYSTEMS AND THE WAYS AHEAD

What are the blind spots and challenges within the country systems presented in this book? We asked authors to identify and point out the critical features, if any, with their systems, and they highlighted quite a few challenges. There are at least four critiques that are shared among most of these countries. The first, and perhaps the most important theme, is a critique of the *legislation and practices associated with voluntary admissions*. In general, voluntary placements are short-term and introduced for family support. There are, however, some weaknesses in these decision-making practices. Almost all authors point out that there is an apparent lack of knowledge, due process procedures, and transparency around voluntary placement systems. Concerns were expressed that these removals may not be as voluntary as they should be; that there is a gray-zone of possible misuse of state power and discretion that may not have been intended by legislators. The essential criteria for sound and legitimate voluntary removals is that parents and children are well informed about what they agree to when they give their consent to a voluntary placement. This is a particular challenge when parents and children live in vulnerable situations—as they normally do when they come into contact with child welfare services. Furthermore, in voluntary processes, parents may not have access to legal advice to ensure that their rights are vindicated.

The second blind spot is *knowledge about the removals*; almost all authors remark on the dearth of scholarship on the removals of children. On a general basis, there is scant original research and the existing literature tells us little about the quality of decision-making in child welfare systems, how decisions are made in courts and court-like bodies, and even less about the use of discretion in child welfare removal cases. Furthermore, as outlined above, for some countries it is difficult to find reliable and accurate statistics and related data on how many children are removed, for how long, on what grounds removals are undertaken, how children participate in decision-making processes, and how the rights of children and parents are protected, to mention a few of the highlighted issues. It is striking that for such an important area of state power, there is such an enormous knowledge gap. This should be of concern to policy-makers, legislators, and those with an interest in human rights and the operation of the rule of law.

This knowledge lacuna also raises questions of how we can know that decisions regarding removals are of high-quality and legitimate. Although child welfare systems are all built on the principles of family preservation and the principle of the "best interests/well-being of the child," there are few systematic empirical studies on how these principles are balanced. One of the main articles of the Convention on the Rights of the Child (CRC) of 1989 reads:

> In all actions concerning children, whether undertaken by public or private social welfare institutions, courts of law, administrative authorities or legislative bodies, the best interests of the child shall be a primary consideration (Article 3).

This means that states that have ratified the CRC are obligated to give children's best interests primary consideration in decisions that concern them. Neither child welfare laws, development theory, or child welfare research provide clear, definitive answers concerning what is in the best interests of children generally, not to mention of individual children in a given set of circumstances. Laws, theories, and research also do not give exact answers in identifying *when* to intervene in a family, *which* services will help, and *when* the risk to a child is so great that the child should be removed from the care of her or his parent(s), and *when* this removal should be permanent. The result is that decision-makers have considerable leeway in exercising discretion as they weigh differing arguments and considerations when making decisions about a child's best interests. More should be known about how they exercise discretion and whether there are any particular groups of children and issues that are not given enough fair attention.

Third, another problematic issue raised by several of the authors is *the lack of transparency and accountability* concerning the removals of children. There are often few established mechanisms for transparency or to review decisions made outside of the court appeal system. Sweden is an exception because all court rulings are public (in anonymized form). In Norway, there is an ambitious goal that about 20 percent of all decisions made by the county boards should be public, but the reality is that only 2 percent to 5 percent are made public. Due to a series of initiatives to bring greater transparency, Ireland's District Court child care proceedings are moving away from being highly secretive (see O'Mahony et al. 2016a,b). There is an obvious need to rethink how the quality of decisions regarding child removals could be evaluated to guarantee trust in the decision-making system among parents, children, policy-makers, and professionals working in the system. There should be multiple ways to support transparency and accountability, given that trust should exist and be strengthened among the families as well as among the professionals and politicians, and the needs of each for monitoring the quality of decision-making systems are different. This is particularly important when decision-making rests on an unsecure knowledge base, due to the very nature of child welfare. Shlonsky and Benbenishty (2014) argue that in child welfare, there may not be a single right answer to what is "evidence"; therefore, multiple sources of information should inform our understanding of "evidence." This is also true of transparency and accountability.

However, having noted the above, and given the levels of public and political accountability associated with child welfare in these countries, it is conceivable that voluntary and involuntary removal systems already aim to operate in a fair and appropriate manner, and that child welfare bodies have implemented sufficiently robust measures to ensure their legitimacy. The contribution of this book is to show that there is insufficient evidence to be comfortable with this position and it is incumbent upon states to do more to make these systems more transparent and accountable.

Fourth, *variations in practice* is a feature that is mentioned as a challenge by many of the authors. Such variations include the many different ways the process can be organized within the same country, differences in how decision-makers exercise their powers and discretion, and differences in how legislation and case practices can be interpreted between agencies and courts and among individual decision-makers. Examples include the organization of decision-making in Switzerland due to its federal system and the racial discrimination highlighted by the U.S. authors. Clearly, these types of critiques raise questions about the fair and equal application of the rule of law and the equal treatment of citizens. States should guarantee equality before the law and that similar cases are treated in the same way. Reports from several of the country authors raise doubts as to whether this principle is sufficiently upheld due to considerable variation in practices within countries and between decision-makers.

RESEARCHING AND REDESIGNING CHILD REMOVAL DECISION-MAKING SYSTEMS

In the first chapter of this book, we argued that there are several reasons why sociolegal decision-making and child welfare removal systems are topical at the moment: the expansion of the child welfare systems in wealthy Western countries, the recent emphasis on children's rights in child welfare systems, child-friendly justice approaches, and new vulnerabilities in childhood and global changes, all of which challenge nation states to ensure their decision-making systems are fair, accountable, transparent, evidence-informed, fit-for-purpose, child-centered, and consistent. Many country authors have reported that their sociolegal decision-making systems, processes, and policies are continually changing, while also arguing that there are elements of these child removal systems that still need to be revisited and revised. Removal decisions are a result of a complex mixture of legal and social organizations, norms, knowledge bases, practices, and ambitions. These decisions should guarantee children and parents access to justice—meaning that the decisions are legally correct—but also guarantee them access to welfare so that children's well-being improves due to the decisions.

If one was to read this edited book with a view to redesigning a country system that decides upon the removal of children from their families, the four key challenges outlined above are clearly elements that might inform such a redesign. We are cautious not to recommend a "best" system, because each system is bounded and underpinned by historical, cultural, legal, economic, social, and relational factors that mean each system "fits" the country. This also means that an uncritical "transplant" of a system, or even parts of a system, to another country, may be both inappropriate and a facile exercise.

Earlier, we argued that there is a need for further research on these systems to assist decision-makers and to support those seeking to reform decision-making systems to improve the quality of these processes and the decisions for children, young people, and their families. This book has focused only on child welfare removal decisions and has ignored the removals of children based on decisions of the criminal justice and health care systems. Such removals also exercise state power to intervene into the relations of parents and children, and the interactions between these systems could be explored more in the future, especially their impact on individual children and parents and their rights.

More research should be carried out with and about children, young people, parents, and practitioners of social work and jurisprudence. Of particular concern is that there is a serious gap in the literature and research reports that give voice to children, young people, and their parents' experiences of these child removal decision-making systems. For ethical, legal, and practical reasons (see, for example, the Ireland chapter) such studies may be hard to design and implement, either within a single country or in a cross-country comparison; however, they should be of the highest priority for future research agendas.

In this book, we did not examine *how* decision-makers reach their decisions (see, for example, O'Sullivan 2011; Taylor 2010; Ward et al. 2012). Ethnographic studies that observe and examine the reasoning processes of decision-makers would be beneficial (see, for example, Klein and Mitchell 2010 on judicial reasoning); however, observational studies of court and decision-making bodies such as CAPAs and boards may be more feasible due to the scheduled nature of their work, rather than unscheduled child welfare voluntary care decision-making, which would be harder to access for observational purposes. Additionally, discourse and content analyses of the small, but growing number of written court judgments could explore how decision-makers reason and explain their decisions. Another avenue to explore would be an analysis of decision-making systems in other parts of Europe and on other continents not, unfortunately, covered in this book. The availability in some countries of large-scale government datasets related to these decision-making systems also may be a fruitful source of "big" data for analysis.

Despite these observations and comments, there is still much to learn from the descriptions herein of country decision-making systems. The analysis provided in each chapter highlights seminal themes of interest for countries and services considering reform. The following questions could be used to scaffold a reflective evaluation of child welfare removal systems in any child welfare system. These questions could either be used for individual/team/professional reflection or form the basis of a larger, root and branch structured reform process:

Setting the scene:

1. What types of child protection removal systems do you have in your country?
2. Who are the decision-makers in these systems?
3. Are the thresholds for removals at an "appropriate" level to ensure that a child's welfare is protected, while also respecting the right to family life?
4. What are the dominant narratives and themes in the media, research, and practice associated with child protection removal systems in your country?
5. What questions arise from these dominant narratives and themes about the strengths and weaknesses of your country's child protection removal systems?

What is known about the wider sociopolitical environment in which these systems operate?

6. In what ways are the prevailing societal and political attitudes toward the welfare state affecting the provision of supports to families who come into contact with child protection removal systems?

7. How would you assess the surrounding political, legal, welfare, and social policy landscape: Is it supportive, risk tolerant, and willing to invest significant resources to support parents under pressure? Or is it risk-adverse, intolerant, blaming, and unwilling to commit sufficient resources?

8. How dominant are family preservation and family reunion as social policy objectives in your country and how do they affect removal and reunification rates?

9. What additional resources could be invested in prevention and early intervention to prevent children from entering state care and to support their parents more effectively to continue parenting? What interventions could effectively target families to prevent children's re-entry to state care?

What is known about the operation of these systems?

10. What is the age profile of children who are received into care on their *first* admission?

11. What is the profile of children who are received into state care on more than one occasion?

12. To what extent do children, young people, and parents meaningfully participate in these removal processes?

13. To what extent are decision-makers trained, resourced, and supported to make timely and child-centered removal decisions?

14. Are child protection removal systems adequately resourced and supported?

Governance and research requirements:

15. What research evidence exists on the functioning and adequacy of your country's removal systems?

16. Is there sufficient statistical and research data in your country on these systems?

17. How can the "legitimacy" of removal decisions be verified?

18. Do all decision-making systems have sufficient independent oversight and mechanisms to ensure transparency?

Implementing and evaluating a reform:

19. What type of consultation process could be designed to facilitate a review of your country's removal systems?

20. Who could convene and fund a consultation process?

21. Who are the stakeholders who should be invited to a consultation process and what type of convening model is most likely to ensure inclusiveness and participation?
22. What are the barriers and facilitators to a meaningful and supported consultation, implementation, and evaluation process?
23. What type of process(es) could be designed to facilitate sensitively the participation of children and young people, parents, and other significant persons (e.g., grandparents, extended family members)?
24. What can be learned from other countries' processes, laws, and system-design decisions?

NOTE

1 We look here at only the decision-makers and ignore the expert witnesses, whom the courts may call to expand their knowledge base.

REFERENCES

European Court of Human Rights (ECtHR). (2014). *ECHR Overview 1959–2013*. Strasburg: European Court of Human Rights.

Gilbert, N. (Ed.) (1997). *Combatting Child Abuse—International Perspectives and Trends*. New York, NY: Oxford University Press.

Gilbert, N., Parton, N., and Skivenes, M. (Eds.) (2011). *Child Protection Systems: International Trends and Emerging Orientations*. New York, NY: Oxford University Press.

Klein, D. E. and Mitchell, G. (2010). *The Psychology of Judicial Decision Making*. New York, NY: Oxford University Press.

O'Mahony, C., Burns, K., Parkes, A., and Shore, C. (2016a). "Representation and participation in child care proceedings: what about the voice of the parents?" *Journal of Social Welfare and Family Law*, Vol. 2 *(Advance Online Edition)*, 1–27, doi: 10.1093/lawfam/ebw001.

O'Mahony, C., Burns, K., Parkes, A., and Shore, C. (2016b). "Child Care Proceedings in Non-Specialist Courts: The Experience in Ireland." *International Journal of Law Policy and The Family (Advance Online Edition)*, 38(3), 1-21, http://dx.doi.org/10.1080/09649069.2016.1176338.

O'Sullivan, T. (2011). *Decision-Making in Social Work*. Basingstoke, United Kingdom: Palgrave Macmillan.

Parkes, A., Shore, C., O'Mahony, C., and Burns, K. (2015). "The Right of the Child to be Heard? Professional Experiences of Child Care Proceedings in the Irish District Court." *Child and Family Law Quarterly*, 27(4): 423–444.

Pösö, T., Hestbæk, A. D., and Skivenes, M. (2014). "Child Protection Systems in the Danish, Finnish and Norwegian Welfare States—Time for a Child Centric Approach?" *European Journal of Social Work* 17(4), 475–490, doi:10.1080/13691457.2013.829802.

Shlonsky, A. and Benbenishty, R. (2014). "From Evidence to Outcomes in Child Welfare." In Shlonsky, A. and Benbenishty, R. (Eds), *From Evidence to Outcomes in Child Welfare*. New York, NY: Oxford University Press, 3–23.

Taylor, B. (2010). *Professional Decision Making and Risk in Social Work*. Exeter, United Kingdom: Learning Matters.

UNHCR Guidelines. (2008). *UNHCR Guidelines on Determining the Best Interests of the Child*.

Ward, H., Brown, R., and Westlake, D. (2012). *Safeguarding Babies and Very Young Children from Abuse and Neglect*. London, United Kingdom: Jessica Kingsley.

INDEX

Page numbers followed by t indicate a table. Italicized page numbers indicate a figure. Page numbers followed by n and another number indicate an endnote.